ABINGDON THEOLOGICAL COMPANION TO THE LECTIONARY

PREACHING
YEAR A

ABINGDON THEOLOGICAL COMPANION TO THE LECTIONARY

PREACHING YEAR A

PAUL SCOTT WILSON
EDITOR

Abingdon theological companion to the lectionary: preaching year A / Paul Scott Wilson, editor

ISBN 978-1-4267-4035-0

Library of Congress Control Number: 2012037975

Printed in the United States of America

1 2 3 4 5 6 7—16 15 14 13

CONTENTS

Series Preface   vii
First Sunday of Advent   1
Second Sunday of Advent   7
Third Sunday of Advent   13
Fourth Sunday of Advent   19

CHRISTMAS

Christmas Eve/Day, Third Proper   25
First Sunday after Christmas Day   31

EPIPHANY

Epiphany of the Lord   37
Baptism of the Lord (First Sunday after the Epiphany) [1]   42
Second Sunday after the Epiphany [2]   47
Third Sunday after the Epiphany [3]   52
Fourth Sunday after the Epiphany [4]   57
Fifth Sunday after the Epiphany [5]   62
Last Sunday after the Epiphany (Transfiguration Sunday)   68

LENT

Ash Wednesday   73
First Sunday in Lent   79
Second Sunday in Lent   85
Third Sunday in Lent   91
Fourth Sunday in Lent   96
Fifth Sunday in Lent   101
Sixth Sunday in Lent   106

HOLY WEEK

Good Friday   112

EASTER

Resurrection of the Lord (Easter Day)   118
Second Sunday of Easter   123

Third Sunday of Easter   128
Fourth Sunday of Easter   133
Fifth Sunday of Easter   138
Sixth Sunday of Easter   143
Seventh Sunday of Easter   148
Day of Pentecost   153

SEASON AFTER PENTECOST

Trinity Sunday (First Sunday after Pentecost)   159
Proper 4 [9] (May 29 to June 4)   165
Proper 5 [10] (June 5 to June 11)   171
Proper 6 [11] (June 12 to June 18)   177
Proper 7 [12] (June 19 to June 25)   183
Proper 8 [13] (June 26 to July 2)   189
Proper 9 [14] (July 3 to July 9)   195
Proper 10 [15] (July 10 to July 16)   200
Proper 11 [16] (July 17 to July 23)   205
Proper 12 [17] (July 24 to July 30)   210
Proper 13 [18] (July 31 to August 6)   215
Proper 14 [19] (August 7 to August 13)   220
Proper 15 [20] (August 14 to August 20)   225
Proper 16 [21] (August 21 to August 27)   231
Proper 17 [22] (August 28 to September 3)   237
Proper 18 [23] (September 4 to September 10)   243
Proper 19 [24] (September 11 to September 17)   249
Proper 20 [25] (September 18 to September 24)   254
Proper 21 [26] (September 25 to October 1)   259
Proper 22 [27] (October 2 to October 8)   264
Proper 23 [28] (October 9 to October 15)   269
Proper 24 [29] (October 16 to October 22)   275
Proper 25 [30] (October 23 to October 29)   280
Proper 26 [31] (October 30 to November 5)   285
Proper 27 [32] (November 6 to November 12)   290
Proper 28 [33] (November 13 to November 19)   295
Proper 29 [34] (Reign of Christ or Christ the King)
    (November 20 to November 26)   300
All Saints Day (November 1 or the first Sunday in November)   305
Thanksgiving Day   310
Contributors   317
Scripture index   319

SERIES PREFACE

Preaching Sunday after Sunday, month by month, is an amazing privilege, opportunity, and trust. It is also a remarkable challenge. Preachers struggle to speak God's word in a fresh way each week that will nurture and sustain the congregation, and in the process they also need to be nurtured by that same word. The steps of preparing a sermon—studying the biblical texts, praying, researching, and writing—are traditional spiritual exercises of preachers. Preachers' lives today are often so demanding that their spirituality gets shortchanged. They desire to climb to the spiritual mountaintop to proclaim God's word, but they may often feel they get only partway up that mountain each week. Of course the Spirit can make a rich treasure out of even a small offering, but how much better are preachers served if the resources they use provide them with clear paths and theological guiderails that help them to reach the inspired summits for which they aim.

Welcome to a unique and exciting ecumenical preaching resource, an offering to the church at large for the enrichment of both preachers and their congregations. It provides important tools not found in other lectionary-based resources. Here preachers will find vital help in specific theological areas where sermons commonly fail or falter. These include: focusing on one key thought that arises from the biblical text/s that can give unity to the sermon, discussing a related theological question that congregational members are likely to ask, connecting the particular reading/s to actual pastoral needs in the congregation, identifying practical things people may do in their lives by way of ethical living and social justice, and linking specific texts to the larger gospel story in the sermon for the purpose of fostering faith.

These various theological matters provide particular lenses with which to think about God and human beings in relationship to God. The demands of faith are explored here, and also the help God graciously gives by way of empowerment in meeting those demands. This essential emphasis on grace, too often missing from preaching resources, is built into each of the theological lenses provided here. The effect of these various lenses can be to radically transform and enhance the sermon-making process. It can mean the difference between creating adequate sermons and creating strong sermons that foster growth and nurture congregational life. These lenses also nurture the preacher, daily providing more ways to see and think about God's gracious love and empowerment.

What further sets this resource apart is that in writing for each worship day, top theologians are paired with top teachers of preaching. The theologians are responsible for addressing a key theological question in clear and simple ways, while the homileticians address the other matters; thus each scholar writes half of the total length. Other lectionary resources typically bypass the systematic or constructive theologians of the church in favor of biblical scholars, even though biblical studies these days are generally less interested in matters of theology, the church, and faith than in history. Here theologians share their important voice with good reason. Throughout history they have been concerned with matters of faith and life, and can provide a key bridge between the Bible and the sermon. This project does not supplant but rather supplements biblical commentaries. It assumes that preachers have already engaged in basic exegetical work. In other words, this volume starts where other resources may leave off, and arguably it takes preachers much further along the journey to sermons that meet deep needs of congregations at several interrelated levels: personal, communal, intellectual, spiritual, pastoral, emotional, missional, and ethical, to name a few.

A final distinctive feature of this project is the help it gives in fostering sermon unity. Some preaching resources offer an array of independent offerings each week that can make the sermon process confusing. They stimulate many thoughts and possible directions, but they offer little help in developing one, and the result can be evident in preached sermons. By contrast here, a natural flow connects the components for each Sunday entry: the assigned Bible readings from the lectionary lead to a theme sentence, and the theme sentence leads to each of the other elements. Because this unity and coherence were built into the process, preachers will find that the various elements readily connect with each other. They support a unified focus from the beginning of the preaching task, and they contribute to the final unity of the sermon.

The weekly entries begin with a précis of each of the assigned lectionary readings (Old Testament, Psalm, Epistle, and Gospel). This provides an overview of the lessons and identifies possible links between them. Nearly every book on homiletics worth its salt speaks to the importance of each sermon having one focus—whether a sermon is inductive or deductive, the listener needs to be able to say in a sentence what the sermon is about. An inductive sermon needs to lead somewhere specific, just as a three-point sermon needs to have a single overarching thrust. This kind of clarity requires discipline on the part of the preacher to do more than identify a single topic (like love or justice), and more than just ask a question about the topic (like what is love?), rather a complete sentence is needed that makes a strong claim about the topic (e.g. God loves without end). A **theme sentence** is required, a complete thought with subject, predicate, and object. For preachers who are imagistic thinkers, finding this kind of clear focus each week can be particularly challenging—they might rather compose the sermon, see where it goes, and then figure out what it is about; but by then it might be too late. Yet all preachers can struggle here, and all may benefit from having a clear direction right from the beginning of their weekly sermon labors.

An additional feature maximizes the potential helpfulness of the theme sentence. It focuses on a key action of God in or implied by the biblical text/s, thus God, in one of the persons of the Trinity, is its subject. This helps to ensure that God has a key role in the sermon and points the preacher and the congregation toward the help that God gives in meeting the challenges of postmodern living. The writers here identify an action of God that focuses on grace and empowerment, in order that the sermon may get to good news. In order for the theme sentence to be memorable, it is generally under six or seven words. The theme sentences are based on one or more of the biblical texts for a Sunday, normally the text/s that seem most in line with the liturgical season. No attempt is made here to harmonize all the lessons for a Sunday to make them say the same thing. A brief explanation connects the theme sentence to the details of a particular text/s.

Concerning **the key theological question**, the systematic theologians identify an issue that arises out of the theme sentence and the text/s. Anselm defined theology as "faith seeking understanding," and that applies no less today when there is so much that engenders puzzlement and confusion in our diverse world with its pluralistic cultures. Where helpful, our theologians identify a traditional theological loci or doctrine to which the theme sentence closely relates. For example, eschatology or teaching about the end times tends to dominate in early Advent. These theologians deal with key ideas in ways that the preacher can easily connect to the experience of the congregation—eschatology provides answers to the anxious question, "What's going to happen?" The theologians refer to the biblical text/s, but they do not write a detailed commentary, per se. Instead, they provide a theological reflection that goes beyond what many biblical commentators might say by engaging matters of faith, God's actions, and faithful life.

Local preachers are in the best position to make connections to pastoral needs, so in identifying **a pastoral need** we make a suggestion for preachers to consider. Who might need to hear a sermon on this theme sentence, and why? If a sermon speaks to one person's need, it is likely to speak to many. By contrast, if a sermon speaks to no one's need, it may not need to be preached. By imagining a person in need during the composition of the sermon, and including in the sermon someone in a similar kind of situation, the preacher can be concrete about what pastoral care to offer—what the biblical text says to such a situation. The pastoral need is a felt need, one that a hearer might identify for himself or herself. It is not one that the writer assigns, as when a preacher decides that on Trinity Sunday the people need to know about the Trinity—the felt need may actually be, "How can I know God?"[1]

God's actions towards humanity have implications for our actions towards God and neighbor. The **ethical implications** of a text are identified out of the theme sentence, inviting faithful discipleship and social justice as part of the mission of the congregation. What difference might this sermon make in individual or congregational living? What outcome or behavioral purpose does the preacher imagine this sermon to have in the lives of the hearers? Ethical considerations normally put a burden upon listeners, setting forth tasks they might do, and one danger is that they can have the effect of reverse miracles: they can turn the wine of the good news in the sermon back into water. In such instances the ethical demands become a new law about what must be done on one's own resources. Thus our writers also speak of God's help and empowerment. The ethical implications thus become invitations to new ways of living in the power of the gospel. They can even become expressions of the good news when connected to God in this manner. They are descriptive of the new creation that through the Spirit is already begun in Christ and will be fulfilled at the end of time. They are concrete examples of the kinds of action that individuals and communities might undertake in their specific contexts, yet they are typically more descriptive than prescriptive.

Finally, our writers address **the gospel implications** of the sermon, namely the specific links between a biblical preaching text and the larger Christian story. Some lectionary texts do this themselves, but they are fewer in number than we might think. This process involves looking for images, ideas, or echoes of God's saving action anywhere in the Bible, like the Exodus, and in particular to the central message of good news as it is found in Jesus Christ. The approach is akin to the ancient practice of typology, but in preaching on Jonah, instead of saying, "Jonah is a type of Jesus," a preacher today might say, "The truth that we find in Jonah's rescue after three days in the belly of the whale is the same that we encounter in Jesus Christ, who on the third day rose to set us free from our bondage." This can help remind listeners of the way in which Jonah's story is their own. Other parts of the worship service, like the hymns and prayers, can make clear the fullness of the gospel of God's saving love. Still, there is value in the sermon doing this.

The issue here is being as clear as possible about who is this God in whom we may trust. One can testify to the power of Jesus by preaching a text like Jesus healing the bleeding woman, but one can also stop short and not clarify for the congregation what that has to do with us. How is Jesus any different from a superhero in a comic book? Our basis for affirming that power lies in the resurrection that each Sunday celebrates: it is not the dead Jesus but the living Christ who encounters worshippers. In other words, the gospel implications clarify how a particular biblical text is a panel in a larger quilt, and they show how it links to the bigger pattern through image, idea, or echo. The gospel implications in the sermon itself might lead to a kind of joy or excitement that testifies to the hope God offers and where it is rooted. Since Jesus' life, death, resurrection, ascension, and Second Coming are central, what does this text lead preachers to say about any one of them?

The tools offered in this resource promise strong help for preachers and their congregations. Preachers able to nurture congregations through theologically grounded sermons are likely to be nurtured by that same Word they proclaim. By the same token, congregations hearing such sermons will find their lives transformed in the Spirit.

The theologians and homileticians who have contributed here have worked hard to establish excellence, drawing upon insights from recent scholarship in various disciplines with a view to enriching the theological contribution of sermons for many years to come. This is their volume and their gift to the church in the hope that preachers will consult it each week. I am very grateful to these writers who have brought not only their skill and knowledge to bear on their tasks, but also their patience and good humor in carrying them out. So much of my joy in working on this project has been interactions with them.

Readers may recognize that the various components structuring each entry have their roots in my homiletical theory, for example, *The Four Pages of the Sermon* (Abingdon Press, 1998). There, for purposes of sermon unity, preachers were encouraged to focus on one text, one theme, one doctrine, one need, one image, and one mission. I have treasured the friendship and guidance of editors Robert Ratcliff, Paul Franklyn, and Michael Stephens at Abingdon Press. They recognized the value of developing a theological companion to the lectionary that built upon those instruments with a view to feed the spirituality of the preacher and to deepen sermons. Their editorial work is a ministry that has been enriching to me and essential in bringing these volumes to completion. As always, I am deeply thankful to my wife, Deanna Wilson, for the patience, advice, and nurture she lovingly provides that helps projects such as this in so many ways. To Derek and Katherine Knoke go many thanks for much hard work in setting up the early stages of this project, sending the invitations, and coordinating the initial submissions. I am also grateful to Principals Peter Wyatt and Mark Toulouse of Emmanuel College, and to President Gooch and the Board of Regents of Victoria University in the University of Toronto for the kind support they have given in this endeavor.

PAUL SCOTT WILSON

GENERAL EDITOR

1. Excellent examples of identifying felt needs in relation to theological doctrines may be found in Shirley C. Guthrie, *Christian Doctrine,* revised edition (Louisville: Westminster John Knox Press, 1994), where each doctrinal issue in the table of contents is introduced by a question (e.g. for the Holy Spirit, "What's new?").

FIRST SUNDAY
OF ADVENT

THE LESSONS IN PRÉCIS

This first Sunday of the Advent season marks the beginning of the church year or liturgical calendar. While commonly thought of as the time of preparation for the Nativity, the Advent readings—with their stark and conflicting images of dark and light, present and future, destruction and reconciliation—point, rather, to a new way of marking time.

> *Isaiah 2:1-5.* The word of the Lord admonishes the people against violence—teaching, instead, the way of peace.

> *Psalm 122.* This hymn of praise for Jerusalem announces the city's security for the people and the prayer that its walls continue to offer peace.

> *Romans 13:11-14.* Paul calls the church of Rome to awaken and "behave appropriately" (v. 13) to be enveloped in the presence of the Risen Savior.

> *Matthew 24:36-44.* Without warning, both death and salvation come to us. Vigilance is required, for the unexpected is inevitable.

THEME SENTENCE

The Coming One awakens us. While violence, injustice, and criminality visit us without warning, the Lord also arrives without prior notice, bringing peace as well as judgment. The church's task is to hear and proclaim the assurance that we live always in close proximity to what ultimately saves us.

1

A KEY THEOLOGICAL QUESTION

First impressions ring true. A gesture, a scent, or a glance gives a clue to character that experience later confirms. Matthew's Gospel begins with Jesus' genealogy, an account guaranteed to induce sleep. Under closer inspection, however, some surprising figures interrupt the largely male litany: Tamar, widow of the wicked Er, who asserted herself against injustice; Rahab, a Canaanite "prostitute" who aided the Israelites; Bathsheba, wife of Uriah the Hittite and raped by David the king; and finally, Mary, mother of Jesus, a young woman pregnant out of wedlock. First impressions? Matthew's Gospel signals there is more going on here than meets the eye.

What should catch the reader's eye in a first encounter with the first Gospel in this first season of the liturgical year? Jesus' family, then and now, is not just for Jews. Just as "all the nations" stream "to the mountain of the LORD's house" (Isa 2:2), so Jesus' family includes outsiders, and the women underscore that openness. Some of them are not Jews at all, much less "good Jewish girls." Moreover, the genealogy leads not to Jesus but to Joseph, who was not even his biological father. First impressions caution readers to be alert when dealing with this Gospel, the guiding text in this new liturgical year. Advent's entire message is to pay attention. A season of vigilance, Advent marks the beginning of God's time.

The texts for Advent's first Sunday invite readers to think of God's time as a drama in four parts, that are like four themes. Act 1: Advent calls us to peace. While ordinary time seems to run in a straight line, liturgical time runs in cycles. While days, months, and years fall like pages torn from a book, the liturgical year follows a circular pattern, beginning with Advent, then moving through Christmas, Epiphany, Lent, Holy Week, and Easter, all of which lean into that long, green, growing season of Pentecost. The liturgical year ends triumphantly in Christ the King Sunday, only to begin anew with a Prince of Peace who comes to us again and again dressed in rags and born in a stable.

The peace that the prophet Isaiah promises keeps coming because people keep needing it. Like rats running a wheel, we circle back to war, resentment, and revenge. The psalmist speaks prophetically: "Pray that Jerusalem has peace" (Ps 122:6), a city still in conflict after centuries. Peace must come to us, because we will never find our way toward peace. We need Advent, because we need relief from our own war-torn souls. Advent returns us to the promise of peace, which comes to us, not as a treaty or command, but as a Person.

Act 2: God's invitation is persistent. God begins with invitation—again and again and again. Treaties dictate negotiation; commands require obedience; invitation asks only for an answer—and that answer is "yes!" The prophet Isaiah is so loved for his images—swords into plows, spears into pruning tools, lions lying down with lambs—that the reader almost misses his invitation. Again and again, Isaiah simply invites people to "Come." His repetition breaks down the resistance of a people too accustomed to conflict. Maybe this time, they will simply say "yes."

Indeed, God will not take "no" for an answer. Custom dictates that if potential guests decline an invitation, the potential host will leave them alone. Not so with God! God keeps coming back, pressing for a positive response. Each of the four weeks of Advent reissues the same invitation: "Come." If the guests could accept right away, perhaps Advent would only occupy a week in the liturgical year—and Christians could go on to other things. But it takes four weeks of repeated invitation to break through the schedules, appointments, jobs, and general busy-ness of people who find all kinds of ways of turning down the divine invitation. Yet, every time they open e-mail, check the answering machine, or go to the mailbox, there's the invitation. Eventually, the only appropriate response is "yes—I'll be there."

Act 3: God comes with urgency. The divine invitation is not just persistent; it is also urgent. If the positive proposal has no traction, God employs a counter-strategy. Gentle invitation comes clothed in negative examples—with consequences. God's speaks in paradox. Although the final message is peace, God's invitation now comes in our terms. The images of God's coming war with one another, and they arrest our attention: darkness and light, sleeping and waking, war and peace, ignorance and knowledge, one taken and one left behind, the coming of the flood—and the coming of the Christ. This summons is bracing, like a shot of espresso, and it catches our attention. Things come hidden beneath their opposite, great training for discerning a "Prince of Peace" who comes as a tiny child.

Advent's journey tutors us in paradox, for it is the first language of Advent's God. Advent dares us to find gentle invitation beneath its apocalyptic opposite.

Act 4: God's coming demands vigilance. Pay attention, stay awake, be alert! Advent has its own AAA membership: people need all of this encouragement simply to stay on the road. Our first language may be

Spanish or English, Bahasa or Swahili; we all need lessons in the language of paradox. We may think we know what God is saying, but Advent reminds us to look more closely. For example, Noah's contemporaries thought they were fluent in God's language. They thought they understood that they could live like there was no tomorrow. Then the flood came, and there was no tomorrow.

Advent pins us in the moment. Will we respond affirmatively? For all of its negative and positive images point to the same message: "Now our salvation is nearer than when we first had faith" (Rom 13:11). Live as those who have Advent's hope!

A PASTORAL NEED

Now is the time of year when people start to buckle under the stress of Christmas preparations, added celebrations, expectations of perfection, worry associated with gift-giving, and the pressure to be joyous. Adding to this weight comes the word of the Lord: "Keep awake . . . be ready . . . !" (Matt 24:42, 44). Too much!

Even more, notice that the three descriptions in Matthew of the day when the Human One (or Son of Man) will come are all negative. The flood came upon them while they were celebrating, suddenly people disappear, and the Coming One is likened to a thief, begging the question to what extent this savior is to be anticipated with dread! (Perhaps the menacing illustrations mean to appeal to the attraction we have for destruction? We perk up our ears more readily over conflict than to good news.) This is a time when the church finds its proclamation coming into its sharpest contrast to the culture's experience. God will do what we cannot do for ourselves.

What—in the needs of *this* community, *this* pastor, *this* time—is addressed by the urgency of these images? The preacher might dwell in meditations over why these frightful experiences are appropriate to the beginning of Advent in order to get at what lies behind the shadow underneath these doom-filled texts. In other words, preacher: Dig deeply into the images. God is concerned about human problems. Setting the jubilance of the "Christmas spirit" next to images that suggest the opposite is, in fact, a way of pastorally caring for the congregation because it does not side-step the realities of life.

ETHICAL IMPLICATIONS

The ominous nature of these texts carries a long history of creating apprehension and confusion. The rapture image in Matthew, in particular, creates divisions between people and churches. When scripture readings offer a familiar and difficult message, people want to hear the preacher's way of seeing it. This would be a good time for a preacher to prepare by reading a book like Barbara Rossing's *The Rapture Exposed* in order to set firmly in mind a larger context for interpreting these troublesome texts.

One aspect of the difficulty in these scripture texts is that the images are strong, decisive, and divisive. Based perhaps on popular theological understandings, it sounds like the "good" people will be taken to "heaven" and the "bad" people will be left behind. That last phrase—"left behind"—calls to mind the popularity of certain novels that have given flesh to a polarized version of reality. No such distinction—the righteous vs. the unrighteous—could be further from the meaning of the cross of Christ Jesus who gave himself for the redemption of the whole world. The wounds that have been driven into Christian witness by judgments based in this text demonstrate the need for continued healing. Because human sin has the capacity to compel us to measure the worth of individuals and render some less valuable than others, the church proclaims again and again that God is inviting all people to a place of mercy.

This is not a day to bypass the tough stuff lest the sermon deprive everyone of the most fruitful insights. The preacher can lead the way by wrestling with the hard questions, letting the meaning of Advent as a whole serve to set what is frightening into the context of God's inclusive love.

GOSPEL IMPLICATIONS

The gospel implications are found in what God is doing in that Sunday's texts. Today in Isaiah, God's word teaches the way of turning violence into what nourishes life. Making swords into plowshares and spears into pruning hooks creates tools for growing food—giving life—instead of tools for destruction. God's judgment and arbitration will "come from Zion" (2:3). There is no hiding from this inevitable shift in relationships between people with regard to technologies that can either harm or serve. God's desire for God's people will prevail.

In Matthew, the inevitable fulfillment of God's word is repeated in the promise that the Human One is coming. Because the images given for this arrival are negative, we may be tempted to think of the "coming" as a threat rather than a promise. But note how much that negative view conflicts with the image of the precious baby in the manger! Here again is precious paradox. The Advent season ushers the people of God into the new reality of the incarnation, which is the unfathomable power of the Infinite to enter into finitude. This awe-filled reality ought, rightly, to give us pause, and this Sunday offers the preacher an opportunity to attend to this coming as God's action, an event beyond our understanding.

Melinda A. Quivik
Martha E. Stortz

SECOND SUNDAY
OF ADVENT

THE LESSONS IN PRÉCIS

Images of earthly things—shoot, branch, root, wolf and lamb, a little child, stones, ax, tree, water, fire, shovel, grain—give heft and form to the themes of peace, hope, and justice.

> *Isaiah 11:1-10.* Peace is coming in a little child, and all the nations will ask who it is that fills the earth with the knowledge of the Lord.

> *Psalm 72:1-7, 18-19.* The psalmist sings a prayer, blessing the Lord who alone creates justice.

> *Romans 15:4-13.* Because disharmony keeps us from welcoming one another and living in hope, Christ Jesus ushers in the way of embracing Jew and Gentile together, those who "belong" and those who are left out.

> *Matthew 3:1-12.* Both the lowly and the presumptuous flee to John to change their hearts and lives and be baptized with water, but John confronts only the religious leaders with their presumptuousness.

THEME SENTENCE

Justice brings peace and makes hope possible. Three themes—justice, peace, and hope—are so intensely interwoven that none can stand alone without losing the thrust of the intent. That the "one who is coming" carries a shovel to sift the wheat from the husks is good news for the oppressed and for all who seek hope (Matt 3:11-12).

A KEY THEOLOGICAL QUESTION

One way to unite justice, peace and hope in preaching is to focus on pneumatology, on the actions of the Holy Spirit. Many people describe themselves as "spiritual but not religious," signaling their distance from organized religion and the fundamentalisms of the Right and the Left. These "cultured despisers of religion" (Schleiermacher) deal with the spiritual realm on their own, without scripture or tradition to help them discern the spirits (1 Cor 12:10). But there are a lot of "spirits" out there, some of them dangerous. How will they know they've latched onto "the LORD's spirit" (Isa 11:2)?

Isaiah offers some defining characteristics of the spirit: wisdom and understanding, counsel and might, knowledge, and the fear of the Lord. Isaiah tells Israel what the spirit does: judges the poor, decides for the meek, kills the wicked. Finally, he describes in vivid detail what life in this spirit looks like: "The wolf will live with the lamb, and the leopard will lie down with the young goat . . ." (11:6). Who would not yearn for that spirit?

This side of the eschaton, yearning is as close as we come. Hope bridges the gap between reality and Isaiah's idyllic vision. Occasionally, we catch a glimpse of "the world according to God," but hope sustains us. As Emily Dickinson put it in the title of her poem, " 'Hope,' is the thing with feathers," capturing both its vulnerability and its strength.

Often, hope gets pegged to concrete outcomes: we hope for that bike for Christmas, we hope for productive talks in the Middle East, we hope the troops will be home by Christmas. Hope for something fixes on outcomes, which change depending on the situation and mood. Christian hope, however, reaches beyond outcomes. Rather than hope *for* something, Christian hope is uniquely hope *in* something, more specifically, hope in someone. We do not so much have this hope, as the product of fierce focus or gritty determination or even deep faith, as this hope has us. The letter to the Colossians puts it perfectly: "Christ living in you, the hope of glory" (Col 1:27).

Christian hope takes getting used to, because it redefines both justice and peace. Peace no longer rests in the removal of settlements or the establishment of an independent security force or the end of genocide, all of which would be good outcomes. The world's peace can only be defined negatively by what is not happening. Biblical peace has the richness of relationship to a Person, who is himself the "Prince of Peace" (Isa

9:6). It's a lot harder to say what this looks like. The only thing to do is follow this person around.

In similar ways, biblical hope redefines justice. Biblical justice comes to us not merely as the end of injustice but through the richness of relationship to a Person, who wears righteousness as a belt (Isa 11:5). In his work among us, Christ took up our sin and gave us the righteousness of God, a life-saving transaction that Luther calls "the happy exchange," and the Apostle Paul describes in full: "God caused the one who didn't know sin to be sin for our sake so that through him we could become the righteousness of God" (2 Cor 5:21). Through faith in Christ and baptism into his body, we are made not simply righteous but "the righteousness of God."

At this point in the story, too many Christians breathe a sigh of relief: "Well, at least I don't have to worry about that any more. My sin is Christ's, his righteousness is mine. I'm home free." Not so fast! Let there be no talk of "my" righteousness in the world according to God. The "happy exchange" means that Christians now bear "the righteousness of God" in the world and to the world. We have work to do. Paul identifies it in his letter to the Romans. He states what has already happened— "Christ also has welcomed you"—then tells people exactly what that means: "So welcome each other" (Rom 15:7). As is so often the case with Paul, command does not come out of the blue. The indicative— the statement of fact, "Christ also has welcomed you"—grounds the imperative, "So welcome each other." Christians are empowered to do what God requires. Grace enables responsibility.

Moreover, the work of welcoming goes beyond cordiality, because we take our cues from Christ, not from expedience or Miss Manners or what feels comfortable to us. Christ's welcome to us was not "Hi, how are you?" It began with an invitation to follow; it forged disciples out of often clueless, unthinking followers; it ended with crucifixion and resurrection. The Greek word for Paul's "welcome," *proslambanesthe*, means to "befriend one another," as Christ has "befriended you." From John's Gospel, we know what this friendship involves: "No one has greater love than to give up one's life for one's friends" (John 15:13). Welcoming one another demands that we show to others the kind of full-body friendship that Jesus himself displayed in calling us "friends." We can never "pay back" what we have been given; we "pay forward" the blessings we have received.

This is the "spirit" behind Christian spirituality, the Spirit of God in Christ Jesus. Did we know what we were getting into at baptism, when we were washed with water and this spirit? We're probably as ignorant as the Pharisees and Sadducees who came to John. John doesn't mince words with them—or us. He uses fierce language and negative images to assure audiences then and now that the kingdom of God brings justice, peace, and hope beyond our wildest imaginings.

Let it be so!

A PASTORAL NEED

Accustomed as we are to defining peace in terms that are as tangible as the imagery in these scripture texts, what individuals, families, neighborhoods, communities, nations, and the world truly need is to know the peace that comes from beyond all understanding, tactile acknowledgment, and proof. This is the peace that God alone offers. It cannot be measured by taking stock of possessions or war budgets or the amount of leisure time one has acquired. In these texts, peace is not about something we can point to with assurance. Instead, it is the peace that Isaiah portrays in his impossible images. A wolf and lamb together? A little child is going to settle our strife? The pastoral need on this day is to imagine relationships without pain: the lion eating straw instead of running its prey to death.

To maintain peace, of course, something else is required, joining our efforts with the Spirit. "If you want peace," the slogan says, "work for justice." Justice manifests itself as right relationship, welcome, inclusivity, fairness, and equitable dealings with creatures and humans. Isaiah plants in our hearts the images that compel us to ask what we must do in order to move toward that peace. Paul offers, "So welcome each other," as an answer (Rom 15:7). And then, in Matthew, we hear the proclamation of the sure and certain baptism of repentance that, at root, is the beginning of answering all pastoral need.

ETHICAL IMPLICATIONS

Paul's prayer in Romans 15 is that those to whom he writes might "live in harmony with one another" (v. 5, NRSV) in order to glorify God. The goal is peace, and the interweaving of this day's themes is paramount in considering the ethical implications of these texts, but we must begin at some point to untangle them in order to know them.

We begin with justice, because harmony requires just relations. If the lion no longer needs to kill to live, and if such were the case with all creatures, the earth would see an end to the violence now required for maintaining life. When the church welcomes the outsider and defends those who are dismissed, ignored or maligned, all God's people are moved one step closer to equity. Being at peace with one another is possible where rights are not being trampled, where mutual respect is practiced, and where life abundant is available to all. Imagine!

Paul's final blessing is that the people might "overflow with hope" (v. 13). The body of Christ week after week is given and offers renewal to others by gathering to open the holy book and hear God's word, knowing that the people can "have hope through endurance and through the encouragement of the scriptures" (v. 4). What we hear this day is the call of John the Baptist to repent and be baptized. Changing hearts and lives is the door to preparing "the way for the Lord" (Matt 3:3). Without acknowledgment of sin and of need, the way of the Lord remains obscure.

GOSPEL IMPLICATIONS

As he calls for repentance, John the Baptist addresses the religious leaders with a question that is, in fact, for all of us: "Who warned you to escape from the angry judgment that is coming soon?" (Matt 3:7). From whom does this warning originate? How did you know to turn toward *this* response to the conundrums of life? Who, indeed, invites us to the cleansing and renewing water, the new beginning promised through repentance and forgiveness, the just reward fervently desired by those who are abused and oppressed? Who commands the in-gathering at the end of time? Who calls us to new life? The answer, as well as the question, is in John's words: one who "is stronger than I . . ." (v. 11). It is the One who invites all people, all creation, to a hope that transcends all our abilities.

Peace arises from the "knowledge of the LORD" (Isa 11:9) and in that, too, there lies a question. From where does this knowledge come? The earth, Isaiah says, will be full of this knowledge, but we do not know how the earth could be so rich with wisdom. How are we to understand this knowledge? Is it knowing *about* or knowing itself? We might be able to grasp everything and everyone knowing *about* the Lord, but can we imagine creation itself owning the Lord's *own* knowledge ("the earth will surely be filled with the knowledge of the LORD . . ." [v. 9]). The earth itself gives witness to God. Creation is a mode for knowing God. What else is the incarnation toward which we look all throughout Advent? Can we, as creatures ourselves, members of this creation, be full of what the Lord owns? By the power of the root of Jesse, all things are possible. This is the gospel of the Lord.

Notes

Emily Dickinson, *The Poems of Emily Dickinson,* Edited by R. W. Franklin, 1999.

Friedrich Schleiermacher, *On Religion: Speeches to Its Cultured Despisers,* 1958.

MELINDA A. QUIVIK

MARTHA E. STORTZ

THIRD SUNDAY
OF ADVENT

THE LESSONS IN PRÉCIS

While waiting and asking for hope, we are given relentless images of estrangement and parched life turned into deep relief.

> *Isaiah 35:1-10.* Sorrow and need are staples of life, but God makes healing and nurture the Holy Way.

> *Psalm 146:5-10.* The goodness of the Lord is extolled in all the ways that wholeness is created for those who are broken: the oppressed are given justice, the hungry are fed, the ill are healed. All of this is the work of the Lord.

> *James 5:7-10.* We await the coming of the Lord with patience, even as the prophets did: speaking "in the name of the Lord," the place of strength that enables patience.

> *Matthew 11:2-11.* We look for someone or something, hoping for deliverance, all the while being sustained by the realities of renewal in every quarter.

THEME SENTENCE

God sends the One who will provide refuge. All of creation lives with infirmities, uncertainties, and fears. Even the desert sands look for water. Need creates weakness, and danger threatens from all sides. But God's Holy Way is a sure refuge proclaimed by the prophets, John the Baptizer, and Jesus, who answers those still looking for evidence of healing and hope.

A KEY THEOLOGICAL QUESTION

The realm or kingdom of heaven is a key notion on this third Sunday in Advent, marking the midpoint of the season. Historically, it was known as "Gaudete" Sunday, a time set aside for some anticipatory rejoicing. The "kingdom of heaven" (Matt 11:11) is at hand. Matthew's talk of the "kingdom of heaven" distinguishes him from the other synoptic evangelists, who speak freely of the "kingdom of God." Speaking of "heaven" instead of "God" respects Jewish Christians who would have been unaccustomed to uttering the name of God aloud.

However, Matthew agrees with the other evangelists that this kingdom turns the world upside down. The texts tell of a series of reversals that the arrival of God's son will bring. A world turned upside down upsets usual expectations, challenges "the way we usually do things," and pours out wonderful surprises. Whatever one calls it, God's kingdom makes all things new.

The first new things are reversals of place. For the prophet Isaiah, the desert "blossom[s]" (35:1) with flowers and trees; wilderness and dry land, usually landscapes that evoke terror, fill with praise. Places of scarcity and danger suddenly become places of rejoicing. Like the psalmist—and all of the Bible's authors—Isaiah writes from a fierce landscape, a desert. In contrast, images of abundance always involve something lush and green. Had the scriptures been written originally in Ireland, for example, images of scarcity and abundance would have been quite different. Everything around the Irish monks was green on green from endless rains. They longed for a little sun. Indeed, when Irish Christians first read the psalms, the difference between the psalmist's desert landscape and their own stunned them. If they were reading these sacred texts, then the gospel had surely "reached the ends of the earth." The eschaton must be at hand!

The second reversal signaled in these Advent texts is a reversal for people, specifically the conditions of people who suffer. And suffering comes in many forms. French philosopher Simone Weil identified three dimensions of suffering: physical, social, and spiritual. In the world turned upside down, each of these dimensions is not only named, but redressed. Physical suffering, so often regarded as a matter of revulsion, receives healing: ". . . the blind receive their sight, the lame walk, the lepers are cleansed . . ."

Social suffering, which segregates people from human community, turns alienation into community: the hungry have food, the oppressed find justice, "the poor have good news proclaimed to them" (Matt 11:5). The psalm singles out three groups of people to whom the Lord pays particular attention: the widow, the orphan, and the immigrant. Again and again, the Hebrew scriptures target this triad of social sufferers as particular targets of God's compassion. This must have been comforting to a people like the Israelites, who were conquered and sent into exile. God had not forgotten them. But once they were restored to their land, they were commanded not to forget the widow, the orphan, and the immigrant. God expected them to show to others the compassion they had experienced: "Remember that you were a slave in Egypt . . ." (e.g., Deut 5:15, 15:15, 16:12).

Spiritual suffering makes God seem "absent," as Weil put it, at infinite remove. The ancients reckoned that physical disease and social alienation were far from the perfection of the divine. The incarnation proved the ancients wrong: God became human precisely to participate in the full range of human experience. Christ even experienced the "absence" of God, as his terrifying cry from the cross demonstrates: "My God, my God, why have you left me?" (Mark 15:34). When anyone suffering reaches this point of utter abandonment, she knows that someone else has been there: God in God-self, through the suffering of his son Jesus.

A third reversal concerns journey or path, and this stretches the imagination of twenty-first century disciples who have streets and highways that are lit, marked, and patrolled. Biblical "highways" were dangerous places indeed. Nothing was lit up, and travelers were easy marks for thieves—and appetizers for wild animals. People avoided leaving the safety of their homes at night or even during the day. Yet, Isaiah promises that the coming kingdom will change everything: " Even fools won't get lost on it; no lion will be there, and no predator will go up on it. . . . only the redeemed will walk on it" (35:8-9). For Christians, quintessentially a "pilgrim people," this is good news indeed.

The fourth and final reversal handles expectations, particularly our own expectations of the "king" of such a kingdom. The Gospel reading is particularly poignant, because Jesus challenges people's expectations of John the Baptist—"What did you go out to the wilderness to see? A stalk blowing in the wind? . . . A man dressed up in refined clothes?" (Matt

11:7-8). Jesus chides the people, even as he knows their expectations of him will also be way off base. They want a warrior, some Rambo from the Desert, who will bring military might to bear on the Roman occupying army. They want a prophet, someone whose words—even if they be words of judgment—would reassure them that God still cares about them, for the voice of the prophets had been silent for centuries before Jesus and John arrived on the scene. They want Elijah, because legend led them to believe Elijah would appear in the Temple heights before the Day of Liberation happened. People keep confusing Jesus with Elijah or one of the prophets (Matt 16:18), but here he echoes Isaiah to identify himself: "Those who were blind are able to see. Those who were crippled are walking. People with skin diseases are cleansed. Those who were deaf now hear. Those who were dead are raised up. The poor have good news proclaimed to them" (Matt 11:5).

Would we recognize Jesus among us today? Advent gives our eyes time to get used to a world turning upside down. Look for the reversals that mark God's inbreaking reign.

A PASTORAL NEED

At this time of year people need a refuge from the busyness of this season. By the third week in Advent, the time of the Christmas celebration is ever closer, and the work of preparing for the joyous time presses more keenly. The church may even be engaging in Christmas activities during the Advent season (not every congregation observes Advent), causing pressure on everyone to be ready with what is still being prepared. In many ways, the imposition of Advent (which is not-yet-Christmas) by its very timing is a gift that brings to the fore a lot of complexity that might otherwise be ignored. We feel in our muscles and bones—and certainly in our daily schedules!—what it is to live as people who have been redeemed and yet struggle with all the difficulties of life. We have been forgiven and promised unending life with our Lord, but we consistently fail to do as we intend and stand, therefore, in need of what we already have.

It is a confounding reality to live in this already-not-yet way. It is the Holy Way, in fact, and the pastoral need on this Sunday is to help the assembly stand in the desert—where water is not flowing—while also bathing in baptismal truth.

ETHICAL IMPLICATIONS

God sends to us One who provides the refuge that is needed, yet waiting permeates the texts for this day. For those who find their situation intolerable, the delay is only more torment. Isaiah and Matthew (through Jesus' words) name people who are blind, deaf, lame, terminally ill, and who do not have enough means to live. There are some people in our time who, having come to terms with a "different" ability (blindness and deafness, for instance) have come to speak of their situation as one that contains gifts other persons—those with sight and hearing, especially—cannot understand. They defend their own abilities as adequate, even special. This fact of our time makes the preacher's task a bit precarious. One cannot speak as if all "differences" are states from which a person is waiting to healed. Yet, death and poverty, oppression of all kinds, uncertainty, fear, pain, and loneliness, to name only a few, are encompassed in the hope that is raised by the prophetic word. That is what must be lifted up.

The sermon might focus, at least in part, on the attention paid to patience in James. The letter names the various gifts in the community that show the shape of waiting. They are common experiences. The farmer awaits crop growth (sure that it will slowly come). Patient people are not burdened by the irritations that arise but, like the prophets who live "in the name of the Lord" see beyond the moment, they work towards what is promised as grace.

The challenge is to speak of patience as a gift already given rather than as a state of mind which has yet to be grasped, and that is a matter of preaching the gospel rather than preaching to insist on behaviors that are very difficult.

GOSPEL IMPLICATIONS

The One who comes is the One whom we already know through the crucifixion and resurrection. The good news proclaimed in these texts is all about healing. The scope of the troubles named is broad enough that everyone who hears it can surely imagine being included in the words of Isaiah, "God will come to save you" (35:4). God will make rivers in the desert—bathing our hurts in cool water. But even more than that, implicit in the reason for the healing God desires for us is Jesus' assertion that the "least" (Matt 11:11) are even greater than the one Jesus holds in highest esteem: John the Baptist. Healing is social as well as physical and spiritual (see the theological discussion above).

The holy scriptures take primary concern for the well-being of the poor and powerless. Who are these "least?" We can readily point to those in greatest need, yet no one escapes the humility of being a creature of dust. "Humus," after all, is soil. The creation story in Genesis tells us God formed us from earth, and twenty-first century physicists add that we are, in fact (as well as legend!) made of matter from the universe. Not even the brashest, richest, most accomplished person can avoid the least-ness of dust.

The message of Jesus' crucifixion and resurrection—poignant for Christians to contemplate as Advent brings the church closer to the Nativity—holds within it, by virtue of Christ's place in the Holy Trinity, the profound implications of the incarnation: that we, poor creatures, are finally honored above all by the One who created, saves, and sustains all of us.

Notes

Simone Weil, "The Lore of God and Affliction," in George A. Panichas (ed.), *Simone Weil Reader*, 1977.

Melinda A. Quivik
Martha E. Stortz

Fourth Sunday
of Advent

The Lessons in Précis

Paradox confronts us most poignantly on this last Sunday of Advent. In the midst of desperation, the power of God to save is identified by Paul as having its source in death.

> *Isaiah 7:10-16.* Despite the fact that King Ahaz refuses to ask God for help through a sign, deliverance will come in Immanuel (God-with-us) and in the destruction of Judah's enemies.

> *Psalm 80:1-7, 17-19.* In a situation of great grieving, the people beg God, "Make your face shine . . ." (v. 3). They are certain the Lord has the power to give them life.

> *Romans 1:1-7.* Paul attests that the power that brought Jesus from death to life is the power that also calls the beloved to faith.

> *Matthew 1:18-25.* Joseph did not readily recognize God's hand in Mary's pregnancy, yet a messenger sent by God appears to him in a dream and rescues him from judgments that kill.

Theme Sentence

God brings life out of death. What occurs in our world appears often frightening and cruel, leaving us desperate for deliverance. God surprises us with varied means for release from impending doom: angels' appearances in dreams, defeat of enemies, and resurrection from death.

A KEY THEOLOGICAL QUESTION

Pilgrims need guidance and in this season of Advent pilgrimage, we might remind the gathered community of all the signs God has given of God's faithfulness, for God fulfills all of the promises and is worthy of all praise. This final week of Advent both summarizes and challenges the desires that draw pilgrims toward the manger. Medieval Christians developed a series of prayers that capture the human longing for a God who knows the depth of the human condition. Chanted for seven nights as darkness fell, the "O Antiphons" draw on images from the prophecies of Isaiah. Then and now, disciples recognize themselves in these prayers— and learn something new about the God they praise and address. These prayers identify for the church the significance of Jesus' birth. Each one speaks to a title of the Messiah and draws on a prophecy of Isaiah.

The prayers began on December 17th, calling for a God who is "Wisdom from on high," for then and now disciples knew ignorance, both the involuntary ignorance of simple naïveté and the deliberate ignorance of prejudice and hatred. This first prayer recalls the promise of a "spirit of wisdom and understanding, a spirit of planning and strength, a spirit of knowledge and fear of the LORD" (Isa 11:2).

The next prayer addresses God as "Master" or "Lord of might," for disciples always experience powerlessness, whether in the exile of the Israelites or the social, economic, and political disenfranchisement of oppressed peoples today. Isaiah assures all that God will "judge the needy with righteousness, and decide with equity for those who suffer in the land" (11:4).

The prayer on December 19 calls out to God as "root of Jesse," a poignant plea from people who find themselves ungrounded, whether they have been run off their ancestral lands or whether they feel psychologically or spiritually adrift. Isaiah promises grounding: "a shoot will grow up from the stump of Jesse" (11:1).

The fifth prayer pleads for liberation, asking for a "key of David" to unlock the doors, whether on a prison cell or the lockdown of addiction, doubt, or despair. Isaiah promises that "the LORD's ransomed ones will return" (35:10).

Calculated to fall on the shortest day of the year, the prayer on the sixth night begs for a "dayspring from on high" to illumine darkness, whether it comes from dead of night or from barriers of injustice. Isaiah invites people to "walk by the LORD's light" (2:5).

Then follows a petition to "the ruler of all nations"—not just this nation or that tribe—but a king who can win every war. The plea echoes Isaiah's prophecy that "peoples will stream" to the mountain of the Lord (2:2).

Finally, on December 23rd, the prayer addresses "Immanuel," God with us, capturing Isaiah's promise for the final week of Advent: "young woman is pregnant and is about to give birth to a son, and she will name him Immanuel" (7:14).

In the original Latin, these seven prayers form a reverse acrostic, the first letter of each word spelling "sarcore," the backwards spelling of the promise *ero cras* that means, "Tomorrow I will be there": *sapientia* or wisdom, *Adonai* or "lord of might," *radix Jesse* or "root of Jesse," *clavis David* or "key of David," *oriens* or "dayspring," *rex gentium* or "ruler of all nations," and *Emmanuel* or "God with us." These ways of calling out for God become suddenly familiar as the verses of the Advent hymn, "O Come, O Come, Emmanuel," a pilgrim's song for the journey of Advent. But beyond the medieval imagination, these prayers identify our deepest human desires today, as they cry out to a God who can address them.

And how God addresses them! We want wisdom and a God with a couple of PhD's, but as the Apostle Paul puts it to the smug, cosmopolitan Corinthians, "This world's wisdom is foolishness to God" (1 Cor 3:19). We want power, a God with clout, but God's "power is made perfect in weakness" (2 Cor 12:9). We get a king, but the "ruler of all nations" winds up crucified under a sign that mocks his royalty. If human desire points the way forward, why are our deepest longings shattered?

Dietrich Bonhoeffer remarked that "only a suffering God can help." God is with us, not so much by eliminating suffering, but by being with us in its midst. Immanuel does not erase human experience, but rather embraces it, blesses it, and offers resurrection. God calls out our deepest desires not to meet them but to transform them, promising "a new heaven and a new earth" (Rev 21:1).

The mystery of incarnation is itself a sign, pointing us toward resurrection. To stop the story at the manger mistakes the sign for the final destination.

Paul is the first evangelist, and he telegraphs the plot line of the rest of the gospels with beautiful concision: "God promised this good news about his Son ahead of time through his prophets in the holy scriptures. His Son was descended from David. He was publicly identified as God's Son with power through his resurrection from the dead, which was based on the Spirit of holiness. This Son is Jesus Christ our Lord" (Rom 1:3-4). Beyond the manger lies the hill outside Jerusalem; beyond the hill, the empty tomb; and beyond the tomb, the Great Commission. We get stuck on the command to "Go . . . and make disciples," but Jesus ends with promise: "remember, I am with you always" (Matt 28:18-20). This promise will be fulfilled in the same manner as the promises anticipating Christ's birth.

A PASTORAL NEED

The preacher can use Joseph's situation to explore how God's unexpected—even unappreciated and intrusive—ways throw God's people off track all the time, yet God brings life out of tough situations. Joseph's situation brings home the disorienting presence of this Savior child whose very existence threatens his mother and his earthly father. As a righteous man, Joseph's religious practice, his cultural expectations, and his notion of what is good and proper do not include this pregnant woman. Even when we are sure of our direction, we may be derailed by God!

Toward the end of December, those who are experiencing their first Advent without a loved one are in special mourning. Because it stands in such stark contrast to the jubilation of party-goers and children eager for presents, the sorrows of mourning are often suffered in loneliness during this time of year. The church has an opportunity on this last Sunday in Advent to hold what some have called a "Blue Christmas" or "Longest Night" service. (Internet resources can direct the liturgist to suggestions for shaping the worship.) It is typically a service of scripture readings, prayers, and hymns acknowledging emptiness and yearning, the memories that come with loss, and God's promises to be with us. It can be scheduled at any time during Advent: on Dec. 17 when the "O Antiphons" begin, the night before the last Sunday of Advent, or the evening of the Fourth Sunday of Advent (if that is not Christmas Eve).

ETHICAL IMPLICATIONS

Not only do our circumstances shift and catch us unawares, but we often speak of God's plans sending us in directions that we didn't dream of facing. Myriad ethical and practical questions surround the problem of amending our lives in order to accommodate these changes. We also wonder whether the changes visited upon us are really what God wants for us—whether they should be accommodated or fought against. Evil, after all, is a power that needs to be resisted. Ahaz questions whether to ask for a sign. For Joseph, the question is the substance of his own righteousness. He thought of a way to do the right thing "quietly" (Matt 1:19) but even that wasn't going to suit God's plan. The ethical question for anyone is, of course, what the right thing might be!

We are a people used to weighing our decisions on the basis of measuring the ethical choice according to what brings about the most freedom, the least damage, the best of something good (health care, education, urban and rural communities). We take surveys and polls, we gather data to compare over years or even centuries, and then we debate.

What, then, are we to do with the story of Joseph's change of heart coming from God in a *dream*? Joseph did not weigh evidence. The story doesn't mention outside consultants. Joseph was moved to stand by his betrothed on the basis of a whisper in the night. Not all ethical matters are suited to the empirically-tested (or politically motivated) strategies common in our time. Sometimes the least efficient—and potentially most painful—path is the most ethical. Sometimes the answer to an ethical conundrum is revealed to us by a sudden, inexplicable, other-worldly insight, perhaps by a voice in the head or the heart, perhaps in prayer.

GOSPEL IMPLICATIONS

Along with the significance of Joseph's change of heart being motivated by a dream, we note that in the dream, the first words of the angel's voice were words of comfort: "Joseph, son of David, don't be afraid . . ." (Matt 1:20). The gospel implications in the story of Mary and Joseph—finding themselves in a very strained, highly dangerous situation—center on Joseph's being undergirded by the assurance that he should fear neither the angel's voice nor the prospect of marrying a pregnant woman. He should fear nothing.

In the season when the scripture readings have enveloped the hearers with warnings and stern realities, a power coming without notice into the world to change it, suggestions of end-times and life arising from death, it is the brilliance of the lectionary choices over the centuries that gives to the assembly on this day the insistence that there need be nothing to fear. Immanu-el/God-with-us is a reality, already resident within finitude, born of a human being. Out of what is given to the human by God comes something "conceived by the Holy Spirit." That Spirit is not unfamiliar to us. That Spirit's grace and peace, as pronounced by Paul to the church at Rome, is ours this day.

MELINDA A. QUIVIK

MARTHA E. STORTZ

CHRISTMAS EVE/DAY, THIRD PROPER

THE LESSONS IN PRÉCIS

At last the awaited moment when eternity has entered, temporal time is upon us, and for a moment, because of God's gift, all is right with the world.

> *Isaiah 9:2-7.* "The people walking in darkness" (v. 2) with warrior boots and bloody garments describes earthly life which, out of its great need, is given the Prince of Peace.
>
> *Psalm 96.* In response to Isaiah's announcement, the assembly sings an ancient hymn of joy for the One who comes to judge with righteousness.
>
> *Titus 2:11-14.* The grace of God trains us to wait in hope through renunciation of all that keeps us from God.
>
> *Luke 2:1-14 (15-20).* Mary and Joseph go to Bethlehem where she gives birth to Jesus and angels reveal to the shepherds his true identity.

THEME SENTENCE

Into the darkness God brings a light of great joy. God addresses our inability to live in accord with what is good, whole, and peaceful in all spheres of human life—political, physical, and spiritual. God both confronts us with the veil that keeps us from understanding how to function and sends a savior who breaks our bonds, transcends the grip of human limitation, and frees us.

A KEY THEOLOGICAL QUESTION

One way to address Christmas is to consider the significance of the Christmas light. Isaiah spoke of a great light come into darkness. The glory of the Lord shines around the angels in Luke. In Matthew, a star guides the Magi. In the northern hemisphere Advent spreads across the darkest days of the year. In the past, without artificial light, people organized their lives around diminishing daylight. Night closed down all activities that demanded light. People either slept or came to "know the dark," as Wendell Berry puts it. The stars illustrated their favorite stories; the darkness teemed with spirits, inviting introspection. The late poet Audre Lorde observed: "The quality of light by which we scrutinize our lives has direct bearing upon the product which we live, and upon the changes we hope to bring about through those lives." What is the quality of Christmas light?

The familiarity of these readings makes Christmas light seem like the friendly twinkle of starlight. In fact, the season's light explodes darkness the way a bolt of lightning explodes the night. Christmas light is blinding, sometimes driving people back into a familiar darkness. The eyes need time to adjust.

Indeed, Isaiah's proclamation may not seem like "good news" to people used to walking in darkness. Once in the wilderness, the Israelites began to long for the "the pots cooking meat [of Egypt]," where at least they had enough to eat (Exod 16:3). They judged hunger worse than slavery, and they preferred their bellies filled, even if their backs ached. Finding themselves in that bright light of freedom, their eyes needed time to adjust. More important, their hearts needed time to adjust.

The shepherds' reaction to the bright light of Christmas, then, tells the truth of Christmas light: "They were terrified" (Luke 2:9).

The angel's comfort comes as a command: "Don't be afraid" (v. 10). These words become an ongoing refrain throughout Jesus' ministry. Again and again, he uses them to comfort followers terrified by the bright light of Christmas: "Fear not!" "Don't be afraid!" The only thing Jesus says more frequently are the words, "Follow me." This is not a coincidence. The balance has now shifted, the days are getting longer, the light will prevail. Then and now, Jesus' voice calls us out of darkness into his light.

Christmas light exposes power. Is this what dazzles us about Christmas light? You can read status in someone's posture, the cut of their clothes, the way they meet your eye, or don't—or can't. As Luke tells it, Jesus' birth comes in the middle of a census, so that "everyone throughout the empire should be enrolled in the tax lists" (2:1). An occupying army ordered the census, and the Romans were an unwelcome presence in a land promised to God's chosen people. Summoned to assemble with their extended families and children for the census, the Jews were vulnerable, gathered like sheep ready for the slaughter. The census reasserted Roman power. In Roman eyes, every male, whether child or adult, was a potential soldier in an army of resistance. The story of the Messiah's birth reflected the contemporary political tension, a reality that played out in the Messiah's death.

Christmas light also exposes particulars: the messiness of a room, dust on surfaces, dirt on windows, things that could be hidden in darkness. Christmas light reveals the scandal of the incarnation, God taking on human flesh. This "savior," the one who is supposed to redeem Israel of the house and lineage of David, does not arrive in Davidic splendor. He is born rather in a stable, probably more of a barnyard than the sanitized crèches we pull out every Christmas. The birthplace of the Christ reeked of ordinary life, and his visitors probably had to cover their noses. Salvation from a pigsty! No wonder everyone was asking Jesus: "Are you the one who is coming, or should we look for someone else?" (Luke 7:19). Christmas light exposes particulars—and the incarnation itself is a scandal of particularity.

In addition, Christmas light exposes people. Joseph's faithfulness shines forth, for he stayed with a fiancée who was already pregnant. Mary steps into the light as someone who trusted in an angel's promise. Despite their fears, the shepherds courageously come to worship a Messiah who shows up in the most unlikely of places and under the most inauspicious circumstances.

Finally, Christmas light exposes who God really is. Psalm 96 counts as one of the "royal psalms," fueling expectations of a king who would come in regal robes with full military accompaniment in order to establish justice among the peoples and peace between the nations.

What Christmas brings is a baby, not a king; who shows up in a manger, not a palace; who's wearing rags, not royal robes. Christmas light exposes a God who wants the full range of human experience from cradle to grave, not only the grown-up version. God takes on the full palette of human emotions, including the primary emotional colors of anger, fear, and despair. God meets us face-to-face and matches us experience-for-experience. The psalmist marvels that God comes to "judge the world with righteousness, and the peoples with his truth" (Ps 96:13, NRSV). Divine truth is present here on Earth; God knows the human condition.

Thanks be to God!

A PASTORAL NEED

On Christmas, the preacher has to consider both the astonishing good news of this time and the state of the assembly. With all of the clutter of this season people may not be aware that the hope for which we long comes from outside of us. The sanctuary may be full of excited and impatient children, parents juggling competing needs, relatives who do or do not like to be together, grandparents with eyes only for their grandchildren or who cannot hear what the preacher says, street people in need of shelter, folks without family, those in mourning, and some who have partied in excess. To preach well in this situation is to gather all of those disparate attentions into the manger with the child so that light of the savior shines on everyone. This baby makes everyone part of one family.

The birth of Jesus—the light of the world, Immanu-el, God-with-us—brings us together for good reason. With all of our differences and difficulties, we are in great need of hearing that none of us is alone in this universe and that God desires us to know the wonders of the incarnation. Most of the time we struggle with problems and answers that make plain the endless further difficulties we don't want to look at. Arriving even at a point where we can acknowledge together the needs in our midst, we are confronted with our helplessness in truly solving them.

So it is that at Christmas we receive joy, practice it, sing and breathe together. People speak of the "Christmas spirit" because it is a palpable experience: one time during the year when we expect blessings and we trust that love is real and eternal and that somehow we do all belong. It is an in-gathering in the best sense, and the sermon needs not only to *say* as much but also to *embody* it.

ETHICAL IMPLICATIONS

About the birth, two ethical matters stand out. First, as the stories tell us, the shepherds go to see the Christ promised by the angels, but instead of a venue befitting a savior, they find a baby born to a couple too poor and unconnected to have afforded a proper room. Christians have mined this story for centuries for the meaning in Mary's youth, Joseph's lineage in the house of David, their long journey to be counted in the census, their poverty and the treacherous situation of a pregnant, unwed teenager. Of all these matters, the humble quality of their experience is of overriding significance.

First, the inelegant circumstances of Jesus' birth find much in common with those who sought him out: shepherds whose work is among the lowliest and loneliest. The story directly aims the location of the holy in that which is not supposed to be anything special: a baby in a hay trough is the Alpha and Omega, the lamb who sits on the throne at the end of time. The homeless and hungry, powerless and voiceless among us are of utmost concern to the Most High God. To them is born this vision.

Second, however small the suggestions of their presence, this story makes clear that animals were present at the miracle as well. The child is laid in the bin that holds food for livestock and angels come to shepherds tending flocks. The birth is surrounded by all of creation—not only human beings but also the creatures who live and breathe beside us and by whose flesh and milk, wool and skins, we are given life. Christ Jesus is born in the place where God's creatures all rest and eat. Christmas, in other words, may be one of the best times for the sermon to speak of God's commitment to the salvation of *all* earth's inhabitants.

GOSPEL IMPLICATIONS

If the incarnation—God become human—is about anything, it establishes the deep connections between all things. Angels speak to earthlings, shepherds meet with a descendant of King David and kneel before a woman who has just given birth, animals give up their meal place, and heaven and earth belong together. This is a bold cry against the notion that heaven and earth shall never meet, that the body has no relation to the soul, that creation itself is irrelevant to God. It is no use to try putting thoughts into the heads of sheep, but there is on Christmas

Eve and Christmas Day a strong impulse toward understanding that the incarnation pulls not only heaven and earth but also *all* of earth together in adoration of the Savior.

The angel's words—"Don't be afraid! Look! I bring good news to you—wonderful, joyous news for all people" (Luke 2:10)—seem to be speaking of the Israelite people. But in the ensuing decades after Jesus' death and resurrection, our ancestors understood that the meaning of God-with-us includes the Gentiles as well as the Israelites. The light that shined in the darkness shines now with the same intensity—enlarged, expansive, encompassing—revealing that the good news has come for *all* of God's beloved creatures. This is the start of God's new creation.

Notes

Wendell Berry, "To Know the Dark," in *Collected Poems: 1957-1982*, 1984.

Audre Lorde, "Poetry Is Not a Luxury," in *Sister Outsider*, 1984.

MELINDA A. QUIVIK

MARTHA E. STORTZ

First Sunday after Christmas Day

The Lessons in Précis

Finally having arrived in the Christmas season itself, and only a few days after singing "Joy to the World," we encounter the slaughter of the Holy Innocents, with Joseph and his little family fleeing for their lives.

> *Isaiah 63:7-9.* God is present with the people of Israel and calls, protects, and saves them.

> *Psalm 148.* All creation—human, animal, vegetable, and earth itself—sings praise to the Lord whose "majesty is over earth and heaven" (v. 13).

> *Hebrews 2:10-18.* The "children" share flesh and blood with each other and also with Jesus Christ who became human, overcame death and continues to help those in need.

> *Matthew 2:13-23.* An angel in a dream warns Joseph and Mary to flee from the Massacre of the Innocents, and another dream warns them, on their return from Egypt, to go to Nazareth.

Theme Sentence

In the midst of the pain and injustice of this world, God calls, protects, and saves. The Nativity of Our Lord does not eliminate the tyranny and bloodshed of those who deal falsely for the sake of their own power. Lies and testing have not come to their end. But the crucified and risen Christ fulfilled the prophets' announcements that God uplifts those in need.

A KEY THEOLOGICAL QUESTION

This first Sunday after Christmas is a ripe time for giving praise. Though suffering and evil are not yet eliminated, in Jesus Christ their end is in sight. However, praise in the midst of trouble can be a difficult issue.

For medieval monasteries, the Great Silence began as the final office of the day ended. No one spoke, as the monks filed out of the chancel, up the night stairs, and into their dormitories. With the first office of the next day, they returned to the chancel, breaking the night's silence with a versicle from Psalm 51:15: "Lord, open my lips, and my mouth will proclaim your praise." They believed that if God opened their lips each morning, praise would pour forth. The last word spoken each night was "Amen"; the first words of the morning were words of praise.

A lot of things open my lips each morning: a call for coffee, loud worries about the weather, and always an awareness of "The List"— things left undone from the day before and tasks for the new day. I need to rediscover a monastic rhythm of silence and praise. These Christmas readings return us to our truest nature. We humans are hard-wired for praise.

The prophet Isaiah bursts out with stories of "the LORD's faithful acts" (63:7). The psalmist gives glory for a creation that includes "sea monsters" and "ocean depths," "fire and hail, snow and smoke," "mountains," and "every single hill" (148:7-9). The detail dazzles and delights: it's full-bodied, full-throated, full-speed-ahead praise. No created thing remains silent.

Yet in the midst of a symphony of praise, the readings register an undercurrent of danger. Christmas light casts shadows, and they are worth noticing. Even as he cheers, Isaiah hints at trouble between God and God's people. In the prophet's audience were people who felt the pain of God's absence; they wondered if God still cared about them. Isaiah's boast sounds so bold—"Truly they are my people . . ." (63:8). But only someone full of doubt would put the matter like that. Hebrews proclaims God's faithfulness, but the author protests too much. Both texts are written to people who fear God has forgotten them.

Matthew's Gospel delivers the starkest challenge to praise. Immediately after Jesus' birth, Joseph receives an angel's command to return to Egypt. This is almost as bad as being told his fiancée is pregnant. The Hebrew people languished in bondage in Egypt; the country represented "the house of slavery" (Deut 5:6). Even if Hosea prophesied of a Messiah who would rise up "out of Egypt" (11:1), the place was no vacation destination for Jews. Egypt neither welcomed nor liked them. The angel's command meant exile in a strange and inhospitable country.

But exile also spared the young family from Herod's cruelty. In an effort to eradicate political resistance, he ordered all firstborn male infants under two years to be executed. Matthew makes sure we remember the carnage, recalling Jeremiah's prophesy about "Rachel weeping for her children" (Matt 2:18).

The liturgical calendar will not let us forget. Christians celebrate the birth of the Christ in a week awash in blood. December 28 commemorates the slaughter of the "Holy Innocents," as they came to be known. Immediately after the birth of Jesus, December 26 marks the stoning of the first Christian martyr, Stephen. December 29 remembers Thomas Becket, the twelfth century archbishop of Canterbury who spoke truth to power and was slain by the king's men. The readings and the liturgical calendar hold together both praise and lament. How can this be "good news?"

So close after Christmas, the commemorations foreshadow crucifixion. They caution against domesticating Christmas and making the Christ over in our own images. Isaiah gets God's agenda exactly right: "My plans aren't your plans, nor are your ways my ways" (55:8). So what are God's plans? What are God's ways?

God's ways embrace both praise and lament, Christmas and the cross. One story interprets the other. The Christmas message plays against the background of cross and resurrection. If the Christmas message stood alone, it would be sweet but trivial because the message would not touch the reality of human suffering. Incarnation is the divine commitment to take on the full range of human experience, not just the good parts. The suffering of dying? God through Christ has "been there, done that," experiencing the slow agony of death by crucifixion. The agony of watching one's own child die? God through the Father has been there, anguishing over the death of his son. Our suffering has already registered on God's body. God is with us in the midst of our anguish. Because of this, Paul writes to the Romans: "I'm convinced that nothing can separate us from God's love in Christ Jesus our Lord: not death or life, not angels or rulers, not present things or future things, not powers or height or depth, or any other thing that is created" (8:38-39). Because of Jesus,

God-made-human, incarnation is the glue holding together both suffering and praise.

Cross and resurrection also have to be read against the background of Christmas, for Christmas clarifies God's incarnational intent. Julian of Norwich put it most succinctly: "Love was his message." God wasn't about substitution or debt or divine child abuse, as theologians across the centuries have argued. Love was God's meaning. God loved us enough to become one of us, a truth we understand only when we have given up all "our ways."

Suffering receives this rough grace because it hollows out the soul, making room for love. A young mother who lost a five-year-old to cancer put it this way: "It changed my life—jelled it in a profound way. I have an image that comes to mind about that time. It's of a white fire roaring through my life and burning out what was superficial, frivolous or unimportant and leaving a core of—I don't think there's any other word for it than love. A core of love" (cited in Ray and Anderson, 2000). That love is the source of our praise.

A PASTORAL NEED

Many people struggle to reconcile suffering in their own or other's lives with a loving God. They need to know that the presence of the one does not negate the other. Pastoral and ethical issues are intertwined in these stories because when we hear of the holy family's deliverance while being simultaneously horrified at the slaughter of the innocents, we must come to terms emotionally and intellectually with a God who does not simply cut down the Herods of the world. Isaiah insists that God knows God's people, calls, protects and redeems them. Yet, the Lord's angelic messenger comes in a dream only to Joseph. What of the parents of the other babies? That we give God praise while God does not stop the bullies, judge them, and make them pay is a huge tangle of contradictions to grasp.

We desire a simple answer, but the church's classic answer is complicated: God is good, God is omnipotent, and there is evil. The problem of theodicy (the origins of evil, which the church's answer means to address) is a theological, ethical, and pastoral matter. The disquiet engendered by images of God that frustrate our desire for justice infects all theological thinking. It drives people away from God, away from worship, and away from God's people.

On this day it is appropriate and necessary to teach about how to image God's deliverance of the holy family from Herod's slaughter. The sermon can speak of how we can give praise to God who seems to notice and defend only some people . . . and not others. This is a time when it would be good to talk about captivity to sin versus free will, and of Christ coming to end that captivity. We might also ponder whether suffering should be welcomed as a "perfecter," and what salvation means, among other matters.

ETHICAL IMPLICATIONS

The obvious problem on this celebratory day (we are *in* the Christmas season at last!) is that on this day we remember a terrible killing of babies. Herod stands for the powers of this world which, in order to keep and exercise their stranglehold on the people, condemn even children to death. Coming so soon after the Nativity, this sobers us up. We have rejoiced in a baby and now we see that this holy birth has meant the blood of others.

Preachers disparage the fact that this Sunday raises the ugly spectacle of a world not simply released from injustice and outrageous tyrants but the world we actually live in, where every day and every hour someone is being trampled by somebody else. How are we to sing our joy when we know what is happening even at this moment? *How* we are to sing is what we are given to practice on this day when joy and terror are juxtaposed with not even a breath to separate them. This day is an embodiment of the life of faith because we stand precisely *in the midst of* this world's injustices to sing of the God who does deliver us. None of us ever gets to sing praise to God from a context of realized and perfect freedom. God calls all people to give thanks *in* this world, where the song of praise transcends the pain even as it fights against oppression. Even in bondage God calls, protects, and delivers us. We do not praise a God who tolerates the oppression but one who feeds us even while troubles abound.

GOSPEL IMPLICATIONS

"He's able to help those who are being tempted, since he himself experienced suffering when he was tempted" (Heb 2:18). In a universe that is unimaginably vast, where we see no end to the struggles endured by humans, creatures, and the earth, and where no uniform understanding exists about what it means to be alive, it is enormous comfort to know that God understands our plight and has acted to address it. What has happened in the Incarnation anticipates both Easter and the Second Coming.

Could it be that that all around each of us are messengers from the One whose name alone is exalted? God speaks into our world not only with ideas and warnings but also with companionship and belonging. The message is always hope and peace. "Do not be afraid," we hear over and over from God's holy word. And it is not just that we hear the word of God calling us to praise and thanksgiving but also the Spirit, through the church—the body of Christ—gathers us, as well, to eat the word in the meal that brings us together around the table of fellowship. The good news is given to us, into us, and we are delivered into joy.

Notes

Julian of Norwich, *Revelations of Divine Love*, 1998.

Paul H. Ray and Sherry Ruth Anderson, *The Cultural Creatives*, 2000.

MELINDA A. QUIVIK

MARTHA E. STORTZ

EPIPHANY OF THE LORD

THE LESSONS IN PRÉCIS

Epiphany marks when the light of God in Christ is revealed to the world.

> *Isaiah 60:1-6.* The light of the glory of the Lord appears, and many nations and kings are drawn to him.

> *Psalm 72:1-7, 10-14.* This is a prayer for the king to flourish and to have all other kings bow down before him because he takes care of the weak and needy.

> *Ephesians 3:1-12.* Paul talks about how the "secret plan" (v. 3) of Christ was revealed to him and how he, as a servant of the gospel, wants to "reveal" (v. 9) this same plan.

> *Matthew 2:1-12.* The magi seek the king of the Jews because they see his star rising in the East, but King Herod is frightened by this.

THEME SENTENCE

Christ's revealed light draws others to him. This is evident through Isaiah, Paul's own experience and desire for his ministry, and the magi seeing his star.

A KEY THEOLOGICAL QUESTION

The Gift of Revelation. The hidden God has been revealed. This is the central theme of these texts for Epiphany. They point to the tremendous gift of God's revelation. That gift brings illumination, direction, and clarity even as it confirms the mystery of God. The idea of revelation captures several important aspects of God's interaction with us, (a) our inability to see and to follow God, (b) the real history of God with us, and (c) the emergence of a new governing reality in our lives through God's Son, Jesus Christ.

The theological conversation about revelation has focused too often on whether or not people have innate abilities to know God when the more decisive point of divine disclosure is on the action of God toward us. God wants to be known, and the knowledge of God is bound up in a real history of deliverance, forgiveness, and redemption. God's presence brings light. This is the truth that was known in and through Israel. It was in a sense hidden in Israel and sometimes hidden to Israel. Israel learned that even when God was present in their midst, God was incomprehensible. God was still mystery. God's ways were not as understandable as human ways, even as God was revealed in protective, merciful, and caring gestures in Israel. God's hiddenness in this regard means more than invisibility. It points to the radical distinction between the creator and the creature, a distinction that shows our inherent weaknesses. We are sometimes blinded by too much light, distracted or lose focus, apprehend poorly what we see, close our hearts when they should be open, and move in the wrong direction. Yet even as Israel struggled to live in the light of divine presence, it was a light to the world, a light to the Gentiles. Israel was a reflecting light that revealed a God who shows us ourselves and who wishes to guide us.

Peoples grope in darkness. This is not a derogatory assertion about any people but recognition that all peoples follow paths they believe best for survival, well-being, and power. Often their leaders lose their way, become blind with power, and oppress their own people or fail to care for the least among their people—the poor and needy. Sometimes peoples follow the path of violence and war, believing that their security and strength demand they take up the power of death to establish their future. Divine revelation speaks precisely to this groping, this hopeless following of our own nationalistic, clannish cunning. God's disclosure, which was woven in stunning mystery first in Israel, was definitively found in a baby born to a young Jewish woman. God's revelation event takes a trickster form—God is found where we would not expect God to be found, where in fact we would have missed, walked by, had not God indicated by a star that here was the beginning of light, clarity, and a way forward for all peoples.

Wise people of other nations have read the signs of God but do not know where God is to be found. This clarifies for us the question of who knows God. All may read the signs of God but only those who follow the star and come to the hidden place of divine presence will find God. Even Israel's leaders are taken by surprise, and they too must search to see the God who is present in their midst. God will of course aid in this search not by divine fiat but through his Son, born of Mary. Here we confront the weakness of revelation and the strength of our blindness. God appears in fragile body, in the proximity of mud and defecation, near offensive smells, among animals, and in an undesirable shelter. God is found in an unimpressive family, as its son who speaks of God his father and with authority beyond that of the rabbis. Most people would and did reject such divine revelation because it looks false, charlatan-like, and certainly not royal.

God's disclosure, therefore, is most often opposed in human lives by false images of how we believe God ought to look and act. These imaginary divinities are powerful. They are pure, seemingly always in control, logical, even clerical, proposing a divine activity that is almost mathematical, formulaic, and governed by eternal principles or laws. These logical gods clothed in cultural and social particularities make sense to peoples and make the real actions of God seem nonsensical and untrustworthy. Thus God's revelation must struggle against gods, not only the gods of this world but also the gods we constantly create in order to find a god who makes sense to us. This was indeed Israel's struggle, and it is our struggle. God, however, was not repulsed by the creature's struggle, and provided light for Israel in the midst of it. The great mystery has been revealed to us. God has also provided for us in our struggle to see, to know, to understand how to live in this world.

Through the weakness of God's Son, guidance has come to us in this world. The ways of nations are now revealed as folly and as failure masquerading as success, vaporous clouds mistaken for solid mountains. No people know where they are going. All are driven by markets and machines, political maneuver and counter-maneuver. Only Jesus Christ can direct us in light toward life and in life toward light. Yet the work of revelation in Jesus is participatory. Just as Joseph and Mary were caught up in this work, so too was Paul and all those who follow the savior. Each gives the gift of revelation as it was given to them.

A PASTORAL NEED

Sometimes life is so dark that one cannot clearly see the light of God. Life's hardships can blind one to God's presence or cause one to think every discerned light is God. A person in the dark may be drawn to a light, only to find it is a car's headlights driving in their direction; they will soon be run over by the weight of the world. At times, people may feel as if they cannot get a break from ongoing pain such that they ask, "Where is God?" They cannot see clearly because their suffering blinds them.

A child who endures constant physical or sexual abuse at the hands of their parents might wonder where God is during their plight. Adults being trafficked for sex across the globe might not see a way out, a light at the end of the tunnel of their existence. God is nowhere to be found through their eyes. Many people suffer from "the strength" of blindness as they live with pain that wearies them.

Rose, a parishioner, and I were sitting in a restaurant sharing a meal together. She began telling me about her relationship with her husband over the years and how he had abused her and her daughter. Yet, she remained married to him. At one point in the conversation, after hearing the horrific stories and seeing the tears of pain drop from her face, I said to her, "that's not living." Rose responded, "I died a long time ago." Her suffering was so great that she joined the contemporary cloud of witnesses who make up the walking dead. She could not see where God was.

For those asking, "Where is God?" it will be important to reveal in the sermon how God reveals God-self in weakness, suffering, fragility, and, in general, in places where one would not expect God to be found. This may shed some light on the presence of the divine light in various experiences of human darkness and suffering.

ETHICAL IMPLICATIONS

The light of God in Christ draws people towards God, and this light can be shared with others, just as the apostle Paul desired. Divine light does not have to be forced on others because it draws others towards truth, justice, and love. The light of Christ is a gift for the world.

On August 28, 1963, before the Lincoln Memorial, Dr. Martin Luther King delivered his now famous speech, "I Have a Dream." This speech was a gift for the world. One of his dreams that he declared was that one day his four little children would "live in a nation where they will not be judged by the color of their skin but by the content of their character." This is probably his most well-known public speech. Why is that? Perhaps, this speech was an expression of the light of God in the world, and that divine light draws people to it. People continue to be drawn to King's dream because it shines with the light of God. People will be drawn to the light of God in Christ, which is truth, justice, and love, like the magi were drawn to the rising star in the East. The gift of the light of God given to us needs to be shared. When a community experiences the light of the glory of God, it should be emboldened to sing with their actions, "This little light of mine, I'm gonna let it shine."

GOSPEL IMPLICATIONS

A sermon focused on the revealed light of God in Christ that draws others might do well to explore the unexpected ways of God. God came as a humble baby among animals. God came as a different kind of king—one that reigns with selfless love, not intimidation tactics. God's light surprised and frightened some people because it was unexpected. Not everyone understood God's revelation, and some wanted to get rid of it. God's apparent weakness in the eyes of some was actually strength. This God did things differently from the norm.

This Light of God shined even in the darkness of a cross on Golgotha's hill. This King came to die and embraced a gory glory. This Light kept shining in hell and shined all the way through the resurrection and ascension. This Light of the world is shining today. But he may not shine and demonstrate his glory and power in the way everyone expects because this Light still has scars in his hands, "standing as if it had been slain" (Rev. 5:6). The revelation of God shows us that what we expect from and of God is not always what we get. But what we get is exactly what we need.

LUKE A. POWERY

WILLIE JENNINGS

BAPTISM OF THE LORD (FIRST SUNDAY AFTER THE EPIPHANY) [1]

THE LESSONS IN PRÉCIS

Baptism points to the baptismal anointing of Jesus Christ as the Son of God.

> *Isaiah 42:1-9.* God anoints God's servant, a light to the nations, with the spirit to do justice.

> *Psalm 29.* This psalm speaks about and depicts "the LORD's voice" as powerful and majestic (vv. 3, 4, 5, 7, 8, 9).

> *Acts 10:34-43.* Peter says that he and others are witnesses to the message of Jesus Christ, about who Christ is and what Christ has done after his baptism by John.

> *Matthew 3:13-17.* John baptizes Jesus with water, but the Holy Spirit also descends on Jesus and baptizes him as a voice from heaven claims him as Son.

THEME SENTENCE

God anoints his servants with the Spirit. In Isaiah, the anointing of the spirit is linked to service. In Acts, Peter links the anointing of Jesus by the Spirit with powerful acts. In Matthew, the descent of the dove will lead to Jesus' temptation and ministry.

A KEY THEOLOGICAL QUESTION

Jesus is baptized. His baptism occasions his anointing by the Spirit, which establishes the baptism of Jesus Christ as the source of our baptism. His baptism draws our lives into the great journey of his life, the purpose of his work, and the power of its effects on the cosmos. His baptism is different from ours, yet together with his death and resurrection, it also makes possible the reshaping of our lives such that our identities are irrevocably bound to his identity. These texts point to God's actions in anointing and God's work that will be done through God's anointed, and in so doing bring us into the inner workings of Christology in association with our justification and sanctification.

God's servants are marked through anointing. The Isaiah passage reminds us that God places the Spirit on the ones God chooses. It is a choice that defies any natural selection. The divine electing is always a matter of grace that unrelentingly points back to the freedom of God for us. Anointing then is a sign of divine condescension in which God commits, even risks holy work by placing it in the hands of fragile flesh. Through anointing, human beings are made bearers of the divine will and are taken on a journey the contours of which they cannot anticipate and the end of which they cannot see. Only faith follows from anointing.

Anointing is bound to the purpose of transformation. God wills to fundamentally change the social order by bringing justice to people and justice between peoples. This divine hope was first pressed into the life of Israel, whose prophetic existence announces the creator's claim on the creation. Indeed divine hope is embodied in incredible contrast—the awesome and powerful voice of the Lord as depicted in Psalm 29 is expressed in small, unintimidating, often unimpressive, anointed voices. Through Israel, God announced a new thing, light for the nations and freedom for those held captive. Such light and freedom seem too good to be true and therefore press our imaginations to see them as hopes for another world, either of a future world or an unseen spiritual state of existence. Yet it is precisely the baptism of Jesus and his anointing by the Spirit that reverse the streams of our imagination toward the real flesh of Israel and the real body of God's Son.

Jesus' baptism was not the first baptism, nor was it an innovation in the ancient ritual. Nor was it an exemplar of baptism in human history. It was the occasion in which God detoured the ritual, drawing it to the life of the Son and forever marking it, when done in acknowledgement of Jesus' life and work, a sign of God's own life. Baptism is the occasion of marking, the sign to us and the Spirit of God that here is a life ready to be led, ready to be guided into its destiny. Baptism says, "A servant is here: Come, Holy Spirit. Take this life and form it into an instrument of righteousness." In baptism we die to our old self and rise to our new. This is the redemptive pattern established in the body of Jesus. This is the redemptive reality enabled by the life of God's Son.

There is a proper selfishness, a necessary exclusivity in God's anointing. It now belongs solely to Jesus. The anointing of the Spirit on Jesus confers less possession and more his position. God the Father acknowledges Jesus the Son as the One who is beloved. From him flows the authentic and pure love of God into the world. From him God's claim on Israel reaches back to its beginning, and from him God will claim afresh a wayward world, a creation held captive to the power and fear of death. Yet the anointing of Jesus in the context of his baptism also introduces us to the triune life of God. God's Son reveals the Spirit as much as the Spirit gives witness to the Son.

We give witness to this life, to God's life in the world. All those who follow Jesus in baptism and do his will enter his anointing, know the presence and power of the Holy Spirit, and yield their bodies to the transforming work of God in the world. It is no accident that many people associate the anointing with the absolute miraculous power of God in the world, because it is precisely under the anointing that Jesus revealed God's power to thwart the machinations of the evil one. And we who have experienced the anointing through baptism are taken up in this redemptive witness. Our lives join Jesus' journey, and here we enter into our justification and sanctification (1 Cor 1:30).

Jesus justifies us and sanctifies us on the journey. Our life journeys inevitably involve the struggles against a false self that wishes to entrap us in histories, purposes that would define the vision of our future, and false systems that wish to channel our energies and hopes toward building that futile future. Yet through his death and resurrection Jesus opened up a new path away from moribund self and death dealing system. So now by the Spirit we too are led by way of the cross to God's emerging new world. In this new world born of the waters of baptism, Jesus judges the quality and character of our lives, adjudicating life-direction and life-strategy. He turns our lives away from becoming fragments of worldly achievement toward the whole witness of disciples who live under the

Spirit's anointing. We live between those who have followed him (saints) and those whom he seeks after (sinners), sharing with them both the forgiveness of sins and the freedom from condemnation.

A PASTORAL NEED

A sermon related to these texts might serve as an opportunity to meet the needs of those who feel disempowered in society. Even baptized Christians at times doubt they can do anything to make a positive difference in the world. They have been sprinkled by or immersed into the waters of baptism but perhaps view it only as a powerless ritual. However, to discuss the baptism of Christ as our baptism and how baptism is linked to empowerment by the Spirit might help one re-envision the spiritual potency of baptism.

The same Spirit that anointed Jesus anoints us in baptism, and this baptism immerses us into service and ministry in the world. To preach baptism as divine empowerment may help those who need to recognize that they can make meaningful contributions in church and society. To preach baptism as God's anointing may help "Christians" to live out that title as the "anointed ones." To be anointed by God's Spirit means that we, with the power of God, can meet real needs in the world as an "instrument of righteousness." To be anointed by God's Spirit means that we have been graced with powerful gifts to challenge those systems that disenfranchise and demoralize the least of these. As baptized Christians, there is a power within us that the world did not give and the world cannot take away.

ETHICAL IMPLICATIONS

God anoints us with the Spirit through baptism, and this anointing is not just for us to hoard in a spiritual social club. Our baptism is linked to mission in the world. We are anointed to do something. Isaiah shows us that the servant is anointed with the spirit *to do* justice. Baptism is not just a little sprinkling of water or full immersion in a pool; baptism is being plunged into a new way of living, being, and acting in the world. It is connected to social responsibility and service towards others. One's conversion to Christianity, signified in baptism, converts; it literally turns one towards God, and this turn to God is also a turn to the other. The invisible grace of baptism becomes visible in outward service.

Our baptism is not just for us, but for others. We are "Holy Ghost" baptized to be a blessing to someone else, to serve church and society. Baptism is interlocked with an ethic of generosity. Thus, it is not just about a baptismal rite but right action, not just heavenly-minded but earthly-good, not just spiritually-ignited but socially-engaged, not just personal piety but social witness, not just the water of the Spirit but the work of the Spirit. The anointing of baptism comes with the Christian responsibility to serve. Dr. Martin Luther King lived out his baptism by dying while fighting on behalf of sanitation workers in Memphis, TN. How will you and your congregation live out your baptism?

GOSPEL IMPLICATIONS

Christ's baptism is akin to our baptism, they both mark anointing by the Spirit. We are not only anointed with the Spirit to serve the world but we are also claimed as God's sons and daughters, as God's servants. Baptism marks us as God's children and makes us witnesses to God's kingdom in the world. The baptism of Christ empowers us to be and do according to God's divine purposes. But we should also be aware that if Christ's baptism is our baptism, death and life are involved. We die in baptism, being crucified and buried with Christ, but also we live through baptism, being raised with him (Rom 6:3-11). In other words, we are "dead . . . but alive" (Rom 6:11).

LUKE A. POWERY

WILLIE JENNINGS

SECOND SUNDAY
AFTER THE EPIPHANY [2]

THE LESSONS IN PRÉCIS

Epiphany is about the revelation of God in Christ, and in these texts, God reveals God's faithfulness to humanity.

> *Isaiah 49:1-7.* God forms the servant in the womb and calls him to be a light to the nations.
>
> *Psalm 40:1-11.* The Lord delivers the psalmist, who therefore testifies about God's faithfulness and asks for continued help.
>
> *1 Corinthians 1:1-9.* Paul gives thanks to God for the grace of Jesus Christ given to the church, and affirms that God is faithful and will strengthen them.
>
> *John 1:29-42.* After John testifies that Jesus is the Lamb of God, the Son of God, Jesus calls the disciples and says "come and see" (v. 39).

THEME SENTENCE

God reveals God's faithfulness. The servant in Isaiah, the psalmist, and the church at Corinth are not forgotten. God's faithfulness is shown to them.

A KEY THEOLOGICAL QUESTION

The Faithful Word of God. God speaks. These texts give witness to the character of the Holy One's faithfulness to humanity through the word. Through word and deed, God interacts with us and in so doing gives us sight of the divine life. These texts touch on the relation between the creator and the creature as well as the role of divine agency in history. They point us away from the ideas that God maintains mechanical-like control over the world or that the world is an autonomous machine lacking divine involvement. The actions of Israel's God powerfully reveal God's desire to come to us, speak with us, and live with us.

The Isaiah passage depicts godly desire that reaches back before our birth. Indeed the life of that prophet was immersed in the calling of God to humanity. Before birth the desire of God to speak to us directed this life. The prophet becomes God's vessel of disclosure. The divine word gives shape to a life, and a destiny is formed in the work of communication. God's desire to speak and be heard by the people of Israel is the basis of election, both of the prophet and of Israel itself. The content of that revelation will always issue in deliverance by inviting the hearers to a place of intimacy with God. The words of the psalmist remind us of the currency of our relationship with God, speaking and hearing, hearing and speaking.

Sacrifice and offering only set the stage for and finally give way to this crucial exchange—words spoken, words heard, and words spoken in response. These are the vital matters. God's desire for communication with us must never be misdirected through ritual. Ritual is in service to the speaking and hearing. Only by that service may we gauge liturgy's holiness and purity. God hears the cries of anguish, despair, and loss. God's response does not mean the end of cries, whether in complaint or anger, but rather their merger with the additional sounds of praise in the mouths of those who suffer and those who live near the sounds of suffering.

The sounds of praise reveal God our creator. They are never inconsequential words. They expose the character of God as faithful and caring, always suitable for anthropomorphic gesture: God leans over with a hand cupping the ear, listening to his creatures. And then God speaks yet again, and then the hearer is compelled to speak. The hearer-turned-speaker is a vital part of an epiphany, the revealing. The hearer tells of God's saving help and sings of undeserved mercy. And yet the hearer also pleads for more help, more grace, and more deliverance. The cycle is complete—praise to plea, to praise to cry, to songs of deliverance, to more calls for help. This is the way of the creature with the Creator, life with the speaking God. We are allowed to be caught up in the continual communication. It is gift, and it is life. It is word bound up with flesh so that flesh might forever carry word.

The heart of this matter brings us to the definitive revealing of the divine speech in Jesus Christ. Jesus of Nazareth portrayed in the Gospel of John presents the world's history as first the Word of God in history. John the Baptist went ahead of him, announcing his imminent appearance. Jesus will be found in and through the speech of John. Here we see the divine condescension. God will be an agent in history who becomes the subject of other's speech even as he speaks, God's words flowing with the words of others. This is risky because the divine word now fully enters into competitive discursive space where other words may contradict, deny, or supplant the words of this man of Nazareth. John, to our great benefit, points to Jesus, this Lamb of God, and John's own disciples are turned toward Jesus. True words of witness always yield to the words of Jesus. They always turn us toward his definitive words. Yet Jesus does not destroy our voice or cover it over with a voice that sounds like majestic streams.

Jesus depends on our voice, our words of witness. The disciples of John become the disciples of Jesus in the precise moment they begin to speak of him and draw others to him. They offer commentary on the body of Jesus: This is the Christ, come and see him. The cycle continues. Jesus speaks, they listen, and then they speak. God, who from the earliest days of ancient Israel was caught up in this cycle of address-hearing-response/confession, now enters the time of greatest weakness. The Son of God will be subject to the currents of speech, of being named and naming, of being spoken about and speaking, of waiting to be heard and hearing. These are the essential elements of epiphany.

The epiphany of our God will take place through these essential elements. In the midst of a cacophony of voices, the divine word will be heard. There is no formula for the Lord's epiphany. It is fundamentally a happening, an event which takes place in the middle of testimony, debate, and appearance. The Apostle Paul confirms this truth for us. He like the other disciples understood his life to be immersed in the cycle of communication. God has been revealed in Jesus and will yet be revealed through the lives of saints who give witness to the grace and peace granted through the Son of God. Even so we seek each day sight of the divine life and wait patiently for the Lord's return.

A PASTORAL NEED

When God reveals God-self, we learn that God is faithful. This is a part of God's character. As is said of Christ, " 'if we are disloyal, he stays faithful' because he can't be anything else than what he is" (2 Tim 2:13). For this sermon, that would be a critical promise to promote—God is faithful eternally. In an age where commitment does not seem to matter much and where promises are not often kept, knowing that God is faithful to promises is good news. Knowing that God will do what God says gives hope to those who have experienced faithlessness on every hand.

Perhaps, faithlessness manifests in a marriage that ends in divorce (though not all people who are divorced have been faithless). Perhaps, it manifests in the economic corruption scandals of big corporations. Perhaps, it shows up when certain "liberation" leaders of countries mistreat their own people in the same manner as the colonizers did when they were in charge. Faithlessness can reveal itself in big or small ways, even when a friend or coworker does not follow through with what they said they would do. People are often let down by others (as Peter in our lesson will eventually let down himself and Jesus), but God is always there to lift us up. God is not like humanity because God remains faithful forever.

ETHICAL IMPLICATIONS

When God speaks, we hear and then respond with speech and action eventually. Our response reveals whether we actually heard rightly. God's word is faithful in that God fulfills promises spoken. God delivers on God's word. In light of this divine faithfulness, disciples of Christ should witness to this faithfulness by following through on our own promises and words. By doing so, we avoid faithless foolishness and demonstrate our faithfulness to God and to others. Just as God embodied or enfleshed his word, we should do the same. If we say we love our neighbor, we should show our words in the flesh, in action, for as with Jesus, the Word of God, "it is word bound up with flesh so that flesh might forever carry word." Christians witness with embodied, fleshy words.

Clackston was a member of the Church of the Holy Comforter in Atlanta. I did not know that was his name at first because when you first met him and asked him his name, he would just say, "Get out of here, get out of here." He said that because he came to believe that was his name as everyone told him—"get out of here." Rather than "get out of here," being faithful to the mission of God in Jesus Christ, one would say, "Come here. God loves you and so do I." Being faithful means that we have to walk the Christian talk and put flesh on our words.

GOSPEL IMPLICATIONS

The faithfulness of the word of God is revealed when God becomes flesh, one of us, human. Divinity takes on the frailty of humanity for the life of the world. This Word is not just spoken but does something, enacts love, grace, and mercy for the whole wide world. Preaching as the Word of God is still a significant sacramental act in the Church and through the hearing of the word spoken, faith comes (Rom 10:17). The Word and words do things. We should not take this for granted and underestimate the power of the Word. This Word heals. This Word delivers. This Word saves. As John the Baptist testifies, "Look! The Lamb of God who takes away the sin of the world!" (John 1:29). This Word died for the world and preached about his love for us with his broken body and dripping blood on a cross. This Word could not be stopped and rose again to speak life to dying humanity. All words can do things, but this Word is divinely distinct in that it will not ever return void (Isa 55:11).

LUKE A. POWERY

WILLIE JENNINGS

THIRD SUNDAY
AFTER THE EPIPHANY [3]

THE LESSONS IN PRÉCIS

During Epiphany, God reveals God's light in Christ, and through these texts, we see that this light has the power to save.

> *Isaiah 9:1-4.* "The people walking in darkness have seen a great light" (v. 2), and their burdens have been lifted.

> *Psalm 27: 1, 4-9.* The Lord is a light of salvation.

> *1 Corinthians 1:10-18.* Paul appeals to the church at Corinth to remain united and to remember that the message of the cross is the power of God, not any other message or person.

> *Matthew 4:12-23.* Jesus is a light to the Gentiles, proclaiming, "Here comes the kingdom of heaven!" as he calls disciples and cures diseases.

THEME SENTENCE

God's light saves. The Lord is light of salvation in the psalm, people have seen a light in Isaiah, Jesus is a light in Matthew, and Paul reminds us that the cross of Christ is where the power of God resides.

A KEY THEOLOGICAL QUESTION

Saving Light. God's light saves us. The idea and image of light are at the heart of these selected readings. They lead us into an important aspect of the doctrine of salvation. They also clarify elements of a doctrine of sanctification. The ideas of light and darkness have a complex history in

Christian tradition. It would be much too facile always to equate light with goodness and darkness with evil, but these texts do make positive use of light. However, what is crucial here is that light is embodied in God. God is not simply a supreme example of goodness as light. God constitutes light. Moreover the life of God revealed is the manifestation of light. God's life shows light not only to be personal, but divine light also creates redemptive events.

God brings light to the peoples of the world, and this exposes the truth that we all lived unable to see a way forward to the fullness of life. The Isaiah passage rehearses this critical theme essential to the difference between Israel and the other nations. God's presence in Israel was the presence of light, and that light would someday also shine on the Gentile nations. It would be easy to see this as a derogatory gesture regarding other peoples as bound up in darkness. That would, however, be an unfruitful way to read this Israel-Gentile difference. The Gentile nations, along with Israel, are the concern of God. God's light in this regard exposes the ways of oppression and violence as unacceptable. God will break open those ways and introduce God's own governance. All humanity walks in darkness, and all peoples with Israel will be drawn together under the guidance of God's own child. Here we see two aspects of redemptive light: liberation and guidance. These aspects may also be combined to be liberation through guidance, as in the words of the psalmist. The Lord is described as the light of salvation who directs the path of those who will listen and follow.

The gift of direction most often comes into view as the central benefit of God's light. God directs us through and around those things of life that would harm us or even destroy us. God will guide us as we face the traps of our enemies and the unanticipated times of trouble. God's delivering hand is also God's guiding hand. Salvation encompasses sanctification. The action of God makes possible the response of humanity. The psalmist's heart speaks the right response to God's gracious direction: seek God. Ask for the help that God gives. The seeking in itself marks sanctification's form. To be sanctified is to be one whose life follows God and goes where God directs. A sanctified life is a life bound to God in fundamental movement toward God. Such movement gives meaning to the ideas of being set apart to God for service. This is the essence of the concept of holiness—a life of movement toward God, a life that follows God's direction.

The Gospel reading in Matthew shows us Jesus of Nazareth as the personification of divine light. He is found among the Gentiles, and because he has come to them, God's great light has come to them. Now with Jesus, divine light is in human form and deliverance from the powers of death walks among us, announcing God's reign. This is light that does not overwhelm but may be clearly seen. It is God's light. However, it might be misidentified as darkness and confusion because it is bound up in the realities of humanity. Those who see this light are those called by the light. This then is light that works through faith. The revelation of light always demands a response. Jesus comes calling the disciples. Light shines on a new path and those whose lives are already committed to another way of life, another direction are asked to abandon that path and follow another, that is, they are called to follow Jesus. Salvation and sanctification come to them in the body of Jesus. In him, they find the way forward in light.

The life of Jesus might be construed as the path of enlightenment. Yet Jesus does not model an enlightened existence and then send us on our way to follow his example. In the body of Jesus light shines, and we may live in this light. This light is always participatory and communal. The disciples—in following Jesus—enter life in the presence of the Holy Spirit, who always gives witness to Christ. This vision of light differs from a vision of enlightenment based in human achievement. God's light that shines in darkness is gift. It is not the result of regimes of human cultivation or the celebration of reason. The danger we face with the use of the ideas of light and enlightenment is precisely the confusion of divine gift with human capacity. We are not capable of saving ourselves.

Paul's admonition to the church in Corinth captures the centrality of Christ's life over against the lives of others held up as exemplars of human excellences and supreme enlightenment. Paul presses the church to resist identifying with leaders who most impress them with their form of enlightened life. These Corinthian saints have been baptized in Christ and the way of Jesus leads directly to his cross. Jesus puts to death on the cross any illusion that we can deliver ourselves from death by our own light. The only light that saves us and leads us to life is the light revealed from the other side of Jesus' cross, the light of his resurrected life. This redemptive light shines on us, giving witness to God's power.

A PASTORAL NEED

Many people in the pews are in need of direction in life. Should I turn left or right? Should I go backward or forward? Many times the way is not clear, and paralysis may set in because of confusion, uncertainty, or fear. Some decisions hold one's life or community's life in the balance. When Dr. Martin Luther King Jr. received a threatening phone call one late night, he was full of fear. He was faced with the decision of whether to carry on or not in his struggle for justice and freedom. He turned to God in prayer, and through that discipline his path became clearer. He experienced God's presence and heard an inner voice that calmed his soul and gave him strength to carry on in the fight for justice. The light of God shone on him in order to see the way forward. People should be reminded and encouraged that God's Word, Jesus, is a "lamp before my feet and a light for my journey" (Ps 119:105). God promises to enlighten the way that we should travel in life, to guide our feet while we run this race.

ETHICAL IMPLICATIONS

The divine light is a gift to us and not something we create out of our own human imagination. God's light saves, illumines, and guides. How might we, as followers of the light, guide others in their various journeys? How might we be receptive to the light that others may have? How can we share the saving light of Christ with others? It may be a simple word of wisdom or a gentle gesture of love, a kind word of encouragement or a hug. It may be offering a listening ear to someone who needs to give voice. Any way that one may relieve another's burdens would reveal the work of the light of God because this light saves. God is a burden-bearer on God's own initiative. This light is a gift for us, and any aspect of this light we can share with another will also be a gift.

Mother Teresa revealed the light of Christ shining in and through her as she taught many street children in Calcutta, India how to read. She felt called to serve the poor and lepers and other outcasts. The light of God leads true disciples to share this light with others. Remembering Jesus' words from the next chapter in Matthew, "You are the light of the world" (5:14), we are to let our "light shine before people, so they can see the good things you do and praise your Father who is in heaven." (5:16).

GOSPEL IMPLICATIONS

There is only one light that saves and lifts our burdens. Whether we realize it or not, that light is Jesus Christ. This light did not come in the form expected, yet it never stopped shining. It shone in the Bethlehem star at Christmas. If one looked closely, that light was shining even on the cross of salvation. That light was strength in weakness and put the spotlight on the cross as a symbol of torture. The light dimmed but never went out and it shone for all other lights that would be unjustly murdered on crosses of various kinds. In the case of Christ, the cross was not necessarily doom and gloom but was God's way to demonstrate that light shines even in extreme darkness, even in a cold, dark tomb. This light never stopped shining, continuing through Easter morning so that others may see and know the light of God's salvation.

LUKE A. POWERY

WILLIE JENNINGS

FOURTH SUNDAY
AFTER THE EPIPHANY [4]

THE LESSONS IN PRÉCIS
God's revelatory teaching is surprising at times and not what we would normally expect.

> *Micah 6:1-8.* God challenges Israel and tells them of the requirements to do justice, love kindness, and walk humbly with God.

> *Psalm 15.* An ethical requirement is revealed by the psalmist—those who walk blameless, do right, and speak truth abide in God's tent and holy hill.

> *1 Corinthians 1:18-31.* Paul reminds the church that no one should boast, except in God, for "it is because of God that you are in Christ Jesus" (v. 30).

> *Matthew 5:1-12.* Jesus preaches a "blessed" sermon, the beatitudes, to say to whom belongs the kingdom of heaven.

THEME SENTENCE
God overturns human expectations. The Old Testament texts reveal an ethical requirement for being in God's presence, not the usual sacrificial offerings. Plus, the New Testament lessons teach that God chooses the foolish, weak, lowly, poor, mourning, and meek, as agents to work and kingdom.

A KEY THEOLOGICAL QUESTION

God's Difference. These texts illustrate a God who surprises us by disrupting our expectations and giving us new ones. These scriptures confront us with a God who is not only found among the lowly, but who also makes humility a prerequisite for understanding divine being and action. These themes are close to the heart of Christology and especially the ideas concerning the relation of the divinity and humanity of Jesus Christ. The Bible witnesses to a God who is constantly on a journey into humiliation, weakness, and lowliness, all the way into the depths of creaturely existence, for the sake of drawing creaturely life toward the divine, toward exaltation.

God suffers patiently with the chosen people. This is a theme that rings out in the Old Testament. In Micah we find God pleading with the people of Israel to turn from their unfaithfulness in worshipping other gods. Unlike other gods depicted in ancient stories, Israel's God seems willing to wait as one caught in the ebb and flow of a relationship, waiting for response and recognition. This Holy One is slow to destroy, but is quick to forgive and often tardy to anger. If ancient Israel knows a deity, they know that their God defies expectations. Their God is different and draws us to this difference. As do other peoples, Israel knows religious ritual and the routine of sacrifice. Yet even with a divinely sanctioned sacrificial system, God seemingly moves against the grain of religious assumptions bound to such a system. Neither great amounts of blood nor spectacular sacrifices are pleasing, but when holy voice comes through prophetic utterance, we encounter an extraordinary desire—that God's people would do justice, love kindness and mercy, and walk with God in humility.

The poetic power of Micah's words in 6:8 helps to capture the unconventional actions that define the character of YHWH. Those who would be associated with this strange God must learn the divine, obsessive concern for those without power, those subject to the powerful, and those disadvantaged by dishonest action. The psalmist, like the prophet Micah, understands that more is at stake in their words than moral instruction to those with power. Something essential to the divine nature is being gestured toward with these words. There is lowliness and a weakness in and of God that is deeply in tune with human lowliness and weakness. This is not any kind of point of contact between the two. What we find here is God marking a way forward in life, that is, a way of faith rooted in love where human existence joins the movement and rhythm of holy life. Just as the weak are in need of justice and to have their voices heard, so too God hopes that human hearts turned away from the divine will might finally give what is owed—devotion, obedience, belief, and love. God waits for God's own justice.

The humility of waiting and hoping meet the humiliation of lacking and wanting in Jesus of Nazareth. The Beatitudes of Matthew 5 have always exhibited an intense Christological character as it exploded messianic expectation. Here, the hoped-for deliverer is clothed in the very hope of God's faithful ones. Moreover, Jesus deepens that hope by locating it in and among those who in every way are not sought after and certainly not emulated. Blessing is announced on those who stand on the losing side of conflict, outside the victor's circle of social accomplishment and achievement and in between warring factions, while seeking the inauguration of a better government not within the reach of any nationalist power. In calling Israel to the most fundamental aspects of its identity as God's people, Jesus is also calling attention to himself as the new space in which that identity will be clarified and intensified in him.

Jesus is the one who will now mark the path to God as the path of this specific lowliness, mourning, meekness, mercy, and peacemaking. This God will be found in no other way, and this way will also be stained by the world's revulsion, rejection, persecution, slander, and purposes of death. The divine dynamic displayed by these texts challenges the dynamic of the world where power flows from the powerful, the socially acceptable, and the beautiful through the circuits of influence they created. God desires to render their power useless, exposing it as that which comes from dust and must eventually return to dust. The theological matter at play in this dynamic is the identity of God, which might mistakenly be equated with worldly power. Unlike worldly power, the power of God will make its home in weak places.

Paul goes so far as to state that the weakness of God is greater than human power. The misidentification of divine power with worldly power constantly plagues Christian thinking because the message of the cross is profoundly difficult to sustain: This crucified human reveals God, a crucified God. This message, however, shows that the revelation of God is an overturning, a theological revolution for all peoples who, like ancient Jews and Greeks, seek signs of power or conceptual devices that will enhance their knowledge. The crucified One draws to himself those who would know God's power through the Son's weakness, and God's wisdom through the Son's pitiful cries. It was precisely this revolution against worldly power that is at the heart of all Christian conversion. Whether we know it or not, understand or not, our redemption destroys our boasting, except in the redeemer himself. This, then, is the place of God's exaltation, precisely in the lives of the humble and lowly, that is, our lives.

A Pastoral Need

Humanity is always at risk of hubris. Human accomplishments in any degree through physical or intellectual abilities may lead down the path of pride. Ongoing technological advancements, creativity in the sciences and arts, and expressing human empathy effectively by serving victims of natural disasters such as the earthquakes in Haiti or Chile may cause one to feel good about oneself. This in and of itself is not detrimental, but what *is* dangerous is if doing good makes one believe they are good.

When one feeds the hungry or clothes the naked in our communities, it may be easy to take credit for these good deeds and praise our human efforts rather than praise God, the fount of every blessing and source of every good gift. When God is replaced by human gods, it is important for the preacher to remind anyone who will listen that God is the source of our lives and that any power we possess comes from God's strength and not our own. To be a human follower of God is to be humble, boasting only in the Lord. If we boast in our power, we deny God's power, but if we acknowledge our weakness, we will see God's wonder-working strength. "When [we're] weak, then [we're] strong" (2 Cor 12:10).

Ethical Implications

God resides in weak places. God tabernacles in weakness. God chooses the foolish, weak, lowly, poor, mourning, and meek, as agents of God's kingdom work in the world. God wields power differently. God's power and strength are used on behalf of the weak and powerless of the world, the disinherited of society, those we think have nothing to offer. But this divine ministry shows us that they, the ones on the margins of society, have much to offer. They may not be glamorous or beautiful or wealthy or powerful according to the world's standards, but they are the ones with whom God dwells. This overturns our usual human ways of thinking and acting.

God's way of being in the world requires followers of God to walk humbly before God, doing justice and loving kindness in places and towards people whom we might normally ignore. Going to church with imperial Christians may not be where God is found because God lives in weak places, not in the rooms of imperial Christianity. This God thrusts us outward into the world to serve the poor, comfort the mourning, encourage the meek, and do justice in the midst of unjust systems. This God of mercy calls us to go on a mercy mission.

GOSPEL IMPLICATIONS

These texts suggest that what we expect of God is not always what we get. God acts differently from the normative, human, worldly powers. God acts in surprising ways, overturning human expectations from the beginning. Divinity takes on the flesh of humanity but comes in the form of a humble baby—weak, lowly, and poor, not strong, high, and rich. God willingly takes on frailty to save finite humanity. What kind of God is this who would choose what is weak and poor to love the world?

God even demonstrates power by dying on a cross, becoming a crucified God. God redefines strength as the weakness of the cross. The cross inverts worldly ideas of power and wisdom, for the cross of Christ is the power and wisdom of God. This is a radical, unconventional way to oppose the demonic powers of the world that aim to destroy the powerless by brute force. Through the cross, God reveals God's solidarity with those on death row. Through the cross, God dies to kill death once and for all. The cross is God's way of reigning—dying to love so that we may live, so that bodies would no longer be broken and innocent blood no longer be spilled. This is the weak strength of the body and blood of the Lord that feeds us every time we celebrate communion.

LUKE A. POWERY

WILLIE JENNINGS

FIFTH SUNDAY
AFTER THE EPIPHANY [5]

THE LESSONS IN PRÉCIS
The epiphany of God leads to acting justly in the world.

> *Isaiah 58:1-9a (9b-12).* God redefines the meaning of fasting to include doing social justice.

> *Psalm 112:1-9 (10).* Those who fear the Lord are lights because they "conduct their affairs with justice" (v. 5) like giving to the poor.

> *1 Corinthians 2:1-12 (13-16).* Paul affirms the demonstration of the Spirit and power and not any form of human wisdom because true wisdom is God's, and can only be taught by the Spirit.

> *Matthew 5:13-20.* Jesus tells the disciples that they are salt of the earth and a light of the world.

THEME SENTENCE
God does justice. Isaiah and the psalmist stress the doing of justice and service to the needy. The psalm links being a "light" with doing justice, which might imply what Jesus means by "light of the world" in Matthew.

A KEY THEOLOGICAL QUESTION
Revealing Justice. These texts bring us to the important connection between two kinds of actions, believing in God and acting justly in the world. They show us that we live in the space between these two kinds of

62

actions, often lacking the follow-through that binds the one action to the other. Reverence for God requires acting justly in the world. Acting justly in the world points us in the direction of the light of the world, Jesus Christ. This connection has also been described more generally as that between doctrine and ethics, and with this connection we are centrally concerned with lives that give consistent witness to the desire of God for a world reconciled.

Our religious rituals often become the stage on which God reveals our contradictions: we say one thing but do another, we pretend to attend to the divine presence when in fact our hearts and minds are on something else, and we use our rituals that pronounce our love for God to sanction injustice and violence. The Isaiah passage highlights the misuse of one of the most intense religious rituals that anyone could engage in, fasting. Fasting, denying oneself life-sustaining food for the purpose of deepening one's commitment to hearing God, should exhibit bodies bound in obedience. Yet the prophet discerns fasting used to serve selfish interests. Divine sight reaches into the depths of our piety and separates truth from illusion. The difference between the real and the lie in our religious devotion is not so hidden that only God may see it. It emerges precisely in the treatment of the oppressed, the hungry, and the homeless poor. If our religious practices, even the most pious practices like fasting, support further oppression or fail to move us to address the suffering of the weak and disadvantaged, then such practices collapse back on themselves and expose nothing more than our hypocrisy.

Authentic, holy reverence draws our lives into God's desire for justice in the world. Religious zeal should move God's people to advocate for those being treated unfairly, to speak for those whose voices are being silenced, and to help those caught in poverty. The psalm for this Sunday traces a similar path around these wider dimensions of holy reverence but also emphasizes the identity of God's people as those who should not be drawn into unjust financial practices. The resources of the righteous come from the Lord, and they should always flow from the righteous to those in need. Here is an economic circuit that not only disavows hoarding those resources but also protects the sanctified from being identified with them.

These texts capture the perennial problem of our identity amnesia. Its roots lie in the ease with which we are distracted and drawn toward false words and worldly wisdom so that we lose sight of who we really are. In the Gospel passage, Jesus tells his disciples that they are in fact the light of the world, the salt of the earth. Yet he presses a question on his disciples in the midst of this declaration of their identity—what happens when salt loses its saltiness or a light is hidden? In such cases, its very existence becomes impossible and incongruous. Jesus is pointing toward actions that deny the reality of God's presence in the lives of those who follow him. By so doing, he displays the divine sight that discerns the difference between truth and lie. However, in this case, Jesus placed his own body in the space between truth and lie and removed the contradiction.

The place of contradiction for the disciples no longer centers on their religious practice, but on their daily life. Now they are in fact something else, something different, living from a different source and reality, and yet they act and sometimes live caught in terrible forgetfulness. They forget they are bound to the body of Jesus and to the reign of God that he announces. They are light in his light, salt in his presence, and vessels of God's power through the Holy Spirit. Now the piety of the disciples is secondary, and their association with Jesus is primary. They give witness to him and thusly if they fail to give witness to the Christ that is itself a witness. Contradiction, like sin and evil, is always a possibility for the disciples of Jesus, yet it need not ever be permanent. Jesus' disciples are lights that simply need to push away those things that conceal their brightness. We are salt that may be reenergized by remembering the waters of our baptism. Like tonal dissonance, contradiction may through the Holy Spirit be moved toward deeper harmony with the life of Jesus. We live in a world shaped through injustice and oppression. Our lives need not be determined by the shape of the world. By grace, we may be conformed to the image of God's Son.

Paul grasps this difference of life bound to Jesus. It is the difference between life built on truth or on a lie. The truth of life builds from the revelation of the crucified savior. This is a life of faith that rests not on the wisdom of this world and of this age but on the wisdom and power of God. The difference between the spiritual and the unspiritual is not a difference of depth in personal piety or of consistency in religious practice. It is a difference that discerns the ways of the world visible in injustice and oppression, ways that seek after worldly power and glory in the cunning of human wisdom. The spiritual choose instead the way of a God who took the form of fallen human flesh and from the spaces of our suffering turned us toward life.

A Pastoral Need

There may be in a congregation those who struggle with selfishness and who need to know the joy of serving others. Even fasting can be done mostly to improve one's own spiritual life and could potentially nurture a selfish life. In Isaiah, Israel engages in fasting, so they abstain from food and wear funeral clothes and ashes as a sign of mourning and penance. They are liturgically literate. They want to draw closer to God, and this is the way they know how to do it. This is how they have done worship for years—singing the right song, saying the right prayer, doing the right dance, saying amen at the right time. But, they seem to move farther away from God as they dive deeper into themselves. They cannot figure out why their fasting won't work. "Why do we fast, and you don't see; why afflict ourselves and you don't notice?" (Isa 58:3). "I have a full worship diet of Christianity. I go to church and church meetings. I sing beautiful hymns, say lovely prayers of confession, serve the communion elements from time to time, and serve special potluck fellowship meals after service. I pray before my meals and even before I go to bed. I read my Bible every day, and sometimes I even fast like Israel. But God where are you?"

Israel cannot figure out what is wrong with their worship until God speaks: "Yet on your fast day you do whatever you want, and oppress all your workers. You quarrel and brawl, and then you fast; you hit each other violently with your fists. . . . Is this the kind of fast I choose, a day of self-affliction . . . ?" (Isa 58:3-5). God brings a serious critique against Israel. Israel's fast is abstention from other people. They delight in God but hate God's people. They abstain from loving their neighbor. They feed on selfish, self-serving, self-interested, individualistic living that regards no one else but "me, myself, and I." Israel is consumed with and worried only about themselves. They neglect serving others. Their spiritual liturgical diet is navel-gazing at their stomachs full of self. They serve their own interests while disregarding others. In light of this perceived need, the sermon on this day would demonstrate how following God means that one is *other*-wise, selfless, caring and helping others, especially the needy. God will then be found because God can be found among society's weak.

Ethical Implications

To be salt and light, we need to be like and in God, who does justice and liberation in the world. God calls for selfless giving. God calls for worship as service in the world. If we are in God's light, we will do and share the love of Jesus, the light of the world, in very concrete, material ways. We will be dissatisfied with selfish, status quo Christian spirituality that has no impact on society. We will be concerned with the liturgy and the *liturgy after the liturgy* because worship includes social witness and justice.

Unfortunately, Israel's liturgical approach, as shown in Isaiah, has been our practical theology of worship. We actually think that just coming to a Sunday service, a Wednesday night prayer meeting, a Bible study or Christian education class is the totality of what it means to worship God. Moreover, if we do not like the preaching, the singing, the praying, the children's sermon, the choir robes, the way communion is administered, we can go somewhere else, window shopping for a church that we like because it better suits us and our needs. This is consumeristic worship engulfed in maximizing the self.

But true worship includes love of neighbor, and without this ingredient one cannot call it worship of God. Lip service must match life service. Thus, we will not neglect others, such as those enchained by a prison industrial complex because of the color of their skin, those targeted by immigration laws because they speak another human language, those attending urban schools with inadequate resources, those so lonely or in such deep depression that they commit suicide because life becomes too much for them to bear. With a clear conscience, we should not neglect the friendless, the jobless, the homeless, and the hopeless while claiming to be disciples of Christ.

God did not say that people have to be Christian in order to be helped. God did not say that they have to have the same skin color as you to be helped. God did not say that they have to believe the same thing you believe or like the same things you like to be helped. Need is no respecter of persons. Instead, God said that the food for God's liturgical fast diet is to loose the bonds of injustice, undo the yokes of the oppressed, let the imprisoned go free, give bread to the hungry, a home to the homeless, clothes to the naked, and love to somebody. God did not say give up something but give something, do something for someone in need. Worship is a verb.

GOSPEL IMPLICATIONS

There was a time when as humans we were unable to overcome our own selfishness and greed, and God in Christ entered our need, dying our death for us, and freed us in the Spirit to act. The good news is that God is present, inhabiting our extended worship as we serve those in need. In light of these texts' emphasis on justice, those whom we are called to serve are now the face of Christ who said, "I was hungry and you gave me food to eat. I was thirsty and you gave me a drink. I was a stranger and you welcomed me. I was naked and you gave me clothes to wear. I was sick and you took care of me. I was in prison and you visited me . . . when you have done it for one of the least of these brothers and sisters of mine, you have done it for me" (Matthew 25:35-40). His light shines brightly in the face of the other.

LUKE A. POWERY

WILLIE JENNINGS

Last Sunday after the Epiphany [Transfiguration Sunday]

The Lessons in Précis

God allows God's glory to be experienced.

> *Exodus 24:12-18.* Moses goes up the mountain of God to receive the commandments, and there he encounters the glory of God in a cloud.

> *Psalm 2.* The psalmist shows how God puts the earthly kings in their place ("my Lord makes fun of them" [v. 4]) and becomes angry but yet promises the anointed ones that God's king will be placed on "my holy mountain" (v. 6).

> *2 Peter 1:16-21.* People witnessed the majesty and glory of Christ as the Son of God when they heard the voice of God from heaven say, "This is my dearly loved Son" (v. 17), when they were on the "holy mountain" (v. 18).

> *Matthew 17:1-9.* Jesus is transfigured on the mountain, and a voice from a cloud says, "This is my dearly loved Son" (v. 5). The disciples were fearful, but Jesus tells them not to be afraid.

Theme Sentence

God reveals God's glory. This is clearly seen in Exodus, 2 Peter, and Matthew.

A KEY THEOLOGICAL QUESTION

The Glory of God. The glory of God is often associated with mountains in the Bible. No one may see God and live, yet God allows humanity to experience glimpses of the divine. Our texts this week highlight this gracious action, through which we encounter a powerful aspect of divine presence. The crucial site for these encounters is the mountain, which aids in the anthropomorphizing of God and the picturing of divine encounter. The Holy One enters time and space and communicates from the mountain. God sits on the mountain and invites people to come to listen to the divine voice. Most importantly, this condescension of God to the mountain leads to the exaltation of humanity, definitively in Jesus of Nazareth. The mountain also announces the coming reign of God through the Son.

If we are attentive to mountaintop experiences in the Bible, we gain insight to the nature of God. Moses led Israel to the mountain and to its God. The mountain has often represented a place of instruction in Jewish and Christian traditions. From the mountain God called Moses, and from the mountain came the law and the commandments for the sake of the people. The mountain was a place of overwhelming fear and life-defining promise. Fear and promise mixed as God spoke out from an unquenchable fire inside an impenetrable cloud, offering guidance for life. The only appropriate response to the voice speaking from the mountain was lifelong reverence and remembrance. Israel was called to remember the true order of things; its God sits high and looks low, ordering their actions in concert with holy communion. If the Holy One lives with Israel, then the mountain experience sets the tone for life in the vicinity of God's glory. Only Moses existed unharmed in the glory of God for an extended time. After forty days and nights, he emerged, establishing the truth that we do not live by bread and water alone but truly by the word that proceeds from the mouth of God. Life is bound up inside instruction, and instruction is tied to life given by God.

The psalmist picks up this order of things revealed on the mountain. The holy mountain mentioned in Psalm 2 connotes not only the absolutely priority of God over earthly kings but also the current and future reign of God. We encounter here the stark difference between nationalist and godly perspectives. Earthy rulers overestimate their wisdom and power. God laughs at them and announces the reign of the Son who is and will be the king of kings and lord of lords. A different vision of time and history emerge from the mountain, one that undermines the hoped-for permanence of nations and the exaltation of their statecraft as signatures of their genius and cunning. A warning rings out from the holy hill—wise rulers must remember the mountain of divine revealing and serve the Lord with reverence or face the wrath of God.

On the mountain, the truth is revealed about who we are as humans. God is God, and we are not. The disciples gain this crucial lesson on location with Jesus. There, with eyes turned toward him, he was transformed. The Lord of time appeared, joining these disciples to Moses and Elijah and showing the present and future to be bound to his body. The transfiguration scene has always schooled Christian theology in humility because it reveals the exhaustion of our words in the presence of God. The disciples were speechless, except for the poorly chosen words of Peter. His honest desire to honor the great voices of Israel's past revealed more than he realized. Even with the incarnate Lord in their midst, his difference from the others was yet unclear. The glory of God may blind in the precise moment it gives sight. Only the second moment clarified the first; that is, only the mighty voice of God thundering from the cloud made clear who must be heard. "This is my dearly loved Son . . . Listen to him!" (Matt 17:5). The clarification of the Son, Jesus of Nazareth, demands the submersion of all other prophetic voices, because the glory of God now shines forever in and through his face.

Now the terror of the holy mountain has been localized. It is hidden in the weak flesh of this son of Mary. He is the intensification of divine instruction, and he draws his disciples away from fear into faith as they follow his own faithfulness to God his father in the presence of the Holy Spirit. God's glory is now tethered to the lowliness of this despised One of Israel, eternally flowing through his nail-marked hands and the echoes of his cries of pain. Fear and promise met in the body of Jesus, and he provided a place where we might no longer be overcome by the former and would embrace more deeply the latter. Here is the glory of God within reach. He is the mountain brought low so that our valleys may be made level ground.

Sight of God's glory does indeed signal divine victory, but for us it is a matter of faith. To know God's glory is to know the walk of enduring trust in the presence of God who will sustain us in the face of life's contradictions. Second Peter (1:16-21) assures the faithful that their lives in Christ are not rooted in cleverly executed myths. The apostle was an eyewitness. He saw God's glory shown on and through Jesus Christ. This in no way eradicates the weakness of witness. The hiddenness of divine majesty is completed in us. Our witness is taken up in the self-revelation of God in Jesus of Nazareth. We become the site for the manifestation of the glory of God, announcing by our life together that a people marked by the mountain have their sights set by it.

A PASTORAL NEED

There may be individuals who have become disillusioned and even distraught over the apparent absence of God. They may not have experienced or sensed God's glory or presence in a very long time. When others appear to speak of experiencing God on a daily basis, they may become even more disheartened by what they consider to be their dry spirituality or lack of faith. They may view their experience of God as something that depends on their efforts. They are in a spiritual wilderness, without any apparent manifestation of glory in their parched land.

People like this may be helped by talking about how God works in time and space in proximity to us. Though God is high, God stoops low to engage us in life. God speaks, moves, and reveals God's glory on divine initiative, when God wants; it is a gift of grace, not manufactured by human hands. Glory is God's gift, and we do not have to ascend to a high mountain to experience it. Through Jesus Christ, the embodied glory of God, we can experience the glory of God within our lives. In fact, our everyday lives can be sites for the manifestation of God's glory. Divine glory may be revealed in unlikely, earthy places, such as a woman giving birth in a tree during devastating floods in the country of Mozambique. This sermon is an opportunity to help those in need to see where God's glory manifests itself in today's world.

ETHICAL IMPLICATIONS

God's voice tells us on whom his glory rests. Jesus Christ is the glory of God enfleshed. Through him, we experience and know God's glory. It is glory in the flesh. God's voice speaks out of glory and should cause us to be speechless and listen to God's voice and words. We should not always feel the necessity to speak or give an answer. Sometimes, we should engage in a holy hush, silence, before the presence of God, the place of God's glory, because in our listening, we come to recognize and remember that God is God alone. Glory belongs to God, not us.

We are not God; yet through Jesus Christ, the glory of God, the divine glory resides in our frail hearts and finite lives. Glory rests in broken vessels. In this way, we become stewards of glory and are effective stewards through listening to the word of God. By listening and hearing God's voice and not our own, we might actually experience God's glory on earth. By listening, we may hear the glorious voice telling us that we are God's sons and daughters, God's beloved children in the world. By listening, we can honor the glory of God resting on others. No words will be necessary, only actions of a loving embrace, welcoming divine glory in our midst.

GOSPEL IMPLICATIONS

The glory of God is within reach. Jesus as the Son of God reveals the glory of God in the flesh, in human proximity. Divine glory is brought near through Christ. His birth, life, death, resurrection, and ascension represent God's glory in motion. We saw it in a little baby lying in a manger. We saw it on the mount of transfiguration as these texts reveal. We saw it on another mountain, the hill of Golgotha on an old, rugged cross. Glory even moved into a grave and came out of it, too. The divine glory embodied in Jesus Christ was gory but also glorious. The glory was wounded but alive, shining all the way up to the right hand of the father. In and through him, God's voice is heard and glory is felt so that the refrain continues to ring out in congregations all over the world: "Shine, Jesus, shine, fill this land with the Father's glory . . ."

LUKE A. POWERY

WILLIE JENNINGS

ASH WEDNESDAY

THE LESSONS IN PRÉCIS

Joel 2:1-2, 12-17. Joel sounds the alarm; the terrible day of the LORD is near. Destruction may be avoided if God's people gather, repent in their hearts, and appeal to God's merciful character and covenant faithfulness.

Psalm 51:1-17. The psalmist, here named as David, recognizes both the depth and duration of his wrong and desires repentance, absolution, and the joy of a recreated heart. Verse 17 is rich existential gospel: a broken spirit and heart is the appropriate "sacrifice."

2 Corinthians 5:20b–6:10. After a proclamation of God's reconciling action, Paul clarifies the relationship between hardship and salvation. The deep mystery is that serenity is found paradoxically in circumstances of its seeming absence.

Matthew 6:1-6, 16-21. The temptation for religious practitioners is to confuse conscious, observable practices with their benefits. Jesus honors the practices of almsgiving, prayer, and fasting but declares that the reward comes from doing them in and with God.

THEME SENTENCE

God breaks our hearts in order to create them anew. Today we begin the journey to the cross, the paradoxical sign where our broken illusions of perfection and immortality are transformed into hopeful obedience. By drawing us into Christ's life, God enacts a repentance that transforms the will (heart), making true worship and obedience a matter of a people's new essential nature.

73

A KEY THEOLOGICAL QUESTION

Ash Wednesday is an opportunity to take an honest look at the conflict-ing realities of human nature. We remember that we are mortal; we also recognize how deeply sinful we are. At the same time, we cannot forget that on the other end of the Lenten season come the Easter promises of everlasting life and the forgiveness of sins. Ash Wednesday puts before us the contrasts and tensions of the Christian life. It is a time to remember that we are simultaneously transformed into a new reality, and yet the old reality in which we were formed still holds sway.

This sense of tension is perhaps most apparent in the second read-ing, where Paul gives a series of contrasting statements: "We were seen as both fake and real, as unknown and well known, as dying—and look, we are alive! We were seen as punished but not killed, as going through pain but always happy, as poor but making many rich, and as having nothing but owning everything" (2 Cor 6:8b-10). Some people in the congregation might think that Paul speaks in contradictions. In fact, this is dialectic tension, where two seemingly opposing realities are held simultaneously as true. Neither quality on either side is, in and of itself, fully descriptive of Paul's vision of Christian life. Rather, each is an essen-tial component of life as an ambassador of Christ, engulfed by the day of salvation. Indeed, this dialectic sense of both/and is essential to the experience of Christ. At the beginning of this pericope, we hear that God made Christ, who knew no sin, to be sin so that in him we might become the righteousness of God. We have something of a dialectic even here, in that the sinless Christ becomes sin. Through this sinless Christ who becomes sin, we are brought into the dialectic life. The day of salvation comes to us as grace, and yet it is not to be accepted in vain. That is, it is a gift that we ought to put to use. The transformed life of grace, then, is simultaneously sorrowful and rejoicing, poor and yet enriching to others, having nothing and yet everything.

Transformation is crucial to entering into the dialectical life in Christ. Here we are met with the highly contested question in Chris-tian theology of the essential nature of humanity. Augustine developed his doctrine of original sin, for instance, to challenge both the excessive pessimism about human nature he found in the Manichean view on the one hand, and the overly optimistic view he found in Pelagianism on the other. The Manichean or Gnostic view held that sin is coincident with human finitude, and is therefore constituently an essential aspect of human nature. The Pelagians, meanwhile, held that humans are born with neither virtue nor vice, but rather are able freely to choose whether or not to act sinfully. Sin, in this view, is a choice for evil, which humans have the capacity to avoid. To put these positions in other terms, one might understand the Manicheans as positing sin as a key ingredient in human nature; to remove it would be to remove the humanity. Pelagians, meanwhile, would see sin as a garnish; it is an optional add-on that is not essential to the recipe. The Manicheans run the risk of understanding sin as inevitable and therefore offering an excuse for human acceptance of evil, while the Pelagian position risks rendering divine action irrelevant.

Augustine rejects both of these positions. He insists, rather, that because creation is good, humans are created good, desire good, and are only truly satisfied when they are attuned to and guided by the ultimate good, God. Therefore sin is not part of the essential nature of humanity, but is rather a choice to turn away from what offers true freedom and satisfaction, that is, God, and towards the transient lures of the world. In this sense sin is voluntary for Augustine. Yet, he goes on, the lower powers of the soul become disoriented by turning away from God's guidance, and soon humans begin to believe that the things of this world are truly good and satisfying. When this happens (and it happens to all people), humanity finds itself in a self-imposed captivity to sin that deforms its goodness. Human nature, then, thus becomes essentially good yet thoroughly sinful. Both realities are true. Sinfulness is not the natural human state and yet is inevitable. Sinfulness is a stain on human nature that requires our attention, and yet we must depend upon divine action to remove it. We have learned to desire ephemeral goods of this world. This worldly formation ultimately leads to disappointment and must be transformed into a renewed desire for God, the true good. When we are thus transformed, we are truly free and joyous, and yet in that freedom our sole desire is to immerse ourselves in God and be obedient to God's commands.

Ash Wednesday is often a time of confession of our sinfulness and a remembrance of our finitude. Yet the two must not be conflated, lest we fall into pessimistic Manicheanism. Rather, it may be more helpful to use these themes as an entryway into the dialectic tensions of the Christian life. We remember that we are dust and to dust we will return so that we are aware of our finitude, and yet we ought not forget that we are also inheritors of eternal life. In the same way, we recall through confession that we are deformed by sin, but through grace we are also transformed and filled by the Holy Spirit to live as holy people. We live with these tensions: deformed yet reformed, deeply sinful yet essentially good, finite yet brought into infinity. The transformative power of God's grace brings the "yet" into our lives of faith. Our hearts, and indeed we ourselves, are broken and yet made new, so that we may seek God with our whole lives.

A Pastoral Need

The laments of Psalm 51 echo those of earnest contemporary believers: "My life is a mess." "I keep trying; why can't I be more Christ-like, joyful, or just *better*?" Such groans are especially troubling in light of the naive expectation that having "Jesus in our hearts" or "God on our side" will yield serenity and spiritual progress.

Today's lessons respond to these existential cries with an invitation to radical unselfconsciousness. Joel reminds us that the sanctified covenant relationship with God is a communal inheritance. The call to join the assembly draws individuals away from even the most private joys (Joel 2:16). *Together* we rend our hearts in lament and appeal to God's fidelity because we know that the capacity for "better" dwells in a place beyond our individual wills.

Jesus affirms sanctifying practices but invites hearers to recalculate how those practices connect to progress and reward. The richest treasure is not others' awareness of our piety (Matt 6:2, 5, and 16) or even our own (Matt 6:3). The richest treasure is in a God-formed heart that provokes actions that have no conscious motive at all (except, perhaps, secrecy!).

Paul testifies that this promise pertains far beyond managing a happy face while fasting. Even when the life impelled by a God-formed will leads to calamity and death, the believer experiences a paradoxical hope and life. "Look, now is the right time" (even if your life is a mess and joy is fleeting); "now is the day of salvation!" (2 Cor 6:2).

Ethical Implications

Paul warns us not to accept the grace of God in vain (2 Cor 6:1) meaning first that we are reconciled for a purpose: to be active in God's mission. But there is a deeper aspect as well. In the context of these readings, vanity (vain-ness) is manifest when we mistake ritual symbols for spiritual action ("tear your hearts and not your clothing"); favor public posturing over true treasure ("that's the only reward they'll get"); and suppose that life should be free of sleepless nights. God graciously invites us to enjoy an unselfconscious integrity and the serene confidence that we own everything.

The culture's charge that "the Church is full of hypocrites" is a cliché that Christians too often discount. But the accusation reveals that even non-believers are tuned to "vanity" and understand Christ's eschatological longing for a seamless unity of faith, will, and action that eclipses the impulse to glance in the mirror or check for our picture in the "Church Doings" column of the local paper.

At one level, those who receive our alms and those for whom we pray care little for our motives or the depth of our faith. And yet in a recent two-day span 16,000,000 users watched a YouTube video entitled "Why I Hate Religion, But Love Jesus." Even the world senses that the church's mission is not coterminous with that of the Red Cross or UNICEF. God's workers, when they give without calculation, fast with clean faces, and flee with courage *toward* places of hardship and affliction, witness to an appealing, mysterious serenity that comes from dwelling in God.

Joel calls us to leave our individual lives behind and to join preparation of an acceptable fast, which we know from the prophetic tradition means to be communally formed for prodigal acts of mercy and justice (cf. Isa 58:5-6).

GOSPEL IMPLICATIONS

Jesus does not want to be a part of our lives; Jesus wants to make us a part of his life.

The Ash Wednesday announcement, "remember you are dust . . ." is spoken while ashes trace the baptismal cross on believers' foreheads. Today we begin the Lenten journey to the cross whose genius empowers us to put death—and all the little deaths Paul mentions in 2 Corinthians 6:4-10—face-to-face with life so that their true proportions can be known.

If Jesus is merely a part of our lives, death wins the showdown; the inescapable reality of frailty, mortality, and the fear they spawn overwhelms our faith. But Jesus wants to make us a part of his life. In his life, cross, and resurrection, frailty and mortality have been accounted for and overcome.

Death is still the enemy. The myriad little deaths we endure still hurt and grieve us. Frailty and mortality are still inescapable. But with confidence the psalmist offers up a troubled and broken heart knowing that this confidence—even more than the troubled heart itself—makes it a sacrifice acceptable to God. And in light of the cross and resurrection Paul trusts that even the worst day is the right time, the day of salvation.

HENRY J. LANGKNECHT

ERIC TROZZO

FIRST SUNDAY IN LENT

THE LESSONS IN PRÉCIS

Genesis 2:15-17; 3:1-7. The first lesson narrates the story of the Fall. Adam and Eve must decide between God's and the crafty serpent's account of what will happen if they eat of the fruit.

Psalm 32. The first part of the psalm (vv. 1-7) celebrates the sheer joy of forgiveness and then, more profoundly, the power of confession to rejuvenate a relationship that has been strained by secrecy. In v. 8 the tone shifts to praise of teaching.

Romans 5:12-19. Paul establishes the iconic polarity between the disobedience of Adam and the obedience of Christ, an obedience that justifies and redeems humankind.

Matthew 4:1-11. In Mark 3, Jesus is baptized and introduced as God's son. Here, in the wilderness temptation, Satan and Jesus establish the terms of the battle between good and evil: dependence, sovereignty, and worthiness to be worshiped.

THEME SENTENCE

Jesus' obedience gives us access to joyous freedom. In the passage from Romans, Paul develops a polarity of mythic proportions between Adam and Christ. This frame invites us to see the disobedience in Eden and the obedience in the wilderness as plot points in the divine narrative of salvation, rather than cautionary or exhortative stories for our day-to-day life of faith. The psalm and Paul both proclaim the happy effects of this cosmic narrative arc: freedom and forgiveness.

A KEY THEOLOGICAL QUESTION

Is there anything more paralyzing than absolute freedom? What do you do when there is nothing that you have to do? You need to make choices that restrict your freedom or you will sit in idle indecision. Making choices is essential to using our freedom, but how do we know what choices to make? In societies that provide a significant degree of personal freedom, many people have no idea how to use that freedom and end up ceding their ability to make choices to others. In particular, people all too easily buy in to the cultural message that they should use their freedom to consume more and more things and demand more and more options. Such consumption and demand for options is a mirage of freedom that makes constant demands on the person, rather than true freedom that allows fundamental choices in the way one lives one's life.

While having some options is essential for a healthy psychological state, having too many can be problematic. For instance, several psychological and sociological studies have tracked how an increase in consumer options since the 1970s among the population of the United States can be correlated with a decrease in general happiness. Writing in a *Scientific American* article summing up these studies, psychology professor Barry Schwartz argues that there comes a point when the benefits of having options becomes outweighed by the increased misery of having to make too many choices. One need not be a psychologist to recognize this phenomenon. Many people who had been content with five television channels find themselves unable to find anything to watch when they have two hundred channels. We are not able to handle such a wide range of options. Too much freedom can be debilitating.

The challenge of freedom is not new. It is an important theme in Paul's writings, for example. Paul proclaims in 2 Corinthians that freedom is a dimension of life in the Spirit (3:17). In Galatians he argues that Christian freedom is founded in Christ. Rather than a freedom for consumption, however, freedom in Christ turns us in love towards others. Indeed, instead of presenting more and more options, freedom in Christ binds us to the service of others out of love. Paul writes, "You were called to freedom, brothers and sisters; only don't let this freedom be an opportunity to indulge your selfish impulses, but serve each other through love" (Gal 5:13). Drawing on this Pauline insight, during the Reformation Martin Luther worked to explain the meaning of freedom in Christ. He famously declared, "A Christian is a perfectly free lord of all, subject to none. A Christian is a perfectly dutiful servant of all, subject to all" (Lull, 596). The resolution of this seeming paradox is that, having received grace, we are free from attempting to earn our salvation. In response to such grace, we are able joyfully to choose to love and serve others as a way of life. We thus willingly turn away from a life of self-centered demands and unthinking dissatisfaction. Instead we can use our freedom to care for others.

In turning to the Gospel reading for today, we find Jesus faced with a choice. In his baptism Jesus had just had an experience of the Spirit descending upon him. Given the freedom of life in the Spirit, Jesus faces the temptation to use this freedom self-indulgently. The temptations start with the simple lure of a meal when he is at the point of starvation, but quickly increase to special divine protection and eventually encompass a promise of all the kingdoms of the world. He resists self-gratification, binding himself instead to the humbler path of service to—and eventual death on behalf of—others. Indeed, he meets each temptation by turning in devotion to God's calling. He counters the temptation for food with trust in God's word, the temptation to receive extraordinary attention from God with humility before God, and the temptation for power with praise for the Lord.

The traditional Lenten practices of simplicity, service, and devotion to the needs of others are guides for appropriately exercising our freedom in response to God's grace. Instead of choosing a lifestyle that demands more and more for ourselves, the Lenten discipline of simplicity reminds us that we are freed and empowered by the Spirit to lead a life of service to others in love. Such a turn to the other is not for the sake of deprivation, but is a joyous celebration of God's goodness. A turn to the other is also a happy imitation of Christ's willingness to use his freedom for the salvation of humanity rather than for his own comfort, special consideration, or sense of control. Freedom in Christ is a call to action and the power to take it up with gladness. We turn away from the paralyzing freedom toward a commitment to others in response to God's freeing love for us.

A PASTORAL NEED

Sometimes the burden of making choices can seem too great, so much rides on them. We need help. Beneath the ordinary question, "What should we do?" lies the deeper question, "Whom do we trust to forecast the consequences of our choices?"

One of the goals of parenting, catechism, and mentoring is helping those in our care "make good choices." And we look to God's revelation (through Scripture, tradition, and experience) for authoritative guidance. We trust that God guides creation and humanity toward the right and good; that God alone has knowledge of choices that lead toward those outcomes; *and* that God seeks to reveal that knowledge to us—ultimately becoming incarnate to do so!

A stunning aspect of the Genesis story is that even when God directly and unambiguously states the consequences of a choice—"eat it and you die"—Adam and Eve are tempted to disobey. Presented with the serpent's confident alternate interpretation of outcomes and enthralled by the fruit's apparent goodness, they eat.

How much more for us? Our choices are rarely as stark as "eat/ don't eat" and appealing fruits surround us. And even if we only consider "Christian" guidance, we will have dozens of alternatives, all of which we seem wired to ignore anyway. No wonder Paul despairs of human ability to choose (Rom 7:14ff).

It is risky to preach Jesus as an example for us to follow. Still, Jesus' wilderness showdown with the devil suggests that the clarity and strength for sorting through tempting options comes not from knowledge but from his intimate relationship with God, a relation that is also available to us.

ETHICAL IMPLICATIONS

One problem with choice is that it opens us to error. From road rage to political acrimony to racism to domestic and sexual violence there is no shortage of evidence of individual brokenness and systemic disease; that is, sin. In spite of the too-often-true caricature of how "good Christians" respond to sin (some mix of incomprehension, tsk-tsking, and horror) the witness of Scripture (including today's readings) and our richest theological tradition is: we *get* it. There is no human or social behavior to which Christians should respond, "how could this happen?" We know how.

Placing the origin of sin in the first chapters of the biblical story shows that we know that sin enters our narrative very near the source. Were we to trace every sinful act back to its genesis, we know it would be rooted in primal fears, hurts, and angers on the one hand and our inability to understand or accept our limits on the other.

The first missional response of Christians to sinners and sinfulness is the gift of acknowledging them with candor, compassion, understanding, and hope. This is not denial or excuse but rather a commitment to remain hopeful for God's way of restoration. To paraphrase Frederick Buechner, the worst thing that happens is never the *last* thing. The second missional response is to open our storehouse of ritual practices. Psalm 32 is the template for one of those; the power of confession and absolution are embedded in its move from "when I kept quiet, my bones wore out" through "so I admitted" to "songs of rescue" (vv. 3-7).

Christians don't sequester sin and sinners. We extend an invitation to candid truth-telling, believing that by speaking aloud what all parties know to be true, chasms can be bridged and relationships—with ourselves, our neighbor, creation, and God—can be restored.

GOSPEL IMPLICATIONS

In light of the typology and logic of Romans 5, the stories of "humanity's fall" and "Jesus' righteous act" are episodes in the cosmic narrative of redemption that ends with "the righteous requirements necessary for life [being] met for everyone" (Rom 5:18). In respect for this frame, the sermon should not exhort us to "resist temptation like Jesus did," but should focus rather on the liberation Jesus' obedience wins for us.

The epigram, "Sin boldly!" is often attributed to Martin Luther. Sometimes it is mistaken as a smug flaunting of freedom from the Law, but the imperative was actually forged in Luther's simultaneous experience of sin's depth and his trust that "the free gift following many trespasses brings justification." All of our actions and choices are tainted by our intrinsic brokenness. We have mixed motives, collude with sinful systems, are trivial, are unconsciously reactive, and show ignorant disdain for consequences. Reflection on this can result in paralysis—leading to sins of omission!

To sin boldly means to claim two aspects of our baptismal birthright. First we trust that when we (inevitably) sin, we have an advocate who knew in advance our dilemma(s). Second, we trust that in the community of faithful practice our lives are being conformed to Christ and that our actions and choices might be incrementally less disobedient today than yesterday.

Notes

Martin Luther, "The Freedom of a Christian" in *Martin Luther's Basic Theological Writings,* edited by Timothy F. Lull, 1989.

Barry Schwartz, "The Tyranny of Choice," *Scientific American,* April 2004.

HENRY J. LANGKNECHT

ERIC TROZZO

SECOND SUNDAY IN LENT

THE LESSONS IN PRÉCIS

Genesis 12:1-4a. In this simple story of God's call and Abram's response, God's mission to bless "all the families of earth" begins. The story also establishes the metaphor of journey or pilgrimage as component of obedience.

Psalm 121. The images of the psalm promise guidance and safety, especially for travelers: surefootedness, shade, and a sentinel who "won't fall asleep on the job."

Romans 4:1-5, 13-17. Paul is concerned here to protect the sovereignty of God against the notion that our righteousness in any way prompts or controls God's action. The "faith of Abraham" is in an autonomous, gracious God.

John 3:1-17. God's mission of cosmic salvation is fully known by the Human One who has descended from heaven and then by those to whom the Spirit freely grants new birth from above. This new birth leads to a life of similar freedom whose quantity _and quality_ are described as _eternal._

THEME SENTENCE

God will bring the entire cosmos to fulfillment . . . and humans, too. Part of traditional Christian practice in Lent is self-examination and repentance in our life of faith. In contrast, the lessons on this day invite us to look far beyond ourselves toward the _land of promise._ We are called to put our lives fully in God's hands and, instead of considering ourselves, to consider the one who is utterly trustworthy (won't fall asleep on the job) and who is busy with sovereignty and mission of universal scope. We are reminded that being a herald of this mission demands humility.

A Key Theological Question

As astronomers bring us pictures of ever more distant reaches of the universe and as the NASA rover Curiosity explores on Mars, we can begin to feel like a tiny, insignificant speck swallowed up by such incomprehensible vastness. What import could we possibly have in a universe of such incredible magnitude? How can we speak of any meaningful role for humanity within the epic scope of the universe's story? At the same time, our talk of God is always from the limited perspective of what the divine means for us. Can we understand God as more than a tribal deity of humanity? Can we understand God as traversing the immensity of the universe while having a tender relationship with humans? In Jesus' discussion with Nicodemus, we find an affirmation of the cosmic stage on which the divine drama unfolds and an affirmation of God's particular love for humanity.

It is easy to fall into divorcing humanity from the rest of creation. Many people assume a fundamental distinction between the "civilized world" and the "natural world," as if human society were not dependent on the rhythms of the land on which we live. Or they speak of the difference between "humans" and "animals" as if humans were not also biologically "animals." These divisions presuppose an independence of human life from the natural cycles of the world. Such a position ignores that humanity is embedded in the fullness of creation. We are dependent on plants and animals for myriad needs, from nourishment to the air we breathe. Indeed, we could trace back how the biological systems on Earth rely on the same physical forces that scientists use to understand intergalactic phenomena like star formation. The theological point in all of this is to recognize the breadth of the claim that God is as much the God of the distant star Alpha Centauri as the God of Adam and Eve. God is not just the creator and redeemer of humanity. God is the creator and redeemer of the entire cosmos, so God's concern encompasses issues of celestial scope.

Christian theology, which has traditionally seen everything non-human as mere backdrop to the divine-human relationship, must recognize that God's work is not all about us. At the same time it should not dismiss the personal aspect of God caring for individuals and for the human family. In this vein, for example, contemporary Reformed theologian Jürgen Moltmann has suggested that salvation must be understood in the context of the entire environment in which we live. He understands our very bodies to be the link between the personal experience of redemption and the redemption of all of creation. The ultimate hope that we claim is, in fact, an affirmation of the physical world. Moltmann says that "the special thing about Christian eschatology is its surmounting of the enmity between soul and body, spirit and matter, and its full affirmation of the body and the matter of which earthly things are composed." (Moltmann, 1993, 259). In other words, human beings are flesh as well as soul. Our bodies are vital to who we are, and so must be included in the redemption and renewal brought about by Christ. Humans are made of the same stuff as the rest of creation, and thus are intrinsically related to all of nature. For Moltmann, then, new creation in one is related to new creation for the other.

Drawing on Moltmann, we can speak of a unique role for humanity even while maintaining an eye on the cosmic scope of God's work. The appointed readings bear witness to the divine action that holds the particular and the universal together. In the story of Abraham we see an example of God working through a promise to an individual as a means of blessing a multitude. God tells Abram that "all the families of earth will be blessed because of you" (Gen 12:3). Thus we encounter the promise of a plan that starts with God's relationship with one individual but has a global reach that will unfold over the course of history, expanding ever farther. The principle that we find here is that God works through the particular to bless the whole.

In the Gospel reading, then, we begin to see hints of the universal scope of God's plan. John has Jesus redirect Nicodemus' focus toward broader realities. Jesus points him to heavenly things (3:12), and then points him to God's plan for the world through sending the Son (3:16-17). We find here an intensification of the blessing of the whole through the individual. Indeed, we find a trajectory of the ever-more expansive realm of God's field of activity that can exceed the farthest reaches of the universe. Moving beyond the blessing for all families that came through the blessing of Abraham, then, we see that new creation is brought about for the entire cosmos through the new creation brought about in Jesus.

Might we understand the baptismal calling that Jesus is pointing to as a call to being reborn as part of the divine drama that extends beyond the human realm? God is bringing about redemption on a cosmic scale that far outstrips our comprehension. Nonetheless, in baptism we are adopted into God's method of working through the individual for the sake of the universal. We may be but a small part of this divine drama, but that by no means suggests an unimportant role. We have a stake as individuals and as humanity in the cosmic plan, with the role of being a blessing to others and a harbinger of a new, redeemed creation that is to come into and transform the old creation.

A Pastoral Need

We appropriately draw on our faith for managing our day-to-day lives. But inward focus can also leave us feeling stuck and unchallenged. In God's call to Abram to "leave your land," in the psalm's assurance of traveling mercies, and even in Jesus' promise that those born from above will be blown by the wind of the Spirit, we hear intimations of the spiritual practice of pilgrimage.

Pilgrimage *can* involve physical movement: congregational service trips, travel to shrines or holy sites, or traditional missionary service. More commonly, pilgrimage involves encountering the new and the other in metaphorical journeys. When seeing couples who are content but feeling stuck, some experienced pastors will suggest that they do more entertaining; seeing each other interact in unpredictable encounters can open undiscovered roads that lead to a deeper relationship. Some spiritual directors, in order to thwart static "navel gazing," will only enter into relationships with those who agree simultaneously to move into unknown territory, often in the form of charity or advocacy work.

The essential dynamic of pilgrimage is that we are prompted by God to encounter new—often disquieting—sights, sounds, tastes, and smells, with the promise that we will be blessed and that we will bless others (Gen 12:3). The gift of pilgrimage is the discovery that the faith we experienced as anemic and moribund is actually resilient and fearless, coming as it does as a gift from our life-giving God.

Ethical Implications

Much Christian reflection on the relationship between God, humanity, and creation begins with the immodest assumption that humankind is the crowning glory of creation and proceeds from the dual commands to "subdue" the earth and "have dominion" over all other life (Gen 1:27-28, KJV). Combining this reflection with strands of tradition that glorify the heavenly at the expense of the material results in a confused interaction between the church and contemporary concerns about creation, nature, and environment.

Today's Gospel reading may not be the clearest prompt for an exploration of how God's purposes and Christ's lordship extend beyond human needs and concerns (cf. Colossians 1:15-20). But by linking the affirmation that "everything came into being" through the creative Word (John 1:3) with the announcement of the incarnate Word that God intends to save the cosmos (John 3:16-17) we can tease out that trajectory. Salvation of the cosmos is more than just peace among nations and getting people safely into heaven; the Church's mission and message should touch that broader vision.

When kudzu vines, termites, raccoons, and ultraviolet rays express their place in God's design, they enter our space. That mosquitoes and grizzly bears see *us* as *food* is part of God's design.

And even if humanity is the crowning glory of creation, we who have been born anew into the eternal life of Christ should require little prompting to lay aside that honor. At the very least we should consider whether human convenience should always determine our response to our environment.

Learning to live with the awareness that all things have been handed over to Christ does not mean an endorsement of environmentalist ideology. It is an invitation to see how God's mission encompasses all the flora and fauna of the universe, including humankind.

GOSPEL IMPLICATIONS

Paul proclaims that God calls Abraham not because of Abraham's fitness but because of God's graciousness (Rom 4:1-5). There is a parallel logic in Jesus' metaphor in John 3: just as we are delivered into earthly life through no initiative of our own, so we are born into (and then travel through) eternal life not by our righteous initiative but by the gift of the Spirit blowing "wherever it wishes."

Scripture later testifies that Abraham set out "without knowing where he was going" and died "without receiving the promises." But he and all those called into God's mission "saw the promises from a distance and welcomed them" (Heb 11:8, 13). In the same way, we who have been filled with the Spirit and then blown into God's saving mission know that God's intended blessing of the world has yet to be fulfilled.

And though the waiting and the longing for fulfillment can be agony, the cross of the resurrected Christ is lifted up and serves as a balm. The cross is the sign of our confidence that our feet will not be moved and that not even death threatens the promised blessing.

Notes

Jürgen Moltmann, *The Way of Jesus Christ*, 1993

HENRY J. LANGKNECHT

ERIC TROZZO

THIRD SUNDAY IN LENT

THE LESSONS IN PRÉCIS

Exodus 17:1-7. In the wilderness the Israelites ask Moses for water and he brings it forth from a rock. By naming the encampment Massah and Meribah, Moses reveals that the people are really anxious about the source of faith.

Psalm 95. After first person plural imperatives ("Let's . . . !") to extol and praise God, the psalm switches to divine warning against testing God.

Romans 5:1-11. Paul expounds one aspect of theodicy: suffering—he seems to mean suffering in discipleship—can be the means by which hope is produced.

John 4:5-42. Jesus reveals himself as Messiah to a Samaritan woman through the metaphor of "living water." Living water reminds readers of John of Cana (John 2:9), being reborn (John 3:5), and Jesus' piercing (John 19:34). With the disciples Jesus echoes the "true bread" image from the temptation stories (Matthew 4:4 and Luke 4:4).

THEME SENTENCE

God seeks and saves the lost—including those lost in their found-ness.
In the first reading, God provides water for a stiff-necked, impossible, and *already saved* people. In the Epistle lesson Paul uses God's salvation of weak, sinful, enemies of God to show the *already and continually saved* that God cares for them.

A KEY THEOLOGICAL QUESTION

In the Exodus reading, the people of Israel have already been freed by God from captivity. They have seen God act. Yet they still thirst for more. In this case, the thirsting is presented quite literally, but we can

91

also take it metaphorically (as Moses' naming of the site implies). Even though the Israelites have further seen God in action with bread from heaven (Exodus 16) they already feel a distance from God. They are on a journey with a route and destination with which they are unfamiliar. In the midst of uncomfortably new circumstances, the people are terrified of being abandoned and long for familiar old ways. It matters little that the old ways were those of slavery; it seems easier to rely on such familiarity even if oppressive than to trust God in these uncertain new circumstances. Thus they are thirsting for a tangible reminder of God's guidance. They feel lost in the desert and want God to act again to save them. They need to experience God's salvific work for them over and over again, to remind them that God never went away, even in the midst of turmoil. Thus the Lord commands Moses to remind the people that God is indeed still among them, leading them through their fears and through the wilderness. The water from the rock is a tangible reminder that God's salvation is always at hand, even when it is hidden from view.

Many people are attracted to being a part of a church as a refuge against the uncertainties that fill their lives. Whether their unease stems from personal relationships and finances, political situations, ecological concerns, or any number of other issues, anxiety over changing circumstances causes people to hold on to familiarity. Sometimes this desire leads to a healthy preservation of tradition. Too often, however, anxiety makes people feel lost and pine for a return to captivity, much as it did for the Israelites in Exodus. Lying behind this desire for retreat is a thirst for a reminder of God's guidance. It is a longing for the assurance, and indeed a tangible sign, that God's salvation leads us forward. We dread being lost and abandoned in the wilderness, and need to be reminded that God never left our side.

The Protestant theologian Paul Tillich helpfully differentiates between "fear" and "anxiety" in his book *The Courage to Be*. Fear, he says, has a clear object that can be faced. Anxiety is a more ambiguous general sense of unease. With anxiety, nothing in particular can be pointed to as threatening, and yet there is a pervasive sense of being menaced. To use the Exodus reading as an example of this distinction, the people express a concrete fear: they need water and there is none. Thus they fear dehydration. God addresses this by giving water from a rock. The unspoken anxiety behind the people's complaints is that God has abandoned them. This is a larger and more diffuse concern than the straightforward need for water. Yet through giving water from the rock

God also addresses this anxiety, as shown in verse 7 when Moses, "called the place Massah and Meribah, because the Israelites argued with and tested the LORD, asking, 'Is the LORD really with us or not?'" The anxiety here stems from the possibility that being freed by God also meant being abandoned. Did God save them only to set them loose on their own, or will God continue to guide them? Is God there at all? God acts again to show them that God will contine to shepherd them. Moses names the location where God provided water as a response to the people's anxious testing, thus recognizing the people's dread and God's response.

For Tillich, having faith is being grasped by the divine so that one can move forward in spite of anxiety that God might not be there after all. As he puts it, "The courage to be is rooted in the God who appears when God has disappeared in the anxiety of doubt" (Tillich, 190). In other words, the deepest form of faith for Tillich is the faith that appears when we continue to trust God despite the anxious sense that we might be on our own. Yet we see from Moses' leadership in naming the people's anxiety that it is also important to have a tangible sign that God is with us in our journey.

Today many people feel that our culture is in the midst of a significant shift. New technologies and forms of communication open new possibilities but also bring new challenges. The image of being in the wilderness can speak to the anxieties that come with living through such unsteady times. It is common to speak of a "Lenten Journey" in referring to our spiritual discernments of the season. This phrase brings to mind the people of Israel journeying through the desert, unsure of where exactly they were going or how they would get there. They thirsted for assurance that God was with them. Today, too, we need a reminder that God journeys with us. God calls us to move forward into unfamiliar territory, trusting in faith that God has already acted to save us and will continue to do so. Yet in leading a community of faith, it is also important to name underlying anxieties and offer tangible signs of God's continuing care. For the preacher this may mean searching for specific examples of God at work in the community.

A PASTORAL NEED

Finding meaning in suffering is perhaps the greatest challenge for our faith. Once found, such meanings give rise to powerful individual and communal testimony. As preachers we may take note, only the one who suffers, gets to find the meaning in suffering; no one should assign meaning to the suffering of another. Gospel preaching about individual suffering inspired by Paul's stirring move from suffering to hope (Rom 5:3-5) or by the Samaritan woman's move from shame to enthusiasm (John 4) should be illustrated by the preacher's own experience. Such vulnerability can move listeners to identify and reframe their own struggles and trials.

Preachers have a different role when interpreting the suffering of the communities to those in their care. "We've come to place with no water; is this a test from God or the result of our inexperience with wilderness camping?" "Our congregation is dying; are we supposed to learn to trust God or refine our skills or both?" And the questions beneath those questions are even harder: "Is a happy solution inevitable?" "Is God *bound* to provide a 'way out of no way' in *every* case?"

Moses exhibits narrative genius when he memorializes Israel's failure of nerve in the names Massah and Meribah—no less than the gritty genius of God's naming of Israel himself in Genesis 32:28. God elects a people and is thus self-consigned to a relationship of contention and ambiguity as the people learn to distinguish God's plans from their own.

ETHICAL IMPLICATIONS

Two things are established in the first act of the encounter between Jesus and the Samaritan woman. First, in violation of cultural norms they are going to have a conversation, and, second, the word "water" means different things to each of them (John 4:7-14). As act two opens, the woman is focused on her personal need: "Sir, give me this water, so that I will never be thirsty." Then the conversation meanders from a revelation of her personal shame, through knowledge about God and true worship, and finally to Jesus' revelation of his identity as Messiah (John 4:15-26). By the end, she has become an invitational evangelist. In echoes of John 1:39 and John 1:46 she invites the people to "Come and see a man who told me everything I've done!" And we can imagine this subtext, ". . . and who didn't turn from me in disgust!"

The curious part of her evangelism script is her vague and indirect question, "Could this man be the Christ?" (John 4:29). Perhaps her caginess is a survival strategy. But it also reveals an invitational wisdom. She demonstrates knowledge of what people are longing for, testifies, but then quickly presents Jesus to them in way that allows them to make their own judgment.

"The inside-out church" is one of the catchphrases of the missional-emergent conversation. It reflects a desire to move away from intramural focus and care, toward missional engagement with world and culture. At a deeper level, becoming "inside-out" signals awareness that though *we* know that in the Body of Christ there is relief for every thirst, "church" is not a known commodity (or that what *is* known is distorted and caricatured).

The Samaritan woman provides a script for us: "Come and see . . . ." Could she be inviting us to the intersection of community and true meaning for which we have longed?"

GOSPEL IMPLICATIONS

The Israelite characters *in* the story really wonder whether God is with them (Exod 17:7). But readers of Exodus experience the question as rhetorical; of *course* God is with them! Similarly in Romans 5, we already "have peace with God" when Paul considers what suffering means. And in terms of the historical sweep of salvation, we believe that through the death and resurrection of Christ, God typifies the assurance that no cross we bear can threaten our eternal life.

But we suffer and bear crosses that shake our faith all the time. What is the right attitude when we ask, "Is the Lord with us or not?" Smug confidence that God will come and strike the rock? Or humility, realizing that just because God is for us does not mean that *this* cockamamie decision won't kill us?

The life of Jesus and the testimony of Paul bear witness that the Christian journey takes us through a *real* wilderness toward *real* crosses. All we *know* of resurrection is that we die; the rest is hope. We trust that God intends for us to keep learning whether the faith we profess has the living God as its object.

Notes

Paul Tillich, *The Courage to Be*, 1952.

HENRY J. LANGKNECHT

ERIC TROZZO

Fourth Sunday in Lent

The Lessons in Précis

1 Samuel 16:1-13. As Saul's failed paranoid reign ends, the prophet Samuel is sent to anoint one of Jesse's sons as king. God keeps God's own counsel about the gifts needed by a king and chooses Jesse's youngest son, David.

Psalm 23. The psalm reflects complete trust in God. This trust is based on the psalmist's experience of God's will and capacity to be always present and leading and to provide absolute serenity and protection.

Ephesians 5:8-14. This passage is an exhortation to an already converted audience to keep living into its conversion. Believers are to live ethically in the light and to *be* light.

John 9:1-41. In addition to reporting a miraculous healing, the story of the man born blind shows that Jesus, the world's light, simultaneously enlightens those wanting sight and confounds those who think they can see.

Theme Sentence

God is the author of God's saving story. The saving works of God speak for themselves in a language that even the enlightened struggle to understand. Samuel is confounded by God's election process. The good shepherd leads the sheep through dark valleys and enemy land. The deepest meaning of the healing of the man born comes into focus slowly and only for some. Yet through it all, God steadfastly works out God's purposes.

A KEY THEOLOGICAL QUESTION

God's ways are not our ways. Indeed God often works in ways that are beyond our capacity to fathom. As we see in our readings for this day, even the deeply faithful cannot always discern the rationale behind God's actions. In the Gospel reading, Jesus' healing of the man born blind throws everyone into confusion. First, after he washes and sight comes to him, those who had known him as a blind beggar are confused about his new identity. Then, more seriously, this healing ignites debate among the Pharisees as to whether a sinner can perform the works of God. That is, they weighed the good of this miracle against the fact that it violated Sabbath laws. Some said that only one who has come from God could perform such signs, while others said that one who comes from God would observe the Sabbath. Pitted against one another in this way, there could be no escape from these circular arguments.

It seems that those who viewed Jesus as a sinner for his healing won the argument. We could read the Pharisees' reaction to this healing as evidence that they were entrenched as Jesus' opponents, looking for any opportunity to make a case against him. Or we could read more sympathetically, seeing instead a group of people struggling faithfully to understand the strange ways in which God works. Recall that the Pharisees are divided over what to make of Jesus' deeds of power (John 9:16). They, or at the least some of them, were trying to take what they knew of God and apply it to a new situation. They knew that God commanded the observance of the Sabbath, and so they were trying to reason out whether someone who breaks God's commandment can be from God. We can see in their debates not trifling arguments over technicalities but rather the attempt of a community to assess reasonably and faithfully a claim of a new way in which God is acting. The challenge for them, and for us, is to maintain the humility to recognize that God may act differently than we expect. Certainly we must balance such openness to divine freedom with a continued trust in what God has revealed to us about the divine nature and ways of acting, yet we ought not forget God's ability to exceed our expectations.

How are we to respond to this God whose works are beyond our understanding? Do we confound ourselves by struggling to explain why God's actions make sense? Or would it be better simply to give up and declare God too mysterious to fathom? Is there a middle way? The relationship of faith and reason has long been debated by Christian theologians. In the middle ages, St. Bonaventure held that the attainment of any truth, even philosophical truth, was possible only when it was approached in faith. In contrast, his contemporary St. Thomas Aquinas argued that while our faith in our eternal salvation demonstrates that we can hold truths that exceed human reason, it is also possible to attain theological truths without faith. Such truths are only incomplete and inferior to revealed truths, however. He called this pairing of revealed and speculative truths a "two-fold truth" about religious claims. Looking back further, St. Augustine believed that Platonic philosophy and other pagan tools should be used to understand scripture. But he also believed that one cannot truly understand God until one loves God. He further argued that the final arbiter for balancing the use of faith and reason is not the individual but rather the church. It is a decision to be made corporately. Yet Augustine also recognized the limits of our human reasoning capabilities and advocated trusting in an experience of the Holy Spirit to help us in our weakness. Indeed many theologians, regardless of their exact stance on the relationship of faith and reason, would echo this reminder for humility when attempting to understand God.

Returning to the Gospel reading, we see the Pharisees who view Jesus as a sinner using the best logic they have to evaluate a new situation based on the truths handed them about God. They know that God commands the Sabbath; therefore anything that contradicts the Sabbath is not of God. It is solid logic that misses the work God is doing right in front of them. They have allowed their reasoning to cloud their ability to see God in action. From an Augustinian viewpoint, we might say that they followed an appropriate process of discernment by weighing matters corporately, but they forgot the humility of trusting the Spirit to guide them in discernment. They trusted their own reasoning too fully rather than acting out of love for God.

In the season of Lent we are called to practice humility. One form of humility is the recognition that faith is a matter of "seeing a reflection in a mirror" (1 Cor 13:12). God's ways are not ours and God does new and unexpected things sometimes. This does not mean that we are not to do our best to discern what is of God and what is not. Indeed we ought to take what we know of God and apply it to whatever situation we face. Nonetheless, our answers are always provisional; God's truth is too elusive for us to ever be sure that we have it in our grasp completely.

A PASTORAL NEED

We believe that God heals, leads, and protects. *And* we know that the people to whom we preach pray for healing, direction, and serenity that never come. Today's readings contain testimonies from the psalmist and the man born blind, both of whom believe that God has acted powerfully in their lives. Both testimonies are sincere and cannot be gainsaid. But neither can we use these testimonies as the basis for doctrine or *specific* promises of God's presence or healing. They can aid faith when signs of God's presence are obscure.

We meet the author of Psalm 23 fully formed, a trusting sheep. But the man who can now see is more complicated. His conversion echoes the movement of the passage from Ephesians—darkness gives way to light, but still with the need for discernment and growth (Eph 5:8 and 10). As he engages skepticism and resistance, he testifies his way into clarity (shown by the evolution of his identifications of Jesus).

Baptism signifies a stark sacramental move from death to life—as if from darkness into light (Eph 5:8). But the darkness of our lives can obscure the blessings. For some hearers, the mature confidence of Psalm 23 provides inspiration that almost in spite of evidence to the contrary, God is present. The man who can now see demonstrates a process of testifying to God's gracious action as the means by which we come to see even more clearly how God is light and life in our lives.

ETHICAL IMPLICATIONS

Ephesians proclaims both that we already are light and that we are discerning what it means to please God living as light. The challenges of that discernment are made clear in the experiences of Samuel and the Pharisees, and the hard words from Jesus in John 9:41. Being close to the engine of God's mission—whether as called, charismatic individuals or as leaders in a religious institution—can give us illusions of insider knowledge, even as that proximity clouds our judgment and puts us at odds with God.

King Saul was God's anointed! But God has a new leadership paradigm. Samuel's grief demonstrates that we will struggle with the very changes God uses us to effect. Honoring the Sabbath is the third commandment and the Pharisees use good-faith interpretation to judge Jesus. But now God is moving on, deepening the meaning of Sabbath observance. God's word to Samuel is a motto for these and many situations: "God doesn't look at things like humans do . . ." (1 Sam 16:7).

The circumstances of the world continually confront God's people with apparent impasses where the way forward is unthinkable . . . even unframeable! Perhaps it is our mortal "short view" that makes us favor the false security of precedents. But God is at work far ahead of our understandings, finding new ways to ply God's mission.

The discipleship implication is twofold. First, the church can be listening carefully for the testimony of the formerly blind who point to evidences of God's work, even from corners we can't believe and through actions we don't quite trust. Second, as we face issues that fit no easy molds of precedent—e.g., climate change, increased cultural heterogeneity—the church might risk "healing on the Sabbath" as an act of deeper obedience.

GOSPEL IMPLICATIONS

In a classic dramatic device someone enters a dark room and turns on the light. Sometimes the light illuminates what has been lost or obscured and the next line of dialogue expresses relief or joy. Other times the light exposes a fearsome danger, but seeing enables dealing with it. The Word of God—in the person of Jesus (John 9:5) and in the work of God's mission community (Eph 5)—functions as light in these ways. Sin is exposed, the way through the valley is illuminated, and the blind see!

Then sometimes the light reveals a compromising scene and we hear a hasty, "It's not what it looks like!" Light does *not* always reveal (as Jesus reminds the Pharisees). Sometimes our eyes deceive us and complex truths are obscured by a confounding appearance. Then, enlightenment—the gift of seeing things in their true proportions and relationships—only comes by God's revelation.

Martin Luther defined "theology of the cross" as daring to "call a thing what it is." God dares to do this, even when we don't. When lit a certain way, the cross is a scandal and death a shroud. But in the light of dawn "everything that becomes visible is light" (Eph 5:14).

HENRY J. LANGKNECHT
ERIC TROZZO

FIFTH SUNDAY IN LENT

THE LESSONS IN PRÉCIS

Ezekiel 37:1-14. In Ezekiel's third vision, he is taken to a valley of "dry bones." God brings brings them to life and commissions Ezekiel to proclaim God's life-giving power.

Psalm 130. Despite being in the depths as a consequence of sin, the psalmist trusts in God's forgiveness. Then, on the basis of that trust, the psalmist proclaims the same forgiveness for the people.

Romans 8:6-11. This passage assumes a stark dualism between setting the mind on the flesh ("selfishness," CEB), death, and immorality on the one hand, and setting the mind on the Spirit, resurrection, and righteousness on the other. But ultimately, the dualism is revealed to be a unity when God, through the Spirit, gives "life to your human bodies."

John 11:1-45. The raising of Lazarus, the last of Jesus' signs, finally provokes the Judean leaders to arrest him. The scene is shrouded in misunderstandings about timeliness, grief, and the deepest meanings of death, life, and resurrection.

THEME SENTENCE

God's life does more than overcome death. God renders death obsolete. The scene in Bethany is filled with people (even disciples of Jesus) who still think of death as God's worthy opponent. But from the same inspiration that gives life to dry bones and calls forth Lazarus, the Psalmist and Paul witness to a faith that mysteriously contains death.

A KEY THEOLOGICAL QUESTION

For many people, death is an alien force. It lies so far outside of our comprehension and experience of life that it is hard to see it as anything other than an evil force lurking and ready to devour us. Death, in this view, is the polar opposite of the God of life. Following this logic, God and death are locked in an eternal struggle. It is a struggle that death seems destined to win, until God, by raising Jesus from the dead, pulls a fast one on death and delivers it a knockout blow.

Yet both our Hebrew scripture and Gospel readings today suggest a different relationship between God and death. It is not so much that God and death are two cagey fighters locked in a grudge match, but rather that God is Lord of all of life, including death. That is, even death is held within the divine. God tells Ezekiel to prophesy, saying, "I'm opening your graves! I will raise you up from your graves, my people; and I will bring you to Israel's fertile land" (Ezek 37:12b). For God to be able to open up graves and restore life indicates that life and death are both within God's dominion. God is the one Lord of all and is able to move between them. This theme is made more explicit in Jesus' raising of Lazarus. Jesus demonstrates that God's power over death extends not just to the last day when the eternal boxing match comes to a conclusion, but rather is available to God when God chooses. For the crowd gathered in Bethany, death seemed an insurmountable obstacle, but Jesus showed them that God's glory is not so bounded. It extends beyond what appears to humans to be an insoluble barrier. God loves life and desires it for all of creation. By raising Lazarus, Jesus shows that death is not an impediment to God's glory.

The fifteenth-century German cardinal Nicholas of Cusa is often associated with the concept of *coincidentia oppositorum,* or the "unity of opposites." This concept refers to a revelatory experience that unveils a hidden unity between two things previously believed to be utterly different from one another. He uses the concept to get at the transcendent infinity of the divine that is also always imminent. That is, he suggests that though the things of this world appear to be radically different from one another, they have an underlying unity within God. God is Lord of all, even things that appear to be conflicting or completely opposite from one another.

Such a sense of the ultimate unity of all things within God suggests that not even death can be separated from God. Death may indeed appear to be something utterly different from the divine life, but it remains an aspect of the vastness of divinity. God need not conquer death because

God rules over death. This would mean that both our life and our death are held within God's embrace. This does not mean that we should conflate the two or understand them to be the same thing. Indeed God calls us to live fully, as Jesus attests in saying, "I came that they could have life—indeed, so that they could live life to the fullest" (John 10:10). Such abundant life is God's aim for creation. Nonetheless, death does not separate us from God, as Paul reminds us in Romans: "I'm convinced that nothing can separate us from God's love in Christ Jesus our Lord: not death or life, not angels or rulers, not present things or future things, not powers or height or depth, or any other thing that is created" (Rom 8:38-39). God's love flows through all things, including life and death, because all things are held together within the divine. Life and death may appear to us as opposing forces, but both are rooted within God. Thus God can bring life even out of death.

It may feel risky to speak of death being rooted in God. It would seem to bring up difficult questions, like, "If God rules over death, why does death still wield so much power? Why isn't death obliterated?" Yet such thinking still conceives of life and death as opposites, rather than intermingled within God. For many Christian traditions, the sacrament of baptism blurs this dividing line. In baptism, we are put to death in Christ so as to live anew (Rom 6:4-5). Thus life, death, and eternal life all converge in baptism.

Lent is often understood as a time of preparation for baptism during the Easter Vigil. Part of the imagery of baptism is the transformation from an old life to a new one through a death to the old self. Affirming that life and death are both held within God allows us to hold that life and death are truly different. As such, a move from one to the other entails a real transformation. To be born again in baptism means living a changed existence. At the same time, we need not infer that prior to this new life in Christ God's love is unable to reach us. God desires more for our life than a life of death, but God loves us even when we are dead in sin (Rom 5:8). Because of this love, God calls us out of death and into new life.

A PASTORAL NEED

In our cultural imagination, crying from the depths usually occurs at 3:00 am. That's the hour for lying awake rehearsing our shortcomings, iniquities, and regrets, and for fretting over all that is unfinished, unresolved, and overwhelming in our lives. At 3 in the morning our lives seem impossible.

In those deep night hours of fret and lament we compose our own versions of "our bones our dried up," "hope is lost," "we are cut off," (Ezek 37:11) and, "Lord, if only you had been here . . ." (John 11:32). In these cries we testify with our biblical sisters and brothers to the experience of the absence of God. At 3:00 am and all other times of lament our souls cry for God's attention and we wait for the Lord "more than the night watch waits for morning." This last turn of phrase signals a hope deeply buried in the lament (and the repetition of the phrase in the psalm stresses this): the morning takes *forever* to come. And it *always* comes.

The Christian philosopher Peter Rollins encourages us to celebrate this paradox of addressing our laments of absence to the "absent one." When, from the depths of dryness, we cry to God that we are cut off and all hope is lost, we give profound testimony to our intimate, committed struggle with God. The accusations of abandonment are contained within a richer affirmation of trust and hope that the God we long for hears us and will come.

ETHICAL IMPLICATIONS

In Ezekiel and John we are faced with the quintessential human limitation: death. As we hear these texts, our mortality makes it natural for us to identity with the dry bones (as we do when we wring our hands over recent church declines); or with Mary and Martha as they try to understand how the promise of resurrection could have meaning even before the last day; or maybe even with Lazarus, believing that the end has come and the only thing left to do is wait in the dark.

These are natural points of identification, but they are eclipsed by our resurrection identity. We who have already been raised from the dead are the Body of Christ. Yes, we still look to God for rejuvenation, healing, assurance, and peace. But we also trust that everything we could possibly need we have already. We are called to be witnesses of the reality of those gifts now in the world. Our points of identification can be with the Spirit who blows through the valley of bones and with Jesus himself coming in confidence to Lazarus's tomb.

By the power of Christ's resurrection and the Spirit's gift, we trust the promises of God to be true, and we bear witness that the Spirit has already blown into our mortal bodies (Rom 8:11). We testify that God's power is already manifest in the world and encourage the unbelief of our neighbor to turn toward trust. We dare to face the stink as the stone is rolled away from the cave, and we stare boldly into the mouth of death in order to call forth life.

The church as the Body of Christ has already been knit together bone to bone and filled with the Spirit. In every act of justice, mercy, and evangelism, we take our stand with Jesus, expecting with a loud voice that Lazarus will come out.

GOSPEL IMPLICATIONS

The phrase "dead men walking" applied to death-row inmates captures the paradox that although the condemned appear to be alive they live under a declared judgment of guilt and an explicit sentence of death.

Those in whom the Spirit of God dwells (Rom 8:9) live under the opposite paradox. We are people who appear to be dying, but who die under a declaration of righteousness and an explicit merciful sentence of life from God. We, the baptized, are *alive* men sinning, *alive* women disbelieving, *alive* children of God suffering and dying.

Without suggesting that it ought to be normative for all Christians, we can say that the practice of infant baptism symbolizes this powerful aspect of resurrection life. By locating our dying and rising with Christ as near as possible to our birth, we bear witness to our trust that the entirety of our lives unfolds within the context of Christ's eternal life. In baptism we face *real* death, not a merely symbolic one, and are raised in Christ (Rom 6:1-6). Everything that follows—our growth, grief, pain, even our mortality and whatever lies beyond—both claims us completely *and* is qualified by being contained in the eternal life of God.

Notes

Peter Rollins, *The Orthodox Heretic and Other Impossible Tales*, 2009.

HENRY J. LANGKNECHT

ERIC TROZZO

SIXTH SUNDAY IN LENT

THE LESSONS IN PRÉCIS

Isaiah 50:4-9a. This servant of God—in contrast to the people described in Isaiah 50:1-3—listens for God's word, obeys God, and trusts in God's help and vindication even in the face of contention and disgrace.

Psalm 31:9-16. This portion of the psalm describes a bleak and overwhelming accumulation of grief, distress, isolation, and disgrace. And yet the psalmist trusts in God's grace and deliverance declaring, "my future is in your hands."

Philippians 2:5-11. This passage extols the nature of Jesus' obedient self-effacement and death and celebrates the reversal wrought by God's exaltation. This story is also an exhortation to us: let Christ's mind of humble obedience be *your* mind, our mind.

Matthew 26:14-27:66. Matthew's passion frames Jesus' obedience and the actions and responses of others as the fulfillment of the scriptures. Matthew also emphasizes that nearly everyone in the story—even Judas, the religious leaders, and Pilate—know that Jesus is innocent.

THEME SENTENCE

Jesus trusts God's intimate power so much he needs neither to cling to it nor defend it. The only way for Jesus to go from his exalted position is down, down into the stark reality of human existence. And, as Isaiah, the psalmist, and Paul testify, our experience of God existentially with us empowers a faith that leads to a life that expands as we pour it out.

106

A Key Theological Question

Too often we confine the doctrine of incarnation to Christmas time. The feel-good image of "God with us" rouses us with hopefulness in narratives of birth and new possibilities for the earth. It is sometimes harder, however, to keep to the theme that God is made flesh as we turn to narratives that remind us of how ugly the realities of this world can be. Indeed, the Passion reading points to the violent darkness that lurks in human existence. It is challenging and perhaps even somewhat offensive for many people to imagine the divine truly incarnated in this episode. Yet even more challenging is the idea that through such participation in the nitty-gritty of life God not only is with us in suffering but might actually move us toward the divine as well.

Within patristic theology, incarnation could be viewed as something of a two-way street. For the Cappadocian Gregory of Nyssa, for example, the incarnation and divinization were closely allied. His writing is dense, "What is impassible by nature did not change into what is passible, but what is mutable and subject to passions was transformed into impassibility through its participation in the immutable" (*Life of Moses*, 2:30). In other words, the bridge between human and divine created by the incarnation effects a greater transformation on the material word, and humans in particular, than on God. Because God took on flesh and participated in the fullness of human experience, God can work in us to move us toward the divine. Because God is infinitely unfolding, however, the more we move toward God the more unfolding of the divine occurs. While reaching unity with the divine is never possible, movement toward the divine is an essential ingredient of the spiritual life for Gregory. The more unfolding of God experienced by us, the greater the excesses of divine love that come into our awareness.

In the reading for today, Jesus experiences much of the worst of human nature. His community of disciples fails him, as Judas betrays him, Peter denies him, and Peter and the sons of Zebedee disappoint him with their failure to recognize the gravity of the moment. Jesus is then crushed by the machinations of power, both through the intrigues of the religious authorities and the abdication of responsibility by the political leaders. He is further mocked, humiliated, and beaten down by the soldiers. Jesus dies isolated and friendless. It is interesting that Mark and Matthew are the two Gospels where Jesus' final articulation from the cross is "My God, my God, why have you left me?" While certainly this is a reference to Psalm 22, it also marks Jesus' despair. In particular, in Mark and Matthew there are no acts of kindness towards Jesus; no appeal from a penitent thief crucified along with him, no touching scene with the beloved disciple and Mary, no women weeping beside him. He is left alone. Nonetheless, the Passion narrative shows Jesus stepping forward in faith, even as his existence crumbles around him. Indeed his cry of despair from Psalm 22 contains echoes of hope, as the psalm that begins with an anguished plea to God ends in watchful expectation. Jesus trusts God's intimate power so much he needs neither to cling to it nor defend it.

Taking the enfleshment of the divine seriously in this text leads us, on the one hand, to find God in the midst of ignominy, isolation, and injustice. In this we find God in solidarity with those who suffer the worst of human existence. This is a welcome message of hope in times when we struggle or despair. Even when we feel most disconnected and despondent, we can trust that God is with us. At the same time, we can draw from Gregory a reminder that God does not simply sit in solidarity with our suffering but also transforms our existence. In holding on to our trust in God even when God appears to be absent, we then sense God working in us to move us deeper into the folds of divinity. As we become wrapped in the billows of the divine depths a desire is awakened in us for God that continues to move us onward toward God. Is it that God is more fully manifested, or indeed incarnated, in our lives, or is it that our lives are more fully immersed in God? Here the image of the two-way street of incarnation and divinization is useful. The two cannot be easily separated, but rather both are true. Nonetheless, because God is infinite love it is not the divine life but rather our lives that are transformed by the encounter of incarnation and divinization.

The spiritual disciplines of Lent, whether understood as giving something up or taking something on, are intended to cultivate the desire for God among the faithful. They are practices intended to invite a space where human existence may be moved toward the divine. The practices of giving up and taking on are no more separable than the concepts of incarnation and divinization; indeed the emptying of our lives and the taking on of the divine within our lives mark the two-way street of the spiritual life. Through practices that turn us to the cross we are enveloped in the mysterious excess of the God who is abundant even in the parched absence and isolation of the worst of human experience.

A PASTORAL NEED

Today's readings, when heard in the context of the liturgical events of palm processions and passion, turn our focus toward Jesus' life, suffering, and death. And while we affirm that Jesus' passion is the cornerstone of salvation, this focus veils the word these readings have for Christian disciples. A prime instance is how the prayerful imperative, "let this same mind be in you . . . ," (Phil 2:5, NRSV), is eclipsed by the rhapsodic Christological hymn that follows even though Paul—in keeping with Jesus' insistence that he came not "to *be* served but rather *to* serve [us!]" (Matt 20:28)—cites the hymn for our sake, not Christ's.

Jesus trusts God's intimate power so much he needs neither to cling to it nor defend it. Transforming our minds into this "same mind" of obedient humility is part of the process by which God draws us into the self-emptying, other-serving, and ultimately exalted mission life of Christ. It is to these ends that we were given strength to undertake the "taking up" or "giving up" for Lent.

Feminist and third-world theologians appropriately question the Western Church's consensus that *pride* is the quintessential human sin and that humbly "becoming a slave" is a free laudable choice for all. For the undervalued and oppressed the inability even to claim a give-able self is sin's primary sign. C. S. Lewis responds by saying that humility is not thinking less of ourselves (overcoming pride) but thinking of ourselves less, irrespective of our ego state. We are empowered to set ourselves aside, consciously and fervently esteem others through prayer and action, and ultimately discover how we have always been fully esteemed, even exalted, by God.

ETHICAL IMPLICATIONS

Holy Week means a smorgasbord of worship events that track in literal time the 168 hours between triumphal entry and empty tomb. One guilty pleasure may be the temporary honor granted to some of us—free worship schedules in the local newspaper!—as we observe our high holy days. The concomitant risk is the hunger we face when we allow the religion business to overshadow God's mission. Today's readings from Isaiah and Philippians keep the challenging mind and heart of mission before us.

Isaiah 50:4-9 counters our inclinations to speak, teach, defend, or protect by urging us to listen, learn, trust, and give over. Trusting God is difficult. Powerful sustaining ministries might arise were we to do what a paraphrased Isaiah suggests we should do, "We turned our ear to our surrounding culture and listened like those who are taught. We gave our Sunday mornings to those who needed them for soccer games and we did not flinch when reminded how our hairsplitting renders us ineffectual and irrelevant. We cared not at all that grocery vouchers might be used for cigarettes or iTunes cards, making us look like fools. The God who vindicates us is near—and shares our humiliation with trust and determination. We are fearless and cannot be put to shame."

In Philippians 2:6, Paul's praise of Christ suggests that a lesser someone *might* consider equality with God as something to be exploited. Could the someone be us? For example, do we exploit our "equality with God" at the expense of the poor when we (in the United States, at least) accept tax breaks in exchange for donations to partisan politics? The arresting invitation to form ourselves into humble slaves so that *we may be exploited by others* reaches into our week of weeks forcing us to consider such provocative and difficult challenges while at the same time reminding us that our crucified challenger is the name above every name. Such trust is difficult but we have nothing to fear.

Gospel Implications

All evidence to the contrary notwithstanding, Christianity is an "all evidence to the contrary notwithstanding" faith. Jesus' trust of God even on the cross is "all evidence to the contrary." For us, there are two levels of contrary evidence to negotiate: what is at faith's heart and our own faith expression.

The evidence to the contrary at faith's heart is the subject of today's readings and the oxymorons they generate: self-emptying savior, servant leader, crucified God, glorified cross. At faith's heart is a savior who seemingly cannot save himself. This is the evidence that Jesus should *not* be faith's object. But this evidence to the contrary *has no standing*; it is not-*with*-standing.

And though our faith is supposed to be all evidence to the contrary notwithstanding, there is plenty of evidence that we live contrary to it. The biblical disciples started it. At the first contrary evidence that Jesus will rightly fill his role, "Satan Peter" dismisses Jesus out of hand (Matt 16:21-23). When Jesus provides contrary evidence that his passion fulfills scriptures, they desert him (Matt 26:56).

We rebuke contrary evidence in our own ways: fleeing to theologies of gratification, laboring to resolve unresolvable ambiguity and confusion through doctrine or rigid biblical interpretations . . . even creating the cross in our own domestic image. But non-contrary evidence always eludes; the contrary cross of Christ stands.

HENRY J. LANGKNECHT

ERIC TROZZO

GOOD FRIDAY

THE LESSONS IN PRÉCIS

Isaiah 52:13–53:12. God vindicates the servant because of his tenaciously obedient service (in spite of being unjustly afflicted, scorned, cut off). Against this haunting, startling vindication, the sinful equivocation and lukewarm trust of the worthy are shown in stark relief.

Psalm 22. On the strengths of the testimony of Israel's praise and a life framed by identity as God's child, the psalmist cries out to God to be present despite apparent absence; to listen despite seeming out of earshot.

Hebrews 10:16-25. Because of Jesus' once-for-all sacrifice, God's people are released from anxious obsession with spiritual accounting. We are free to live boldly, trusting that God is forming us into lovers and doers of good.

John 18:1-19:42. In John's rendition of the passion, Jesus is the divine "I am" who controls every scene until he is enthroned on the cross where he declares his reign complete: "It is completed!"

THEME SENTENCE

Jesus' obedience summons truth from the fabric of existence. Isaiah prophesies that rulers will see things they have not been told and contemplate things they have not heard. The prophecy is fulfilled as both Caiaphas ("it was better for one person to die for the people") and Pilate (inscribing "The king of the Jews" over the cross) unwittingly tell the truth about God's servant, Jesus.

A KEY THEOLOGICAL QUESTION

The events of the Gospel narrative today are small in scale but cosmic in significance. We have a recounting of an episode that is in many ways commonplace: a man in a provincial town finds himself at odds with the local religious authorities and caught up in the particular tensions of local political intrigue. The man is easily expendable and so executed. Such events are not only un-extraordinary, but generally what significance they may have would be confined to a small geographic area for a short amount of time. Yet the Gospel tells us that the particular experience of this particular man, Jesus, signifies cosmic truth. It is not just the particularity of the man Jesus who is arrested, tried, convicted and executed, but also the cosmic Christ. We find here, then, the tension between particularity and universality.

Indeed, whether the particularity of Jesus crucified can have cosmic significance is one of the intense debates in Christian thought. Often called the "Scandal of Particularity," the details of the debate have shifted over the centuries, but the central question still haunts Christianity: how can the infinite God be known to us in one particular and therefore limited person? It is scandalous to say that in one person we can see a fullness of God; it is even more scandalous to suggest that in looking at a man who is powerless in the face of a Roman governor we could also encounter the God who is the creative force of the universe. Indeed, in the second century Justin Martyr described how his surrounding culture viewed Christians: "They say that our madness consists in the fact that we put a crucified man in second place after the unchangeable and eternal God, the creator of the world" (*Apology* I, 13.4).

Later, in the third century, the theologian Arius tried to avoid such outrageous claims of the connection between the crucified particular and the divine universal by saying that Jesus is not exactly the same as God, but is, rather, similar to God. The Church, at the Council of Nicaea in 325, decided against Arius, instead upholding that the Jesus who suffered under Pontius Pilate was indeed of the "same stuff" (*homoousios*) as God. In other times and settings debates have sprung up over which aspects of Jesus' particularity are ones in which the divine is encountered. For instance, heated debates continue today over whether cosmic truth is revealed in Jesus' humanity in general or in his gender particularly.

In the Gospel reading for today, we find that the particular events leading up to Jesus' crucifixion unveil universal truths. Some of these truths are unwittingly unveiled. Caiaphas and Pilate tell truths about the nature of the universe and the God who creates and loves it, just as Isaiah foretold. As Caiaphas says, one man does indeed die for all of the people. Jesus' particular death has universal consequences: the Almighty God is manifested in and works through the meekness of this crucified one. The truth of God's identity as one who is compassionate towards creation and known especially in those who are weak and lowly is revealed in Jesus' crucifixion. Indeed, in obediently dying such a disgraced death, Jesus is marked not only as king of the Jews, as Pilate's inscription declares, but as king of the cosmos created by the God who cares for the disregarded. Such a claim brings to mind the cosmic Christ hymn in Colossians 1:15-20 that sees Christ as the foundation of all things. In this passage we hear that God created everything on heaven and earth through Christ. Thus through the particularity of Jesus the Christ we have a lens for encountering God the creator of the universe. The particular and the universal are tied together through Christ. Therefore in Jesus' obedience in the midst of degradation and crucifixion a window is opened to the cosmic truths that carry universal significance.

If in the cross we encounter God's love for the lowly, that means it transcends its historical particularities. Certainly the historical details of Jesus' crucifixion and the social stigmas and connotations associated with crucifixion in the ancient Mediterranean world more generally are important for our understanding of the depth of the meaning of the events, but they are not the limit of its significance. Rather, through the collision of the particular and the universal in the cross, it continues to affect our lives today. When we look to the cross today we can still encounter cosmic meaning. We can be grasped by God's compassion for creation and embraced by this truth. Even stronger, as our theme sentence above reads, **Jesus' obedience summons truth from the fabric of existence.** Further, we are empowered by the truth of the cross to participate in God's concern for the lowly. This compassion and concern were not one-time events tied to the particularity of Jesus' crucifixion, but are instead continuing truths about the nature of the divine that we encounter in the cross. The story of the cross is not only about the specifics of Jesus' suffering, but also envelops us in its narrative and calls us to be part of the universal truth of God's concern for the weak and downtrodden.

Good Friday worship is generally somber in tone, for good reason. There is much to mourn in the story of the events leading up to and including Jesus' crucifixion. Indeed, the cross is not lovable or comforting.

Yet the cross also discloses something of the nature of the cosmos. The creative force of the divine is inextricably tied to the integrity, compassion, and suffering known through Christ in Jesus. Through the cross the grandeur of the universal and the gritty reality of the struggles of the particular are bound together. This unbreakable connection of the two means that even as we grieve on Good Friday, we are also called forth to take part in the work of love revealed to us in the cross.

A PASTORAL NEED

The Good Friday lectionary gives central place to John's passion narrative in which Jesus is at his most divine, seemingly distanced from human existence. In fact, from this gospel's genesis "in the beginning" (John 1:1) to the penultimate climax of Jesus' victorious "it is completed" (John 19:30), John strives to assert the cosmic significance of Jesus' life. Even with this seeming distance, Jesus summons truth from existence. Even those people who do not want to testify to Jesus do so, namely Caiaphas and Pilate. In John, Good Friday is a day of victory, the world has done its worst and has not been able to destroy Jesus. The victory of Christ over the forces of death and destruction is clear. All they have been able to do is to kill the innocent one.

But poetic theological metaphysics are tough to sell to our pragmatic, evidence-based, rational, cause-and-effect, Western mindset. When faced with real-life troubles, contemporary people want step-by-step programs and clinically tested therapies. We, the church, believe with John that the cross is not just one religious image among many; the cross symbolizes truth that is woven into the very fabric of creation. But we must frankly acknowledge that there is no way to isolate that truth on a microscope slide.

What the people may need is not the proofs they ask for, they need rather to name for themselves who confronts them in these texts and in their lives, who it is who calls forth witness to his truth. They need to name for themselves who or what they trust in the face of evil and death. The God we trust is evidenced by a web of testimony that has sustained *real people*. In the same way, we put our brokenness into the care of God whose ostensive presence on earth is an unbroken succession of real-person-to-real-person testimony that stretches back millennia.

Yes, there is always an immaterial gap that must be crossed by a leap of faith. Only in making that leap does one discover that it was at the invitation of the living God who summons witnesses to the truth.

ETHICAL IMPLICATIONS

Most of us know the gratifying—if fleeting—feeling of righteous indignation. We've been falsely accused and look forward to our accusers' humiliation on our day in court. Our wisdom is ignored for some flashy but untested innovation, and we relish the chance, eventually, to say, "I told you so." The pleasure of righteous indignation comes from the anticipation of public vindication. We are not attractive to *others* when we are righteously indignant; the satisfactions are selfish and belong to us alone.

However, there is an attractive alternative righteousness. In Isaiah's description of the "suffering servant," the psalmist's paradoxical trust when God is absent, and John's portrayal of Jesus through his trial and passion we are invited to consider the haunting allure of those who are righteous *without* the indignation. To be righteous without indignation at the unrighteous, that is, to allow righteousness to be its own witness, is a bold ethical challenge.

We see it in a scene from the 1982 film *Gandhi*. Gandhi (portrayed by Ben Kingsley) still lives in South Africa and seeks to protest apartheid by burning his discriminatory government identification in a public demonstration. Respectful and calm, he approaches the fire. Each time a uniformed soldier beats him down; each time he rises, calm, and approaches again.

We saw it in newsreel footage of voting actions during the civil rights era. Calm, peaceful African American men and women lined up in Sunday clothes to exercise their right to vote and were assaulted by fire hoses, dogs, and clubs. They were righteous *without* the indignation—and hauntingly alluring.

A church that rests securely in Christ's vindication and that emulates the suffering servant's unswerving, selfless obedience to God's desired mercy, justice, and peace will be the means by which "many are astonished" and "kings shall shut their mouths." More importantly, such righteousness *without* the indignation points beyond itself to God who is the source of healing and enlightenment for the world.

GOSPEL IMPLICATIONS

When God created the first creation, God had nothing to work with. Unless chaos counts as something, there was nothing. But God brought order and made chaos into cosmos. And it was very good.

When God set out to create the new creation, God had less than nothing to work with: death, sin, shame, and evil. Yet **Jesus' obedience summons truth from the fabric of existence.** God worked through Incarnate Word to bring order again.

After six days of the first creation, God rested for a whole day. Saturday. And the cosmos held its breath to see how it would go on Sunday, the first day of the first new week.

Prior to the days of the new creation, God rested again for a whole day. Saturday. And the cosmos held its breath to see how it would go on Sunday, the "eighth day," the first new day of a new creation? Is the creative power of God's love sufficient to overcome evil, sin, and death? Is the creative power of God's love sufficient to overcome how much we make of ourselves and how little?

God's first words of the first creation have become the prayer of those who faithfully participate in God's new creation, "Let there be light."

HENRY J. LANGKNECHT

ERIC TROZZO

Resurrection of the Lord (Easter Day)

The Lessons in Précis

Acts 10:34-43. The proclamation begins with a sermon from Peter to the household of Cornelius. Jesus was raised for all. This is a stunning confession: God does not play favorites when it comes to redemptive activity and the desire to save. Jew, Gentile, and all are raised with Christ, because he is Lord of all. Peter is coming to see, and proclaim, that Jesus' resurrection casts a definitive light on all that they had come to know about God.

Psalm 118:1-2, 14-24. In its original Jewish context, this psalm functioned as an entrance liturgy to the temple, used at the festival of Passover. It proclaimed God's deliverance from Egypt and from exile. The tone is jubilation. In the resurrection, we too are delivered by God, so now Christ empowers us, transforms us, and pulls us out of death's grip.

Colossians 3:1-4. The claim here is that those who are being addressed by the letter have also been raised with Christ. The letter is written to people who have "died" (v. 3), and their "life is hidden with Christ in God" (v. 3). Christ is their life. They are in him—with him—and he is "above" (v. 1), "sitting at God's right side" (v. 1)! This text connects believers to the resurrection and guides them to an ethical response.

John 20:1-18. All three disciples see the empty tomb, but Mary stays long enough to "turn around" (v. 14) and see Jesus standing there. She turns away from the desire to find him in the tomb, and then Jesus encounters her. Jesus guides her away from the desire to cling to him, so that she might go and tell others what has happened, following him into the new creation.

118

THEME SENTENCE

God raised Jesus from the dead. God the Father raised the crucified Son Jesus from the dead. The Easter celebrations are the high point of the church year, but even the seasoned preacher can be surprised by the difficulty of preparing for this day. Isn't every Sunday a little Easter? Didn't we preach Easter at every funeral, every wedding, and every baptism over the past 364 days? So how do we up the ante for the actual feast? Perhaps we don't. Perhaps the challenge is simply to be awestruck.

A KEY THEOLOGICAL QUESTION

The theological challenge is several-fold, one must attempt to explain the unique nature of this event and not reduce it to something tame and familiar. Theologically speaking, it is too easy to run (as did the disciples) to the empty tomb expecting one thing and finding another, and then to lapse into the familiar again. After all, don't the disciples themselves need to be reminded, even by Paul years later, of the meaning of God raising Jesus from the dead? Part of the problem is that the resurrection has no real analogue. The event defies logic. It remains outside of human expectation, religious interpretation, and even subsequent reduction in something mystical or supra-natural in Word and Sacrament. But perhaps that is the theo-logic that is needed. In God raising Jesus of Nazareth there is something that uniquely remains mysterious, or unknown in God. Nonetheless, God, in sovereign pleasure and as a manifestation of God's mercy, extends that mysterious grace to material, finite, and human life. Thus, Easter morning is indeed the model of God's dealings with materiality, finitude, and human life.

On Easter morning, with the resurrection of Jesus of Nazareth, God demonstrates that the Immaterial Creator is not disinterested in the material but is joined with it through overcoming it. What is natural is superseded by the supra-natural. Likewise, the "end," in this case Jesus' death, is not the final word but instead he is sustained by the eternal Word. And finally, God declares that it is now impossible to speak of humanity without God and God without humanity, because the resurrection, as the disciples would come to know, is the proper form of that relationship between God and humanity. Neither humanity nor God can accurately be described without reference to the other. God is no longer completely Other, nor is humanity completely God-forsaken, but in the resurrection, with the destruction of the enemies of God in sin, death, and Satan, God and humanity are found to be fundamentally intertwined, thus deepening the story God initiated with Jews centuries before in the election of Abraham.

That someone is raised from the dead in itself is an astounding but not unique event, as others in the Biblical narratives have indeed been raised. But God raising Jesus from the dead stands unique, as it validates the distinctive life, ministry, and work of Jesus of Nazareth such that he is understood to be the Christ, defying the pious, hopeful, and even skeptical. This is the uniqueness of his resurrection—not only is Jesus raised, but Jesus will not die again, and the enemies of God, particularly death and finitude, are now defeated by the work of God. In a very real way, humanity and God are changed that Easter Sunday.

Of course, part of this must necessarily remain a mystery. The eventual understanding of God as Triune begs consideration of Jesus' death and his relationship in life to his deity. Is it even possible for God to die or experience death? Can the Father experience the Son's death, or are they sealed in two distinct compartments in the Incarnation? Does Jesus' human side die but his divinity remain somehow intact does he experience a pseudo-death? However these questions are answered, they seem to highlight both the mystery and the limits of theological thought. The death and resurrection of Jesus of Nazareth is interpreted as an affirmation that: (1) God is eternally Triune; (2) Jesus the Son is differentiated from God the Father and God the Spirit in his joining of humanity to Himself.; (3) and the death of Jesus is also a victory in God.

God raising Jesus of Nazareth from the dead shows God overcoming everything that seems to be anti-God—death, sin and the Devil—and that occupies a space of non-being in terms of God's purposes for created reality. All creaturely realities live only in the permission of Divine Will, but more importantly are found judged and naked so that everything anti-God can be defeated by God. Humans are reminded in the resurrection that reality, including sin, death, and the Devil, is actually theo-logical – a reflection of the truth that God reveals about Himself. The Church, in Word and Sacrament, testifies to this theo-logic but must also remain humble in what it can claim to know and instead allow itself to be lifted into the mystery of God in Christ.

A Pastoral Need

Our aching need is for the wild and merciful God to bring to fullness this reconciling work. In the face of death—hurricane, tsunami, flood, drought, earthquake, war, disease, disorder—the victory of Easter can be difficult to "see." We cannot see the full promise of the empty tomb, yet. At times there is a Holy Saturday quality to the life lived in faith (Lewis, 2003). Easter preaching can address this need by pointing to the silence of God while Jesus is dead in the tomb, which precedes the utterance-for-life which raised Jesus from the dead.

There is very little explaining needed. A gift from the pulpit on Easter Sunday might be to strike the Passion Narrative gem in a way that allows it to break open anew. Evoke the full promise of an empty tomb. The disciples find new life in God, a new creation in the risen Lord, by *not* finding what they were looking for. Maybe the preacher can help worshippers not to find what they are looking for as well.

What do they not find? A corpse. After such a loss, hope clings to the idea that we can see the loved one "one more time." Hope clings to the idea that once more we can touch him, see him, find him. But no such luck. God doesn't want our hopes to be that small.

What do we not find? What desires are frustrated by this action of God then and now, and how does this open totally new possibilities *ex nihilo*, "out of nothing."

Ethical Implications

In Colossians 3:1-4, the baptized are reminded that we have "died", and our "life is hidden with Christ in God" (v. 3). We are in him, and he is "above," "sitting at God's right side" (v. 1). The mark of this reality, and the means by which it becomes a practical reality, is the human heart transformed to love. The aspects of our character and behavior that do not conform to the love of Christ are stripped away. In the resurrection of Jesus, the new world has already broken in, and we are given a hope that will not tolerate anything outside of this new reality. This takes continuing conversion to the fullness of the Easter good news. Our response to the Easter proclamation can be to plunge into the struggle against evil knowing that *in Christ* victory is possible, probable, assured! This is the strongest kind of hope because it gives the strength, courage, and endurance necessary to follow Christ through the fray. A struggle continues, but Jesus is Lord and someday even the powers of evil will admit (confess!) this. So we do not have to "cling" to the Lord, we simply run out to meet him in the new creation. Our response is to trust what we hear and live accordingly.

Gospel Implications

Of course, the cross is the central Christian symbol around which the faithful gather to find the presence of the Lord. God took the dead Jesus and raised him to life. God wants to do the same thing with us—to encounter us and to raise every kind of deadness to life. Not only does God want to—but also God has done and will do this. It is our hope; it defines a life lived in Christ's name; it opens to all a "world" of salvation. Easter is the day which the Lord has made; let us rejoice and be glad in it!

Notes

Alan E. Lewis, *Between Cross and Resurrection: A Theology of Holy Saturday*, 2003.

TODD TOWNSHEND

DARREN C. MARKS

SECOND SUNDAY
OF EASTER

THE LESSONS IN PRÉCIS

Acts 2:14a, 22-32. Here, on the second Sunday of Easter, we have a Pentecost sermon. When the followers of Jesus were filled with the Holy Spirit, they were perplexed, asking, "What does this mean?" (v. 12). Peter speaks; he proclaims the Christ-event and the meaning of Jesus' life, death, and resurrection (the *kerygma*), addressing the people who have had their lives changed by that event and the sending of the Spirit.

Psalm 16. A song of trust and a confession of faith in YHWH alone, this psalm becomes an expression of confidence through its descriptions of God's providence. There is fullness of life in this trust. Those who utter the psalm promise to have nothing to do with other gods.

1 Peter 1:3-9. An expression of awe, blessing, and praise for the mercy God has shown in giving new birth and a living hope in the resurrection of Jesus. Encouragement in suffering is given through the promise that the inheritance is "pure and enduring" and "cannot perish" (v. 4). More precious than gold is the faith that without seeing him still allows the faithful one to "love him", "trust him", and "rejoice with a glorious joy that is too much for words" (v. 8).

John 20:19-31. On the evening of the day that Jesus rose from the dead, he enters a room filled with disciples who are trying to lock out all that threatened them in the aftermath of Jesus' execution. He appears twice amid their doubt and believing, brings them his peace, breathes the Holy Spirit on them, and sends them out again in his name.

THEME SENTENCE

Jesus invades his followers' fear and gives them a future. Unlike last Sunday, in John 20:1-18, Jesus now allows his followers to touch and see him. The good news of Easter is still primarily *heard*, but the incarnate and risen One condescends once more out of compassion and the desire to save. Jesus invites them to touch his wounds and to taste the goodness of his risen life. This appearance of Jesus is astonishing. The disciples are locked away in a room of fear. They've lost hope and are looking for a way out. Without Jesus, they are nobodies again. Threatened nobodies. They are confused and bewildered, not just by the appearance itself, but also by the fact that Jesus did not come through the door! Nothing is happening the way it's supposed to happen. Nothing seems real. The physical evidence of his suffering helps to identify him, but it is his command "Shalom!" that reignites the whole biblical witness for them, especially the promise of life made in the face of death. The words "receive the Holy Spirit" (John 20:22), along with the breath of life upon them, bring them to a new creation moment when the dust of the earth is formed into flesh, when dry bones are knitted together into life. Jesus establishes a new humanity from the people he loves, thereby giving all people a future in God. They have been re-membered. The future is God's future, and God's future involves God's people in Shalom and in Spirit.

A KEY THEOLOGICAL QUESTION

The future is already promised in the act of Creation itself. God decides, in Triune Being, to create an-Other and to join with that which is not God. The future is also seen in the history of God with Abraham and Israel and its prophets. God alone elects to save and creates a people for God-self which has never wavered in promise. Although the disciples are not yet completely aware that the saving promise would extend beyond the election of Israel, Christ opens a new future by giving God's peace and Spirit (John 20).

In accepting God's future does one also to find God's peace? Certainly there are enough Christian platitudes, plaques of saintly prayers to support this point of view. But does this even accurately reflect the experience of Jesus? How much "peace" did he feel during the passion because of the promise of a future with God? How much at peace were the disciples following this event?—they hid back in the wilds of

Galilee. Clearly, the equation of peace and future is false. So what is the connection?

The Spirit is key, and the doctrine of pneumatology (largely left to Pentecostals and neo-Charismatics) helps us to understand any link between future and peace. The Spirit is given in baptism and continues to nourish the baptized in every sacrament. If this were not the case, and if the gift of the Spirit was instead the completion of one's humanity such that a person is now "seen" by God, then one might conclude that the future will be a smooth journey on the rough roads of life. Such was the docetic understanding, to reproduce "Christs" who seemingly float above human life and its complications. Rather, Christ was fully God and fully human, and that means he experienced the complete spectrum of human existence. The Spirit is not a kind of generic principle of love. Instead, the gift of the Spirit is the intrusion of God's future upon each one of us. We live in hope and future rather than being bound by the limits of the present.

The Spirit is the foreshadowing of life as seen by God, and that is promised and ultimately elected by God. In this, Christians are re-linked to Israel, allowing us to see what Jews call the *Tikkun Olam*—the mending of the world, including ourselves, by the Messiah. Peace, then, is not inner calm or piety; it is about learning to live in the promise that God is indeed active and real, bringing all things unto God's own self, and mending the world. Despite evidences to the contrary, the future is God's and God's action brings that future. The fruit of this future is the gift of the Spirit. To think more deeply on the Spirit is to think more deeply on the future and the reality of peace.

A PASTORAL NEED

Jesus meets all people at their point of need. He meets the disciples in their fear, he meets Thomas in his doubts, and next week we will hear that he stirs up fire in the disheartened Cleopas. After Peter denies Jesus three times, he forgives him and calls him three times, restoring him. Jesus meets Paul and changes him from persecutor to apostle. Jesus meets and changes people. He redeems the past and opens the future. He was good at knowing the nature of each person's need. What was the nature of the disciples' fear—what was the threat? What was the nature of Thomas's doubt? For many of us, the deep *nature* of our need is the last thing we want anyone to know. Most of us would prefer to have people believe that we need nothing. Walled off from those who would discern our need, we wonder why there is a lack of peace, a lack of Spirit, in life. Preachers may find this an opportunity to proclaim that Christ has already come inside the walls, past the locked door, asking hearers to put away their self-protecting resources. The Holy Spirit of God has already been given, breathed upon all of the baptized, and that same Spirit nourishes continually in the sacraments. Knowing our needs before we know them ourselves, Jesus brings a peace and a Spirit that enables us to ask questions. What makes me sad or afraid? What makes me hurt? What threatens? What needs to change? What stands in the way of faith? When Jesus meets us at our point of need, he sees us as God would have us be. Just as God mends the whole of creation in Christ, Christ mends us too, making the way for our future with him.

ETHICAL IMPLICATIONS

Sometimes the ethical implications of proclamation are more directly related to the things we should stop doing, rather than things we should start doing. The effort to live a holy or "ethical" life can be nothing more than an effort to *manage* our fears and desires, or worse, it can be an effort to manage God. But if the resurrection of Jesus from the dead shows anything, it is that God will not be managed. Jesus invades the disciples' effort to "manage" his death by holding out his wounded hands and giving them his peace. Perhaps the mission of this sermon is to help listeners recognize the ways they might be avoiding God—even by means of their religious patterns of life! The ethical imperative here is to trust the One standing before you. This is faith-work. We are full of mistrust because of the many times we've been put at the mercy of someone else's agenda. But when the agenda, or the purpose, is God's, we trust that, like the disciples, we will be recipients of the peace bestowed by the Spirit—a peace that results in the surprising confession that Jesus is our Lord and our God. That confession has implications for a way of life.

GOSPEL IMPLICATIONS

We are freed from our fears and our unhealthy desires not by knowledge or understanding but by flesh—crucified and resurrected flesh. The wounds of Jesus remain even though he is glorified. The wounds are transformed

Sell your books a

sellbackyourBook.c

Go to sellbackyourBook.c

and get an instant price qu

We even pay the shipping - s

what your old books are wor

today!

into signs of forgiveness, sources of healing, places of compassion and faith-confession. The gospel prevents us from hiding our own wounds, partly because what is hidden may not get healed, and what is not healed cannot be a blessing to others. God continually mends and renews us through the risen and ascended One.

Todd Townshend

Darren C. Marks

THIRD SUNDAY
OF EASTER

THE LESSONS IN PRÉCIS

Acts 2:14a, 36-41. Hearing the conclusion of the Pentecost sermon Peter preached (last week), the followers are "deeply troubled" (v. 37). Their query has been transformed from "what does this mean?" (v. 12) to "what should we do?" (v. 37). That is a *significant* shift. The response to the sermon, guided by Peter, is a response to the question: they repent—they turn to God—and they are baptized. Reception of the gift of the Holy Spirit, in the name of "this Jesus, whom you crucified" (v. 36), is the key to receiving *the promise.*

Psalm 116:1-4, 12-19. A song of thanks, this psalm moves from an expression of distress, to YHWH's deliverance, to an expression of faith and a claim to "keep the promises I made to the LORD" (v. 14) who "hears my requests for mercy" (v. 1).

1 Peter 1:17-23. Those who have a living hope in Christ are summoned to holy living, reminded that they have been "liberated" (v. 18) with something more precious than imperishable things—the precious blood of Christ. Raised up from the dead, the blood of Christ is now a non-perishable! The exhortation is to love deeply and constantly from the heart.

Luke 24:13-35. Jesus was active on the day that he rose from the dead. Here, he comes alongside two disciples who walk away from Jerusalem looking sad. They thought they knew everything there was to know about Jesus of Nazareth—he gave them hope, but now he is dead. They could not recognize that he was walking with them, alive, until they invited him to stay with them and allowed him to be the host in their own home. They recognized him in the breaking of the bread, and in that recognition Jesus disappears, requiring them to become witnesses to his appearing. They go and tell, returning to Jerusalem in great joy.

THEME SENTENCE

Jesus frees his followers for faith. One of the great turn-arounds in the Christian story, the road to Emmaus is a round trip. Revealing the dynamics of the post-resurrection church, it is a story of encounter and witness. There are several steps in the movement to faith. Jesus initiates the encounter, and his own witness allows the disciples to accede to faith. Jesus reveals that his death and resurrection is the "key" to understanding the whole witness of scripture, and he demonstrates that his disciples need guidance in order to "see" this. The sacramental gesture of recognition and reception is essential in the movement to faith (at the breaking of the bread), as is the mission of the believers to make the witness their own. They travel from no-faith to faith, from Emmaus (before Jesus) to Jerusalem (with Jesus), from "Jesus is dead." to "Jesus is alive!" Together with Jesus the Risen One, they unwittingly "perform" each element of this conversion experience, and as a result they increasingly gain competence for witness.

A KEY THEOLOGICAL QUESTION

Faith is a word commonly used in theological works but rarely explored. Faith, as understood by Martin Luther, is as simple as confidence in an agent to fulfill a promise, understanding that the agent is sufficiently powerful to deliver. This is a helpful definition, as it underscores two important ideas: first, that the one in whom faith is placed must be worthy of such faith, and second, its correlation, that the one in whom faith is placed must be able to fulfill the promise given. Of course, for Luther, the question would ever remain: how does one know a gracious God is exactly that? For Luther, it would be folly to trust one's own merit and thus, as with most of the Reformers, he needed to add that ultimately faith is a gift of God and by God. God's grace is known only after God is self-revealed to be gracious. Our witness is merely to point towards the character of God who makes a promise. This too is God's self-revelation.

According to the Emmaus narrative (and its strong foreshadowing of the Eucharistic meal), the power of revelation and faith is seen in conversion. Conversion is not a conviction that we derive based on evidence, but rather is a gift of God opening one's eyes and heart to the declaration of God in Christ. In other words, God is the agent of conversion and the subject of faith. What is asked of the Christian is to witness—not to persuade or coerce but to point to God, trusting that God is sufficiently powerful and trustworthy to be able to do what God promises. If God's promise in Christ is to be *for* humans, then it follows that the church has a special kind of activism as its witness. Its activism is its theological existence, proclaiming the future of God without usurping that future (and thus becoming an enemy of God or at least an idolater). It does this obliquely by being converted by Christ. Just as Emmaus redefined what is the nature of witness, so Word and Sacrament redefine how we witness. But faith and conversion are key.

A PASTORAL NEED

It is important to know what faith is (and what it is not), and it can be helpful to extend the question further to include, "how does a person pass from no-faith to faith?" Faith is a gift, and we might ask about the dynamics of this gift. Many people want faith, but barriers stand in the way. Is there a certain *competence* required, even for the reception of the gift? The Emmaus narrative demonstrates the interplay of what God provides for us and what God requires of us in order for us to be transformed, converted to believers.

How does faith come to believers? Their eyes are closed to faith initially. When the narrative begins, the Lord is no longer visible. In fact, his followers are sure he is dead and gone. Second, there is an initiative from God. The disciples do not initiate the revelation. But revelation must be received, and thus participation in the conversation is required. In this case it requires that they reveal their needs. Then, through four actions, the disciples are "turned around." Faith begins to come through speech (we need a guide for scriptural interpretation), through a response "stay with us," (Luke 24:29), and through recognition of Christ's identity (this is the same Jesus who was crucified).

There is one final element that is easily missed: the eyes must open on an absence (Jesus vanishes from their sight). Now, because this presence has become invisible (again), the witness is urged make proclamation of the gospel his or her mission—the witness is urged to embody it, to make it visible again. The passage to faith, which relies so heavily on the divine initiative and the Word's interpretation, is incomplete without the gesture of reception and the act of witness, both of which are empowered by the Spirit. A pastoral response to need takes seriously the various "required" elements in the passage to faith.

ETHICAL IMPLICATIONS

The Christian is asked to give allegiance to God, putting the character and wisdom of God at the center of life and giving witness to the goodness of God. Witnesses do not merely speak, they also enact the word as they live in the world. "Jesus is risen" is not merely an announcement, it is also an appropriation of the new reality—that God has defeated the last enemy, and the Word and Spirit of God are doing the work of realigning a world of disordered and disempowered relationships. These relationships are being made right. When one's eyes and heart are opened to this, the act of witness rises up and overflows. It does not require effort. Faithful discipleship starts with this overflow of joy, generated by the surprise of Christ's presence. What a difference this makes in individual or congregational attempts to live faithfully! The challenge for sustaining the healthy character of our witness comes in the moments when the excitement wanes, the times when we have to wait, and we walk along, and we get sad again. The news gets old, and self-interest sets in again. In those times we look around for the One who walks with us, and we again implore him to "stay with us" (Luke 24:29). In those times we recognize the need to develop the wisdom that remembers and anticipates the eyes-open moments, so that they sustain us between the times.

GOSPEL IMPLICATIONS

The two disciples were heading home, thinking that they knew all there was to know about Jesus of Nazareth. But an understanding that reaches only as far as yesterday's events may be a misunderstanding. Yesterday Jesus was dead.

But this is the first day of the week, and at early dawn this morning, something happened. They didn't know it. So this person came to them, opened the scriptures to them, and freed them. Jesus freed them from old, bad news. But they didn't know it. So they invited him to stay with them. When you have someone like this with you, you keep it going. And over the meal their eyes were opened, so that they could enter into a new understanding, a new creation. Jesus was with them—Jesus was not dead! And then . . . he vanished from their sight. Right while they were enjoying it. Right while it was dawning on them that Jesus was alive and that he was sitting at their table! Right where they wanted him! Right when they thought they had it all figured out, Jesus vanished.

Their eyes were opened, but on emptiness.

Kind of like when the other disciples came to the tomb that morning. They did not find a corpse, which is what they expected to find. But their eyes opened on emptiness. However, this emptiness was full of a presence, and they could not wait to go tell. They dropped their utensils and rushed out the door to Jerusalem, full of faith in him.

God sends the Risen One. At the Father's word, the Word comes. "Go to the distressed, go to the faithless, don't assume their faith is always strong. Go to them and walk with them." And the Risen One comes. In the absence comes his presence, and he walks with us, and demands that we listen to his interpretation of things. He ought to know! He's been to the dead! He's been raised up from dead! He sits at the right hand of God, for God's sake. He was in the beginning, and he'll be at the end. He's been in your fishing boat, and he's been at your table, and he will welcome you, in the end, to his table. But for now he comes to you as you walk along. And you've got to ask for something. You've got to pipe up in prayer, saying, "Stay with us." Lord, stay with us.

TODD TOWNSHEND

DARREN C. MARKS

FOURTH SUNDAY
OF EASTER

THE LESSONS IN PRÉCIS

Acts 2:42-47. After the Pentecost event, after the search for the meaning of it, after hearing Peter proclaim the *kerygma* and point them to baptism into Christ, the followers are now fully converted to a new way of being: "the believers devoted themselves to the apostles' teaching, to the community, to their shared meals, and to their prayers" (v. 42). Awe came upon *everyone* as a result of this new "way," and the Lord added to their number those who were being saved. The Holy Spirit is driving and enlivening the young church.

Psalm 23. Tied to this week's Gospel text, this well-beloved psalm is drawn towards the image of Christ as the shepherd, when originally this image evoked a different royalty. The shepherd was the king of the nation. In Christian proclamation the tensions involved can become very meaningful.

1 Peter 2:19-25. Endurance is the opponent of suffering, especially if it is unjust suffering. The example of Christ is offered so that his followers might not return abuse with more abuse, or threats of abuse, but rather that they might entrust themselves "to the one who judges justly" (v. 23).

John 10:1-10. In the middle of the Easter season, the lectionary leaps from resurrection appearances to the tenth chapter of John and faith statements about Jesus. We hear Jesus saying, "I assure you that I am the gate of the sheep" (v. 7). "I am the gate" (v. 9). "I am the good shepherd" (v.11). "I came so that they could have life—indeed so that could live life to the fullest" (v. 10). These statements are taken from his life and applied to the time of his resurrection life. It makes a difference to hear them in the season of Easter, now that Jesus has been crucified, raised from the dead, and seated at the right hand of God in glory.

THEME SENTENCE

Jesus knows his followers and gives them life in abundance. Jesus and the Father are one (John 10:30). Together with the Spirit, the intimacy between them is unparalleled, and the "I am" sayings in John attest to this from many different angles. Preaching from John 10 does not call for simplifying summaries. A straightforward statement is juxtaposed with deeply symbolic ones. God chooses to give life to sheep and shepherd freely, persistently, and in the face of every challenge. An emphasis on the shepherd might help preachers to avoid allegories unsupported by these texts. This shepherd provides all and promises all. He knows his sheep by name, and is so desperate to give them life that he would lay down his own life so that shepherd and sheep might rise together. This is the way to abundance.

A KEY THEOLOGICAL QUESTION

Could we think of this abundance of life as a conversion to the pneumatic/Spiritual life promised, won and given in Christ's resurrection and ascension? If a sense of abundant life marks our conversion to God, we no longer seek some other kind of fulfillment or existential peace. How does this affect our mission as Christians? Is God's focus merely me as "the sheep" or is it really the flock, or both? Our Western sense of individualism is not to be confused with God's global intent. God is not merely "this person's" or even "this community's" pet god but is always cosmic if only because the scale of creation, incarnation, and redemption is cosmic. That God created, was incarnated, and redeems affects everything, and the stage for this work is everywhere. The works of God are all one and the same, and nothing can be left outside the work of God. God is in the business of complete renovation, not merely repairing. Abundance, conversion, peace, and so forth are symbols of something or someOne always larger than us. But that is also good news.

It is good news because, if a sense of abundant life is not possibly won or worked out by us as a community, even the church, then it follows that abundance means to stop striving, to stop becoming idolaters by setting up pet gods and instead accept the Shepherd's care and presence, trusting the Shepherd to find pastures and protect the life of the flock. This is also good news because abundance requires not striving and programs but instead a joyful worship of God in Christ. Christ can then come in unique ways, even in the ordinary ways of the Word and Sacrament. God, theologians tell us, is in the be-coming of God in which God's work as Creator, Redeemer, and Sustainer brings about God's future. Abundant life is living in the be-coming of God.

A PASTORAL NEED

Pastoral needs arise when we think of abundance in material terms and immediately want more stuff, or want our way, or want fulfillment and satisfaction in every hour. Abundance is turning to God and living in God. The task of finding and naming genuine need often involves stripping away perceived need. It also involves taking the focus off the things we lack and the ways we are lacking. These are realities, but we can stop cherishing them. God sees them. Jesus is not fooled, but he also sees past them. Jesus would have us believe that God sees us and thinks, "Look at this beautiful person I have created! Look at this work of art; this ongoing work of art. I know this one! This is my beloved." Are we to protest, saying, "Oh Lord, what about all the other things you know about me? What about this thing I did. What about that thing I said. What about all the ugly stuff I hide away. What about the distortions, the worn out parts, the failed parts?" "Oh I see those," says the Lord, "and I've redeemed them. I've healed them. They are visible to me, but they are nothing to me." "Remember," says the Lord, "I know you—you are mine. I saw you in the womb. I guided you as a child. I lived with you in the drama of teen life. I provided through your work. I know the 'outcome' for you and for the whole cosmos. Nothing can snatch any of it away from me. I want to make you just like Jesus, whom I adore. And I want to give you everything, an abundance of life."

ETHICAL IMPLICATIONS

Mission in the abundant life is rooted in the action of God, and our burden is light. What we find is that our newfound abundance is a conversion, as an immersion into the pneumatic life of Christ we enter into a world much larger than ourselves. God is in the business of complete renovation, and we embrace this work of God wholeheartedly. How can we help? What to do? Stop striving for anything that does not serve God's work. Stop setting up pet gods, and self-made empires. Accept the Shepherd's care and presence. Invite God to work through you to find pasture and protection for the flock. Who are your fellow sheep? What does the Lord require? Worship joyfully in the expectation of Christ's coming in unique and ordinary ways.

All of this is done joyfully but without forgetting that most people in the world do not live with material abundance and most often this is a sign of injustice. Those who plunge into this life "in Christ" find Christ at every turn, and very often the "turn" is found as we relate to the people who do not know abundance in any form. The divine provision of abundance always requires provision for those whom Jesus calls "the least of these brothers and sisters of mine" (Matt 25:40). Christian mission and identity is found, and divine grace is experienced, as we serve, protect, feed and love these beloved creatures and children of God.

GOSPEL IMPLICATIONS

John's Gospel seems to tell us what we can know about Christ. Jesus repeatedly is saying, "I am this, I am that. I am the good shepherd. I am resurrection. I am the way, the truth, and the life. I am the true vine. I am the doorway, the gateway to safety in God." The first two words of those phrases must be significant. *I am.* This takes us all the way back to the "I am" spoken when God sends Moses back to Egypt to free the slaves (Exod 3). Moses asks, "Who should I say sent me?" And God said to Moses, "My name is I am." So Moses went, saying, "The great I am has sent me." Not was, not will be, but everlastingly now. And here Jesus speaks of his divine sonship, "I am the bread of life. I am the light of the world." They wanted to know who Jesus was. So he said, "I am."

Right after the part of the text appointed for this Sunday, in John 10:27, Jesus says, "My sheep listen to my voice. I know them and they follow me." You'd almost expect Jesus to say, "My sheep listen to my voice. *They know me.*" But no. He says, "I know them. And they follow me." He is claiming to know us. We're his sheep, so we're not supposed to do all the knowing; we're supposed to do the following. If you don't believe it, I want to assure you that every baptized person is a lamb of the Lamb of God. They are the sheep of Jesus the Great Shepherd. He knows you. He claimed you. He is making you like him. And he says that nothing can snatch you out of his hand.

That's different. It goes the other direction. He knows us. We don't examine the sun going over our heads and decide whether we believe in the sun or not. We don't examine the earth below our feet and decide if we believe in the earth or not. No, the sun is warming us even while we examine it, or even while we're oblivious to it. It makes the day light, and its rays make the earth bring forth life. It's almost like God's creation believes, reaching out like glorious sunflowers toward the sun. So all the more, God knows the creation, and all of us. God does the knowing.

We do the believing, the following, the praising, the serving. We only have to know enough to recognize that.

Maybe the mission statement above our door should read: we are a people known by Christ, and we believe that he's working on us! We're a work in process. Don't be put off by that! He's got us to the point that we're really listening for his voice. He's got us that far, at least, and He's promised to give us everything, in time. There is enough for all. Come join us!

Todd Townshend

Darren C. Marks

FIFTH SUNDAY
OF EASTER

THE LESSONS IN PRÉCIS

Acts 7:55-60. As we hear the story of Stephen, we recall, among other things, that not every sermon is well received. Leading up to this passage, Stephen has been falsely accused, and in his defense he recites the story of salvation, culminating with his judgment that those standing before him are opposing the Holy Spirit as their ancestors did. The response to Stephen is murderous, but even in the stoning pit Stephen remains faithful and sees Jesus *standing* for him at God's right side.

Psalm 31:1-5, 15-16. A song of lament, this psalm rehearses the elements of lament often overlooked (even obscured or omitted by the lectionary divisions)—prayer (vv. 2-5), expression of trust (vv. 6-9), lament (vv. 10-13), "but" another expression of trust (v. 14, 15), and prayer (v.16). It is important to note the "but" in verse 14 as a key to our human capacity (a gift) for praise and prayer.

1 Peter 2:2-10. Compare the use of the word "stone" here with its use in Acts 7:55-60. Far from being "a stone that makes people stumble" (1 Pet 2:8), or worse a stone that brings death, Christ is a living stone, the cornerstone, on whom our life is built, and through whom we are "called . . . out of darkness into his amazing light" (v. 10). The people of God receive mercy through this living stone, the stone that brings life and light.

John 14:1-14. Jesus advises the disciples not to let their hearts be troubled, but to believe. Not easy: in fact without God's grace it is impossible. However, Jesus gives them the way, the means, to be lifted from their anxious, directionless, fearful state. The cross of death is coming, but the difficulties will not last forever; they will give way to God's will and future. Jesus himself is the route to God, the path, the mode of transportation, the fuel, the navigation, the destination, the reason for the voyage—the way, the truth, and the life.

THEME SENTENCE

Jesus stands up for us and brings us to himself. Our preachers and hymn writers exhort us to "stand up, stand up for Jesus!" (George Duffield Jr., 1858). Yet in the stoning pit of life, those who look in faith will see him standing for them—and acting for them, on their behalf—at the right hand of God in glory. As the hymn says, "We stand in his strength alone." Far better for the Christian to proclaim where *we* stand, and where we believe Jesus stands, than to proclaim an exclusive "one-way-to-God-as-described-here" path upon which everyone should stand. We have found Jesus on that path, and we expect that everyone can find him there too. It is a narrow gate, but it is open and offered graciously and persistently: it is not dictated as a command. But why wouldn't *everyone* desire a God who hears our lament, stands up for us in our trouble, comes to us in our joy and in our sorrow, and finally brings us to himself so that where he is, we may be also!? We stand on this living stone, and he stands for all.

A KEY THEOLOGICAL QUESTION

In a multicultural and pluralistic society, Christian mission seems almost oxymoronic. To be "Christian" is to be tolerant and this, by extension, can mean that "mission" is self-defeating. Being Christian can mean being theologically and culturally neutral. The "foundation" of Christ can be like a lukewarm "Hallmark card" moment of ethics, certainly not unique and most certainly found in any reasonable human reflection, religion, and philosophy. Christ might seem to be a highly able but certainly not unique teacher of this kind of Christian tolerance. But this raises an important theological question and a most important ecclesiological question: what then is the role of the church? Is it only to be a Jiminy Cricket providing a conscience to the Pinocchio of culture?

Perhaps a clue to what the church *ought* to be is found in the simple action of Jesus. He stands up for us and brings the church to himself, which often means that the church is to stand in polar opposition to its dominant culture. This is a matter of freedom for the church, witnessing to its risen Lord who calls it to stand with him in proclaiming God's in-breaking future. That can mean a stoning, a stormy reception, or perhaps being outside the simplistic moral aphorisms that swamp the boat of Western culture. Most important, Christian service will be costly and not "cheap grace," as Bonhoeffer reminds us.

Cheap grace is classically understood as forgiveness without cost on the part of God. It can be seen in a kind of selfish, self-affirming, and inward acceptance of Christ that asks only Sunday morning to be unique in the life of a Christian. But Bonhoeffer pushes the idea more radically. He critiques not only a smug and easy Christianity that costs little culturally. Some might see the implications of cheap grace in the seeming contradiction between some kinds of advocacy, on the one hand, and not risking losing tax breaks or social status. Or some might point to Christians claiming to stand against poverty when there is nothing to distinguish between Christians and the general culture in terms of wealth. One of the charges against the first Christians was that their civic life was so exemplary, particularly in supporting the poor of Rome, that they embarrassed the Roman civic leaders!

Costly grace originates in the price God paid for our liberty in Christ. It can be reflected in the way in which the church stands with its Lord, calls the church to a deeper commitment of resources and time, and reconsiders its privileged place in culture. Costly grace invites the church to hear, pray, and then act in order to find its theological mission. It invites the church to see Jesus as Stephen did—majestic in God's future and not as our "buddy Christ" who reinforces our cultural expectations, however noble. This is not easy by any means, as the gate is narrow, but it may be necessary.

If the church were to engage in a rediscovery of "mission" theologically speaking, it might mean a shift from conversion or advocacy to the witness of God's future. It involves a rediscovery of spiritual habits of grace within the church. Before witness and mission, faithfulness and vision must come. This may mean in turn a rediscovery of ecclesiology to ensure that the doctrine of the church is not a doctrine of cultural reification.

A Pastoral Need

We are being made just as the world is being made new. This means change. God is making, molding, and pruning us, not trying to make us feel comfortable. If anything, we are being made *conformable* to Christ's death and rising. The nature of our going down reflects the nature of our rising up. So through the sighing, crying, and sorrow, through the hurt, anguish, and anxiety, our prayer can only be, "Your will be done." This is a statement of praise and joy, because God is bringing us into the fullness of Christ's stature. We do not suggest that suffering is the will of God, but transformation is, reconciliation is, gracious saving is. These things can hurt. God sees the hurt and stands up for us through it.

Ethical Implications

A rediscovery of mission is a rediscovery of faithfulness and vision. Vision is not understood here as an attempt to empower yourself or your organization with strategic tools, techniques, and to-do lists, but rather, the act or power of anticipating what will or may come to be in Christ and through the Holy Spirit.

Faithfulness is a way of being, complete with habits, practices, commitments, vows, and knowledge of God's help in keeping them. God calls the church to a deeper commitment not to tire us out and stretch us beyond our limit but to take us to that liminal place where God's glory is revealed. There, we see that nothing is impossible with God, even as our feet are planted firmly in such a worldly place as a stoning pit.

Gospel Implications

The interpretation here is influenced by a passage from a sermon by Gardner Taylor (2000), *"Seeing Our Hurts with God's Eyes."* The gospel implications may be revealed in what Taylor preaches about Stephen and Stephen's death. Taylor describes how it was an awful death; Stephen died in the stoning pit. There he saw mean faces and trembling hands ready to throw stones which were meant to break his bones and draw his blood. But even in the most hateful pit, Stephen was able to see what he had never seen before. As Taylor says, "he said he saw what you cannot see when the weather is fair, saw what bright days will never show you, saw what calm seas never reveal . . ." (Taylor, 2000. p. 90). In the stoning pit Stephen saw the glory of God. He saw the Human One <u>standing</u>. And in a moment that brings his preaching to a crescendo, Taylor helps the listener to see what Stephen saw. Acknowledging the newness of this vision Taylor says, "I know the New Testament says that the Lord Christ has sat down at the right hand of the majesty on high, but in the stoning pit, Stephen said he saw Jesus standing at the right hand of God, saw him on tiptoe, saw him standing up. 'That it might bear more fruit.' 'My God,' you say, 'what fruit after the stoning pit?'" (Taylor, 2000. p. 90).

Taylor preaches, "Well, there was a young man standing there who held the cloaks of those who held the stones. He saw Stephen die." (Taylor, 2000. p. 90-91). Saul saw a glimpse of the light in Stephen's eyes before he met the Light on the Damascus road where he became Paul, apostle to the Gentiles. In Stephen's death, Paul saw a man die praising God, he saw a man die forgiving. This was a reflection of Jesus' death and a vision of Jesus' resurrection. It bore fruit in the life of Paul, who through his own conversion, through his own vision of the Glory of God in the Son of Man, saw this Jesus stand up for him.

With Taylor, we get a glimpse of Jesus as Stephen saw him in his vision, majestic in God's future. Up on tiptoe, for us. If there is a gift to give—if there is a gift to receive—it is to know that this Jesus, from his childhood to his glory, is the way, the truth, and the life. He's not the *only* way; there are other ways through life, but if you need to find a way through something difficult or beyond your resources, He's your way. He's not the *only* truth, but if you seek the truth behind all that is, He's the face of it. He's not the *only* life, but if you want an abundant life, a holy life, an eternal life, He's the source of it.

Notes

Gardner C. Taylor, *The Words of Gardner Taylor*, vol. 2, compiled by Edward L. Taylor, 2000.

TODD TOWNSHEND

DARREN C. MARKS

SIXTH SUNDAY OF EASTER

THE LESSONS IN PRÉCIS

Acts 17:22-31. Paul, who witnessed the stoning of Stephen, and who by the Spirit became the holy fruit of that terrible act, is shown here in Athens bearing witness to Christ in a very different context. Paul recites the story of Jesus (the *kerygma*) in a manner attuned to the interests and commitments of the Athenians, offering them a better hope.

Psalm 66:8-20. Both a communal and an individual thanksgiving for deliverance, this psalm is a remembrance of God's help through every kind of difficulty.

1 Peter 3:13-22. Christ suffered to bring us to God, and in the face of suffering the letter encourages the church, "whenever anyone asks you to speak of your hope, [to]be ready to defend it" (v. 15).

John 14:15-21. A requirement is placed in loving Jesus, and that is to keep his commandments. Mutual love and the help of an Advocate is promised. The Spirit of truth, the Holy Spirit, will abide with those who love Jesus as he intercedes for us with the Father.

THEME SENTENCE

Christ suffers to bring us to God. God is near, and yet in our weakness we still need Christ to bring about reconciliation and communion with the Creator. This is a hope for preaching on the sixth Sunday of Easter: that the Word and Spirit will rekindle our hope through the act of proclamation and celebration. As the preacher gives an account of her or his

Christian hope, the congregation may gain, or reclaim, a sense of what real hope, a better hope, can be. A quest for genuine hope, however, leads us through the challenging terrain of "trouble," where hope seems all but dead, and it probes out into a future clouded by the unknown. But the Christian gospel offers Christ, the person who is our reason for hope and the person who goes to astonishing lengths to bring us to God.

A KEY THEOLOGICAL QUESTION

Again we are faced with a fundamental question: what does Christ mean *for us*. In Protestant theology, the idea of *"Christus pro nobis"* (Christ for us) is often associated with medieval Catholicism and a monolithic, impersonal church. It tended to be replaced by the much more personal and intimate *"Christus pro me,"* in which our personal relationships are linked to the work of God. In part, this makes a lot of sense given the theological and ecclesial applications on the eve of the Reformation. However, it also can create a kind of individualism in which the love, work, and suffering of Christ *for us* gets reduced to an example we are to emulate. Take the movie *The Passion of the Christ* and its widespread reception amongst individuals of *pro me* theology. For them, the passion of Christ is a demonstration of Christ's care for *this* individual. Such a muscular, vital Christianity seemingly encourages us to be "all that we can be." Here, God in Christ can become merely a form of our self-actualization, a graphic demonstration of how much commitment we should muster, given the ultimate demonstration of individual sacrifice on the cross. Is there anything wrong with this?

The answer must be "yes." It must be "yes" because the cross changes the nature of reality by bringing God's judgment on it. Reality cannot be merely personal. The suffering of Christ brings "us" to God in a cosmologically important event in which the entire created order is fundamentally altered. It does include individuals, but it is more than "me" and is "all" by its very nature. Nothing is left outside the judgment of God, and it is by divine grace alone that Israel and the church are lifted into this mystery as witnesses to God's future and the peace and abundance therein. By the same token, nothing is left outside of God's redeeming grace and purposes. This is a *"pro nobis"* theology, a passion that brings structural alterations in creation into which the church finds itself living as a kind of divine interstice or seam/faultline. The church is, as Bonhoeffer notes, the "hidden centre of Creation," and is given the privilege of possibly living in that "now and not yet" of God's future won in the passion.

But there are some important boundaries in this idea: the *Israel-church* event is primarily one in which the community living in word and sacrament is joined to its Lord in order to find its mission. It is not a one-time event in which the church could be conceived to be left to act in the place of its Lord, to bring about its own future, a position that would be idolatrous. Christ's passion is a cosmic event, a defeat and judgment on the enemies of God—sin, death, and the devil—who raise idols for the creation to worship. Christ suffers to bring creation to God, to make all things new, and the church acts between the passion and the parousia. It is a *pro nobis*, for us all.

A PASTORAL NEED

Preaching always functions in contexts of change. However, some needs never change. "Loss of hope" strikes human beings at their core, and represents a pastoral need present in every context. It seems to rise up in at least one member of a congregation, most of the time. Of course, the gospel has the power to address it.

We are inclined to place hope in the wrong things. Those whose hope is waning—whose hope is all but dead—often do not know it because in last-ditch attempts, they have transferred their hope to "something" else. When these "somethings" are other than God, they become idols, raised by the enemies of God. We find ourselves in deep trouble. We are wandering away from God. We are wandering, or running, away from life.

This may be why Paul is so willing to wade into the fray at Mars Hill. The people there are following many idols. His mission is to offer people a better hope, a living hope, and to have Christ bring them to God.

Paul's sermon at the council on Mars Hill (Acts 17:16-34) is similar to Peter's sermon at Pentecost (Acts 2:14-36, from the Second Sunday of Easter). Like Peter, he addresses his context with the *kerygma*—the story of the life, death, resurrection, and ascension of Jesus. Paul adapts the message for different hearers, recognizing a familiar need for hope. He is addressing people who know their way around philosophical debate, have an interest in personal religious experience, and are tasters at the smorgasbord of religious choices. However, Paul preached what they deeply needed when he spoke of Jesus being raised from the dead. Some rejected his message, perhaps they thought it was too superstitious, below them, or just plain gross. Nonetheless, this scandal of the cross and resurrection remained the center of Paul's message and some believed. He knew that as long as we remain low-hoping, sin-sick people, we risk losing life.

ETHICAL IMPLICATIONS

The church is given the privilege of possibly living in that "now and not yet" of God's future won in the passion. Among other things, this implies that we know that God will win and we must be ready to answer anyone who demands an explanation for the hope that is in us. What is your hope? This is a huge question, and when the response is addressed from one human being to another, it cannot be answered in formulaic language. The formulas of our faith, the theological language of scripture and tradition, must form and inform our response to the question, but the answer combines proclamation and personal witness, confession in conversation. With an emphasis on how Christ has acted for us all, indeed for the whole created order, we include our personal, unique, immediate claim of hope *in Christ.*

Hope is *expectant* longing. It lives within us, and, because it generates life, we believe that God in the Spirit has placed it there. It is more than mere desire or wishing things to be true; it is faithful, even reasonable, expectation based on God's promises. The foundation of my hope is always that we are "in Christ," and this takes on different expression, depending on context. Writing here, I am moved to say that I hope my children, as they grow and learn about life, will struggle with me to find God. They already do, and they both find God and reveal God to me. I hope the people in our congregation who are dying before my eyes while I'm preaching will reach out and take the hand of Christ as it is offered. I have seen what happens when they do, and it is a glimpse of glory. I hope Christ, working with and beyond the church, will overturn the horrors of this world, even as I know that every enemy has already been defeated in Him. I hope I will have the opportunity today to help God in the mission to reconcile all things in Christ. I hope God will not abandon us, so I take Jesus at his word when he says, "I won't leave you as orphans. I will come to you" (John 14:18). He suffers to do so. We trust this to be true, and we live in that hope; otherwise, we die.

What is the hope within you?

GOSPEL IMPLICATIONS

Christ suffers to bring *creation* to God, and the Church acts as a sign of what it is to live in God. Christ will make all things new. So we worship, we glorify God, and we expand our capacity to enjoy the Father's love by loving Jesus and telling other people why we love him. We keep his commandments, which all seem to involve loving one another in the same way that he loves us. The best news is that as we attempt to do what we are commanded, we come to know the help of the promised Advocate, the Holy Spirit of God.

TODD TOWNSHEND

DARREN C. MARKS

SEVENTH SUNDAY
OF EASTER

THE LESSONS IN PRÉCIS

Acts 1:1-11. Luke returns here to the ascension of the Lord. Jesus cautions his followers that they cannot know when the end times will come, but they will receive power when the Holy Spirit comes upon them. Jesus ascends blessing them (Luke 24:50-51) and he promises to return doing the same.

Psalm 47. An expression of the kingship of God, this psalm recognizes YHWH on the throne over heaven and earth. God has gone up with a shout of praise to the throne after the conquests of David. Christians traditionally hear in this the conquest of this son-of-David, Jesus.

Ephesians 1:15-23. This letter is a prayer for the church— that "the eyes of your heart will have enough light to see what is the hope of God's call" (v. 18). This prayer is to see an ambivalent, ambiguous reality: Christ's body, the church, is the fullness of him who fills all in all. We ought not put our hope in the church any more than God does, but the power of God is somehow at work in this *ecclesial milieu,* making it a place where resurrection life happens. It is still a broken place, but God has a hope for us.

Luke 24:44-53. Luke's first book ends with Jesus saying, "Everything written about me in the Law from Moses, the Prophets, and the Psalms must be fulfilled" (v. 44). He opened their minds to understand the scriptures and reminded them that he was to suffer and rise from the dead. Repentance and forgiveness of sins is to be proclaimed by the witnesses of these things. Finally, Jesus promised to send the Spirit and power, and he blessed them as he went. They worshiped and returned with great joy.

THEME SENTENCE

Christ blesses the church. Can two opposite things be true at the same time? Are we residents in the world or in the kingdom of God? Is death conquered even while people still die? Can we be as busy as a bee and still accomplish nothing? Can the church be broken and still be a blessing?

There is an "already realized" quality to the eschatology in the text from Ephesians. It speaks as though it is patently obvious that the glory of God has spilled over into the church and the church is full of that glory. Disciples of Jesus know that this is both untrue and true. It is unrealized and yet realized. There is a sense that disciples must continually hear Jesus say, "I am sending upon you what my Father promised; so stay here . . . until you have been clothed with power from on high." At the same time, be busy! Be faithful! Let your faith bear fruit. Live according to the kingdom of God. Desire the reign of God, for it is the really-real. While we do these things and wait, the Spirit initiates the Father's will and finds someone to clothe with power so that it may be accomplished. The Spirit finds a vessel ready to sail. The Spirit finds a clearing into which God can come to be seen, heard, and encountered. The Word and the Spirit lift the willing, faithful church into the reality of God, here and now, and someday in fullness. Wait, stay, expect, and be busy. What a gift to know the right kind of busy to be.

A KEY THEOLOGICAL QUESTION

Everything written in this section would be theory if not for the ascension of Christ and the sending of the Spirit. So often the story of Jesus stops on the resurrection and ignores the ascension, but the ascension is also the sending of the Spirit to the community of faith, so that in its enactment of faith through Word and Sacrament, the church can live its mission. Without the ascension of Christ and the sending of the Spirit, there is no church, only a society of philanthropists and philosophers whose individual interests are joined in common society. The church without ascension is merely another society, like the Optimists.

The ascension is simultaneously the absence and presence of Christ. Christ is truly with God but in the sending of the Spirit he also blesses his church into that reality as the be-coming or in-coming of God's future. The ascension is the dialectic of the church itself and its mystery of "being here" of this world and its frailties and at the same time belonging to "the

Lord's certainty." The church cannot think of itself *as* Christ but only *in* Christ. Only because of the ascension and the sending of the Spirit is the Church more than a group remembering a sage teacher, honoring a truly heroic sacrifice for principles. The ascension allows the church to participate in divine time, but always in the wild spaces of God's mystery.

But the absence/presence of Jesus is also a lesson to be learned for the church. It must, by default, take care to cultivate humility in its life of Word and Sacrament in order to hear the Spirit and perform the gospel. It requires much in terms of Christian habits—not morality, per se, or piety, but the willingness to follow where the Spirit leads.

The ascension is also a promise of Christ's return, as witnessed by the "two men in white robes" in Acts 1:10. Jesus "will come in the same way that you saw him go into heaven" (v. 11). If Christ has not ascended, if he is still on earth in his resurrected form, then he cannot return for he has not departed. The Second Coming, however we may understand it, is an assurance that just as God has been faithful in raising Jesus Christ from the dead, so too at the end of time, all of God's promises through the ages will be fulfilled through Christ. Justice, peace, and mercy will rule, and all creation will be renewed. That renewal is already happening in and through the Spirit.

A Pastoral Need

Much of "the world" just wants to smack folks down. Sometimes out of cruelty, sometimes out of hurt, people push others down to exalt themselves, even just a little bit. It's not just people but also systems, institutions, and bureaucracies that draw energy and dignity from others and reduce them to a number and a statistic. Then there are the machines of death, carrying out war of every kind. There is plenty of pain associated with the dehumanization that happens around us and to us. So we try harder to fight it and fix it, or we try to make a name for ourselves, striving further to lift ourselves up from the ground.

We need to hear that there is someone at the right hand of God, the almighty power of the universe, who knows our names and understands our lives. We recognize that any desire to escape this world, with all of its pain and struggle, is misplaced. Rather than longing for escape, we can luxuriate in hope exactly *because* we remain here waiting with God and for God. The angels said, "Why are you standing here, looking toward heaven? This Jesus, who was taken up from you into heaven, will come in the same way that you saw him go into heaven" (Acts 1:11). That is a promise. The one who will consummate history is a person who knows us; he knows where we are and what it's like here. There is compassion and forgiveness with him. He returns with his wounds still visible. So we lean away from the fantasy of escape and the busyness of production as we wait in hope, and we lean toward a posture and attitude of gracious hospitality. We welcome the animating, humanizing Spirit, as we watch the gospel happening powerfully all around us. Remember Jesus saying, "You will receive power when the Holy Spirit has come upon you; and you will be my witnesses . . ." (Acts 1:8). This raises us up to be his body, as we wait.

ETHICAL IMPLICATIONS

If the Advent bumper sticker says, "Jesus is coming, look busy!" then one might expect the ascension bumper sticker to say, "Jesus left the building, work it out for yourselves!" But, as has already been suggested, the ascension of Jesus is as much about coming as it is about going. It is about the promised coming of the Spirit at Pentecost, and the difficult and wonderful waiting on the Spirit that this entails.

In these final days of the season of Easter, there are three things to do: worship the ascended and enthroned Christ, rejoice in the presence of promised Spirit, and remember our calling to be witnesses. In short, we are to hear the Spirit and perform the gospel. We are to go about the work of the Lord.

GOSPEL IMPLICATIONS

Performing the gospel starts with the struggle to hear and speak truthfully to one another. While we imagine what it would look like to see Christ enthroned, high and lofty at the right hand of God, and to hear the angels singing, "holy, holy, holy," we recognize that our life, even now, is lived out in front of that throne in the face and presence of God. In a conversation about the challenges of living faithfully as church in this time, a friend asked rhetorically, "Why do we try so hard; why do we bother?" The answer came back from another, "Because we stand before the Lord." I did not hear this as a heavy, worried, afraid-of-being-judged statement. It was said with excitement and joy—we live with God! And God lives within sight of us, within reach of us. We are within *God's* reach. There at the right hand of God is the one who will intercede for creation, the one in whom all things will be reconciled, and the one who sent to us the Advocate, the Spirit, until he comes for us himself and lifts us into the fullness of him who fills all in all.

Barbara Brown Taylor uses a beautiful image for the ambiguity of life in the church today and through time. Drawn from what can be seen east of the Black Sea, in the mountains between modern day Turkey and Georgia, Armenia, and Russia, she describes the Byzantine churches as "monuments full of exquisite arches, frescos, and stonework, many of which survive today, but only as ruins or museums, because the age of Christianity is over in Turkey . . . If you go there today, you can still find the wrecks of those great churches deep in the countryside . . . The roofs are gone; so are the doors, the floors, the altars. All that are left are the walls, the graceful arches, and here and there the trace of an old fresco that has somehow survived the years—half a face, with one wide eye looking right at you, one raised arm, the fingers curled in the distinct constellation: it is Christ the Lord still giving his blessing to a ruined church" (Taylor, video, 1997).

This image hangs over Paul's letter to the Ephesians, and in the end Taylor speaks of the power of God to work among the ruins and to bring about "your basic raising the dead kind of stuff, stuff that happens in the church all the time" (Taylor, 1997).

Notes

Barbara Brown Taylor, "Great Preachers, Series 1", The Odyssey Channel, 1997.

———————

Todd Townshend

Darren C. Marks

DAY OF PENTECOST

THE LESSONS IN PRÉCIS

Pentecost celebrates the coming of the Holy Spirit and the birth of the church.

> *Acts 2:1-21.* Jesus' followers are "filled with the Holy Spirit" (v. 4), speak in other languages, and draw a diverse crowd of gawkers. Peter addresses the crowd, interpreting the day's dramatic events as fulfillment of God's promise to "pour out my Spirit on all people" (v. 17).

> *Psalm 104:24-34, 35b.* All creatures are dependent upon God and are fed by God's hand, face, breath, and spirit: "When you let loose your breath, they are created" (v. 30).

> *1 Corinthians 12:3b-13.* "There are different spiritual gifts but the same Spirit" (v. 4). Paul describes the Spirit's many ways of working in believers, stressing the Spirit's unity.

> *John 20:19-23.* On the evening of the resurrection, Christ appears to his disciples, apparently undeterred by their locked doors. He shows them his wounds, bids them peace, and breathes on them saying, "Receive the Holy Spirit" (v. 22).

THEME SENTENCE

The Spirit gives birth to the Church. The texts provide an overview of the Spirit's gifts and their uses. Acts shows them getting the attention of potential converts. First Corinthians suggests several ways they build up the church. All four lessons remind us of the Spirit's mysterious, generative power.

A KEY THEOLOGICAL QUESTION

The Spirit Gives Life. While Jesus exudes "the breath of the resurrection" (Barth, 1960, 336-37), it is the Spirit who spreads and fulfills the quickening of all things—the mark of the new creation.

The Spirit creates the church—a new form of community, one whose unity is based not on domination and submission but on mutuality, reciprocity, and equality. Filled with the Spirit, this new community is the fulfillment of Jesus' prophecy and those of the prophets for the redemption of Israel (see Acts 1:4-8; 2:1-4; Jer 31:31-34; Joel 2:28-32; Acts 2:16-21). As God constituted them as a people at Sinai, so this new outpouring of the Spirit begins Israel's reconstitution. God keeps God's promises.

The Spirit brings not retributive justice (Acts 2:19-20) but creative reclamation, a reversal of the tower of Babel's split of humanity into tribalism and chaotic warfare. As with John's and Paul's communities (see John 20:19-23; 1 Cor 12:3b-13), cohesion is not founded on divine charisma given to a few who then enforce unity through coercion—the pattern throughout history of societies ruled by military leaders and charismatic politicians. Rather, the Spirit descends upon all and gives charismata to each (Acts 2:17-18; see also 8:17; 10:44–11:18; 19:1-6). Instead of an oligarchy of powerful males, all "were given one Spirit to drink" (1 Cor 12:12-13). Social cohesion is thus based upon the presence of the Spirit (who cannot be controlled by any individual or faction), and upon the Spirit's unifying act through baptism of believers to one another, to Christ and to God the Mother/Father (Acts 2:37-38, 19:5-6; 1 Cor 12:13). Such a conception of unity has social-revolutionary import.

Carrying the Spirit's powers of the new life, Jesus gives life to the dead. Jesus breathes this Spirit on people (John 20:22) to transfer to the church the same powers found in the new creation. The same Spirit who gives all things breath and sustenance (Ps 104:27-30; see also Gen 1:2, 2:7; Job 34:14-15; Ps 146:4; Wis 15:11) dwells within individuals and the united body, distinct from the human and communal spirit yet holding them up, and now present permanently (see Ezek 37:9; John 3:1-10; Rom 8:2). This mothering Spirit heals brokenness and opens new capacities for intimacy.

This formation of healed individuals and communities is a gracious end in itself, but more deeply, a means to a greater goal: empowering humans to aid God in restoring wholeness to the created order. The Spirit "fills" those in the church, orienting them simultaneously to Jesus as center (1 Cor 12:3b, 5, 12) and to the world Jesus loves. In the believers, the Spirit gives the ability to interpret the scriptures in light of Jesus' ministry, death, and resurrection, as well as to speak with bold, persuasive rhetoric (Acts 2:4, 11-47; 1 Cor 12:8). The first task of the church is to act as a witness (to Jews [Acts 2:5, 9-11, 22], then to Gentiles [Acts 15:6-18]) that the crucified one is the risen Jesus (Acts 2:22-24, 32), the messianic figure through whom God has restored Israel. The second task is to continue Jesus' work of revealing a God of love and mercy who restores all things (John 20:21-22), a task accomplished not only by pointing to Jesus who embodies such divine mercy, but also by loving one another (John 13:34-35).

These are bold texts. The divine Spirit bursts down upon believers with the force of storm winds and "with fire," giving them abilities they could never get on their own. Yet many wonder how they can know the Spirit is present with them if they do not have such dramatic experiences. As an improviser, the Spirit's acts are mysterious (see John 3:8), yet also concrete: the Spirit brings power, freedom to breathe, and important choices to make. For those whose life and hope are dissipating, the Spirit gives new energies for living and a reason to live, as was seen with the fear-filled followers of Christ in Acts and the new converts in Corinth who found new purpose. This innovative Spirit enhances distinctive traits in each individual, then weaves the particular efforts into a community in which the good of each is lifted up simultaneously (1 Cor 12:3b-13, especially vv. 7, 11; see also 1 Thess 5:11). The Spirit thereby creates personal and shared "free spaces" in which people can breathe. Further, the Spirit who opens space for agency brings individuals and the community to key moments of choice. The Spirit enables the church to perceive true choices and their implications: Will one support the powers of death or the forces of life (see Rom 8)? However, the Spirit's power is non-coercive, inviting us to fight for life and against the demonic, but not forcing us. The choice remains ours.

In a multi-religious world, the texts may also offend, for the Spirit's work may seem too exclusively oriented to Christ, church, and Israel. The Spirit-infused believers speak to faithful Jews about the true nature of their longed-for Messiah and Israel's restoration (Acts 2:29-36). Gentiles will join this restored Israel. Those who believe in this Messiah receive the Spirit of new life (see John 3:3-10, 20:17; 1 Cor 12:3b), and the church seems to have power over divine forgiveness of sins (John 20:23). However, the church has the center of its life outside of itself: in the living, risen Jesus and the life-giving Spirit who seek to create the new reign of wholeness for all things; in its service to this broad-working Trinitarian God; and in the courage for hospitality and love, which marks truly human life in the new community. The Spirit is first the world's, and only because of that, the church's.

A PASTORAL NEED

Everybody is touched by death, even the most fortunate of us. "In the midst of life we are in death," the funeral liturgy says. Age, war, illness, and accidents produce the literal kind. Fear and guilt give rise to the metaphorical. Death and the fear of it overwhelm all kinds of people.

Whether we encounter death at mid-life in what have been called the "Three M's"—mortgage, menopause, and mortality—or standing under a cemetery canopy, one of the worst things about it is the way it sucks life out of us. We become paralyzed or exhausted, unable to do for ourselves the one thing that is needed. It's a time when willpower, bootstraps, and strategic plans are powerless, and only spiritual CPR will do. Most people and many churches know a good bit about these times.

One of the most important things a Pentecost sermon can do is point to the ways God breathes life into God's people. Examples abound:

- The unexpected birth of a baby restores life to a family who believes its gene pool is at its end.

- A depleted congregation features the use of iPads in its after-school program and suddenly is "discovered" by its neighbors.

- A married couple overcomes the stress created by long-term unemployment and finds a new capacity for intimacy.

- Church factions reach détente on the strength of a surprising new insight.

ETHICAL IMPLICATIONS

Saying that God is the author of life is another way of saying that we are not. What the Spirit does is beyond what we can do. Life is not ours to create, restore, or control. When it comes to ultimate matters, we are not inventors—not Frankensteins, Oppenheimers, or Salks. Apart from the dance of ovum and sperm, we can claim little credit. We are not life's inventors; we are its stewards—stewards of both its spiritual and physiological mysteries. We guard and nourish life partly because it is something we are not able to replace. We are a little like the prehistoric woman who is not able to make fire. Because that is the case, she focuses all her energy on keeping the kindling dry.

Over the sweep of human history, keeping the kindling dry has led to remarkable achievements. Christianity has contributed countless hospitals and schools to the world; innumerable cups of water and bowls of soup have been served in its name. But maintenance is only one aspect of stewardship. The grateful steward will go further still, aiming to enhance life wherever he or she finds opportunity. Peacemakers like George Mitchell and Mohamed ElBaradei (winner of the 2005 Nobel Peace Prize for his work preventing the military use of nuclear energy) as well as human rights advocates like China's Liu Xiaobo offer excellent examples of the kind of stewardship that enhances God's gift of life. The stories of women's advocates like Mukhtar Mai of Pakistan stir our passions and rekindle our own commitments. Artists like Gerard Manley Hopkins ("Glory be to God for dappled things . . .") and mystics like Annie Dillard (*Pilgrim at Tinker Creek*) inspire reverence and a joyful appreciation for life's mystery. Wise counselors, those who care for the elderly, people who create jobs . . . there are many ways to enhance life.

GOSPEL IMPLICATIONS

The life-giving work of the Spirit runs like a ribbon through the gospel story. From the murky beginning to the triumphant end, the Spirit murmurs, breathes, and broods with ah! bright wings over it all. Life is the Spirit's business; giving, tending, and fulfilling it. But make no mistake, the life the Spirit superintends is no mere physiological phenomenon. It is won for us by Christ. For Christians, it does not make sense to speak of life apart from the death and resurrection of Jesus Christ.

Selecting any two of today's texts will help focus a very broad theme ("Life"—surely the largest theme available to the preacher or anyone else!) on one point of Christian experience. The Gospel lesson and the text from Acts 2 might be combined, for example, in a sermon that emphasizes an "emboldened to witness" theme, narrowing the theme to show one aspect of the life the Spirit gives. Or the psalm and the 1 Corinthians text taken together might produce a sermon with a theme that shows "the one God who feeds every blade of grass, every believer's faith" and that emphasizes the unity of God and of God's church in the world.

Notes

Karl Barth, *Church Dogmatics III/2*, 1960.

JANA CHILDERS

GREGORY ANDERSON LOVE

TRINITY SUNDAY

THE LESSONS IN PRÉCIS

Trinity Sunday marks the end of the liturgical calendar's focus on the life of Christ and the coming of the Holy Spirit, with a celebration of all three Persons.

> *Genesis 1:1-2:4a.* The seven days of creation are described as the work of God-the-Creator. The work of God-the-Spirit may be alluded to in verse 2.

> *Psalm 8.* The hymn celebrates God's majesty and creativity (the skies are "what [God's] fingers made" [v. 3]). Humanity's place in the created order is suggested: "You've made them only slightly less than divine" (v. 5).

> *2 Corinthians 13:11-13.* "The grace of the Lord Jesus Christ, the love of God, and the fellowship of the Holy Spirit . . ." (v. 13). Paul closes his letter with the Trinitarian benediction.

> *Matthew 28:16-20.* Jesus commissions the eleven to "make disciples of all nations, baptizing them in the name of the Father and of the Son and of the Holy Spirit" (v. 19).

THEME SENTENCE

God chooses the ways God will be revealed. The riddle-wrapped-in-enigma is seen from various angles. The Old Testament texts picture a vastly Creative single God and praise the majesty of God's name. Matthew and Second Corinthians suggest Trinitarian ways of thinking of God's unity.

A KEY THEOLOGICAL QUESTION

The Fulfillment of All Things by the Triune God. Trinity Sunday is summative. Beginning with the first words of the Bible and moving to the final words of Matthew, the day culminates the themes of the entire liturgical year: the world-altering life of Jesus, the descent of the Spirit who births the church and the new creation, and the founding and receiving acts of the one whom Jesus calls "Abba."

The Source of All is not an impersonal force, but a personal God who creates and acts with purpose. God sends forth God's Spirit to change the earth towards life (see Gen 1:1-2; 8:1; Job 33:4; Ps 104:30). This God who shapes such beauty is not a mere influencer, but the One who is Sovereign over all things in heaven and on earth (Ps 8:1-4, 9).

According to Matthew, this One who is Sovereign is represented fully in Jesus of Nazareth (Matt 28:18). Jesus tells the disciples to draw all people toward the new creation, baptizing them in the name of the Father who initiates both creation and the new creation, of the Son who incarnates them, and of the Spirit who completes them (Matt 28:19). As Paul says in his last words to the Corinthians, the blessing—the healing—of the entire world comes to fruition through these actions of the Abba, Jesus, and the Spirit (2 Cor 13:13).

The texts for today bring both problems and promise. The first problem is that of seeming idolatry in relation to Jesus. While Genesis 1 and Psalm 8 present God in the singular as ruler of heaven and earth, the texts in Matthew and 2 Corinthians complicate things. The eleven disciples, seeing the risen, living Jesus again in Galilee, "worshipped him" (Matt 28:17). The Matthean author quotes Jesus as saying, "All authority in heaven and on earth has been given to me" (v. 18). While the Hebrew Scriptures make it clear that YHWH alone is to be worshipped (Exod 20:1-6) and is the One Sovereign (Gen 1, Ps 8), the Matthean author has the disciples worshipping Jesus, and seeing sovereign authority in him, alongside YHWH.

Further, instead of baptizing in the name of YHWH, the disciples are to baptize also in Jesus' name (see also Acts 2:38; 8:16; 10:48; 19:5; 1 Cor 6:11), and in the name of the Holy Spirit. Being baptized "in the name of" the Father, Son, and Holy Spirit places believers under the possession and protection not just of the Father, but now also and equally of the Son and the Spirit (see Ps 124:8). This reverberation of care and protection beyond God the Mother/Father is reflected in Jesus' final words to the disciples, that he will be with them (v. 20).

Paul's message coheres with Matthew's. The blessings of grace, love, and fellowship once looked for from Yahweh, now are to be sought in Jesus, God, and the Holy Spirit (2 Cor 13:13).

The Christian Scriptures contain no worked-out Trinitarian conception. (This would come only with the later councils.) However, without denying the Jewish affirmation of monotheism, they follow a threefold pattern in their references to God. In that nascent conceptuality is the promise of something new: A view of sovereign rule marked not by the historically-assumed traits of divine impassibility, invulnerability, and the aggressive possession of power, but by the willingness to share power for the sake of freely-given love. Jesus is the Lord of heaven and earth, the one who represents God's cosmic rule, and also "the king of the Jews" (Matt 2:1; 27:11, 29, 37), for God the Mother/Father, not holding power jealously, shares all that God has with Jesus, making him the exact counterpart and representative of God (see Matt 11:27). While Jesus himself declared that only God may be worshipped (Matt 4:9-10), there is no idolatry in worshipping Jesus or in seeing him as sovereign over all things, for Jesus and God the Mother/Father share such authority without competition. Such a view of God models egalitarian patterns of power and reciprocal, inter-subjective views of selfhood. While each of the three—Father, Son, and Spirit—has distinctive roles in bringing the new creation to fruition, they share a unity of mind, will, and purpose.

A second problem emerges from the texts in Matthew and 2 Corinthians. Jesus is the king over all things, and his followers are sent into all nations to make disciples—to baptize people into the name of the triune God, bringing them into the Christian fold. By suggesting that salvation comes through a connection to Christ alone, the texts clarify Jesus' role as comprehensive savior. For some readers, however, such a comprehensive saving role for Jesus may imply a religious exclusivism that seems problematic in a world of religious pluralism.

While God is represented by the figures of the Father, Son and Holy Spirit in Matthew and 2 Corinthians—an essential particularity of the Christian faith—several things qualify a seemingly harsh exclusivism. Jesus' place at God's right hand after the resurrection is not only due to his divinity, but surprisingly, also to his humanity. He is exalted as the

"Son of Man," the truly human being who is the first fruit of the new creation and who, by his obedience to God's ways throughout his life, restores the image of God in human beings (see Dan 7:13-14). And he is the first of many "daughters and sons of God" to come (see Rom 8:19).

The community into which Jesus invites people is an inclusive one. Persons from all nations are invited, overturning the usual religious identity markers based upon tribe or ethnicity (see Gal 3:28-29).

Finally, this new community gains its unity not from relations of super- and subordination, but from the very same unifying movements of gracious hospitality, love, and bonds of fellowship that mark the relations between the three persons of the Trinity (2 Cor 13:11b, 13).

A PASTORAL NEED

The recent bestseller *Unbroken* tells of WWII veteran Lou Zamperini's 47-day ordeal adrift in the Pacific Ocean. It's a classic foxhole conversion story minus the foxhole. Instead of dirt and trenches, Zamperini was driven to prayer by two thousand miles of open water and circling twelve-foot sharks. Most of us come looking for God under much less pressure, but almost everybody comes. Eventually almost everybody has a moment of realizing their need for a higher power's help.

Foxhole and canvas raft moments are not limited to seekers. People of faith have crisis moments, too. Life "tumbles in," faith is tested, and we find ourselves wondering what God is really like, how God works, and whether God is disposed to heed our prayers. Anne Lamott says that there really are only two kinds of prayers, "Help me, help me, help me" and "Thank you, thank you, thank you." For many people, the time between the two is a time of wondering about whether God is *powerful enough, available enough,* or *willing enough* to help.

Is God big enough to finish what God started? Does God want to be known? Does God care enough to bestir God-self? Is God present or distant or something in between? Answers to these and other similar questions are suggested by the distinct natures of the three Divine Persons, the promise of sufficiency and intimacy hinted at in their mysterious union as one. As Jesus' commission and Paul's benediction suggest, the work of the Three has tremendous power to encompass and bless.

ETHICAL IMPLICATIONS

If we take the relationship between the three Persons of the Trinity as the model for Christian community, the terms of our charge are perfectly clear. We know what we should do. We should build radically democratic communities where self-giving is the norm and power-sharing is realized. Inclusivity should be our watchword and mutuality our way of life. The problem, of course, is that in two thousand years of trying, no community has lived up to the charge. Few have even come close. Surely one of the reasons for this is that when we concentrate on the pattern of the divine relationship, we often miss the power that drives it. What is essential in the Trinitarian nature of God is not understanding the mysteries of perichoretic union but availing ourselves of the energy that funds it. The agape power that flows among and between the Divine Persons is what fuels and funds the church.

Theologian Kim Young Bok tells the story of a congregation who knows something about that power. During the 1970s resistance movement in Korea, a young member of the congregation was arrested. Under torture he gave up all the information and names he had. Other members were arrested as a result. After his release, the young man did what few if any others in his position had ever done, he found his way back to his congregation and asked to be readmitted. Through the night the congregation met to discuss scripture, debate, and pray. By dawn the voices who argued for forgiveness had been heard and heeded. The congregation opened their arms and accepted their young brother back in. Such things do not happen as much as we would hope. But that they happen at all is a miracle and testimony to the power of God's love.

GOSPEL IMPLICATIONS

Judaism speaks of the 72 names of God. The prophet Mohammed exhorts his followers to praise "the 99 Names." Hindu scripture refers to "a thousand names of Vishnu." Christianity, too, uses many names for God. However, Christian theology also goes to great lengths to recognize the unity of God. Why? Why try for a resolution of a thorny problem? Why not chalk up the differences in today's texts to different aspects or faces of God? Why not make God's identity at any given point a question of emphasis or perspective? Why not let all the brain bending go and think of God simply as "a God of many names"?

At the heart of the gospel we preach is the claim that "Our God is the LORD! Only the LORD!" (Deut 6:4). It's more than a poetic thought. If God is one actor in human history, God's saving, redeeming, and sanctifying works are one. If God has integrity, so does God's work; God's works may be distinguished but not divided from each other. God can never be pitted against God-self. God is tender and just, loving and chastening, wooing and distant—all at the same time.

_____

JANA CHILDERS

GREGORY ANDERSON LOVE

PROPER 4 [9]

THE LESSONS IN PRÉCIS
The righteous live by faith, they do what God commands.

> *Genesis 6:9-22; 7:24; 8:14-19.* After directions for the construction of the ark and the gathering of the animals are spelled out in detail, the text declares, "Noah did everything exactly as God commanded him" (6:22).

> *Psalm 46.* The psalmist celebrates God's faithfulness. In all kinds of upheaval—in the cosmos (v.2), the natural world (v.4), and history (v.6)—God is our "refuge and strength" (v. 1).

> *Romans 1:16-17; 3:22b-28 (29-31).* "The righteous person will live by faith" (1:17). And God "makes right" the one who has faith.

> *Matthew 7:21-29.* Those who hear but do not do can say "Lord, Lord" all they want, but it will be to no avail. They are like a fool who builds a house upon the sand. Those who hear and do are like a wise builder who builds a house upon a rock.

THEME SENTENCE
God justifies the faithful. Three of the texts show the link between faith and faithfulness, or obedience. The passage from Romans leaves no doubt that faith is what is important to God. But, as the cases of Noah and the wise home builder remind us, faith is often shown in obedience.

A KEY THEOLOGICAL QUESTION

The Fidelity of God and of Human Beings. This combination of texts seems to present huge theological problems. On the one hand, the Genesis and Matthean texts suggest that both God and the risen Jesus will judge us according to our deeds. Mere words are insufficient (Matt 7:21-24). Coming at the end of Jesus' sermon filled with detailed instructions of dos and don'ts (chs. 5–7), and with warnings about the "narrow gate" that leads to life (7:13-14) and about vines and trees that do not produce grapes and fruit being "chopped down and thrown into the fire" (7:16-20), the intent seems clear: The righteous do the will of God. Certainly such persons exist, for was not Noah one of them (Gen 6:8-9, 22; 15:6)?

Romans seems to slam head-on into this argument that we will be judged by our deeds. Romans seems to present the classic Reformation belief in justification by faith, arguing that believers are "treated as righteous by faith, apart from what is accomplished under the Law" (Rom 3:28), and gain "God's righteousness" "through the faithfulness of Jesus Christ" (3:22; see also 1:17). All boasting based upon works is gone (3:27); only faith survives.

The combination of texts, however, coheres. Justification by faith, while included, is the minor theme. Paul speaks not about human beings, but about what God has done in Jesus Christ to transform the world. Within this context of divine fidelity, the Matthean theme of human fidelity finds its rightful place.

Here, Paul is not speaking of a righteousness given by God to human beings; he is talking about God's righteousness, about God's goodness. To the patriarchs, God had promised a nation and as many descendants as the stars. Through the prophets, God had promised to vindicate Israel, who suffered oppression under pagan rulers. More comprehensively, God had promised through Israel to restore justice to the human order (see Isa 40–55; Pss 67:4; 82:8). Given the sufferings of the Jews in Paul's day and the genocides of our twentieth century, is this God trustworthy? Or is God, like fallen human beings, without integrity (see Rom 3:1-8; 9–11)?

Within this context of painful doubt, Paul trumpets the fidelity or "righteousness of God" (Rom 1:16-17; 3:21-26). God had at last acted within history to vindicate Israel and counter the evil that threatens God's good creation. In Christ, God overcame the problem of sin in humanity, which is what the covenant was set up to do (Rom 3:24-26; see also 1:3-4, 18; 3:1-20; 4:24-25; 5:6-10, 15-21; 8:3-4; and 1 Cor 15:17). The new age having dawned, the principalities and powers, including death, had been defeated and were summoned to pay allegiance to God. Most significantly, Christ and the Spirit had forged a new community whose unity was based on equality, reciprocity, and mutual forgiveness. This new community of former enemies, Jews and Gentiles, had a unity rooted in allegiance to a crucified Messiah whom nobody had wanted (see 1 Cor 1:18–2:5). In history, there was finally one "family of Abraham" worshipping the one God. Though parties may have disagreed on food taboos and culture, they shared a common worship life and mission (Rom 14:1–15:13).

This overcoming of sin and tribalism is not brought about through humans trying to be faithful. (That is not the point of the Noah story.) The universal impossibility of such self-transformation is clear (Rom 1:18–3:20; 3:23). Human idolatry distorts individual and communal life with violence, leading to the loss of the human ability to image God. God chose Israel to reverse idolatry and embody faithfulness, thus shining a light to the Gentiles to beckon them home. Yet they failed at this (3:2-3).

The fall is reversed through the surrogate faithfulness of Jesus the Messiah. (See the alternate rendering of Rom 3:22; 3:26; Gal 2:16, 20; 3:22; Phil 3:9.) For in this one person, God's faithfulness is met with an answering human faithfulness (see Rom 1:17; 4:18-22; 5:12-21). He believes God, believes that God will fulfill God's promises of redemption (Rom 3:21-22; Gal 3:22; see Hab 2:4). Not that Jesus' obedience is meritorious; rather, he lives every moment within the free space of hope in God's promise.

Within this sphere of grace, the question then becomes: What will we humans do? In none of today's texts is this a question of works-righteousness. However, the only response that fits God's invitation to participate in the sphere of grace is a holistic one: faith, which involves a new, basic act in which one shifts from fundamental doubt to fundamental trust in God. One believes, "God has my interest at heart, and God can deliver on God's promises." In this basic shift, one overcomes idolatry and tribalism.

This shift brings an integrity which overcomes hypocrisy (see Matt 6:1-18; 7:1-5; 23:25-28). Words and deeds cohere with a person's inner nature (Matt 3:8-10; 7:15-23; 12:33). Integrity or its lack is revealed by one's deeds: Whether one gives one's whole self to the ethic of the new community, summarized in the Sermon on the Mount and the love commandment (Matt 7:12; 22:34-40; 24:12).

A person of integrity believes that God is trustworthy, as the psalmist and Noah both do, as the wise builder does (Matt 7:24-27), and as Jesus encourages the disciples to do (Matt 7:7-11). This act of trust and loyalty is the "Torah of faith," the sole sign of one's inclusion in the family of Abraham (see Rom 2:27; 3:21-22; 4:18-22; 9:30-10:13; 14:1–15:13; 1 Cor 7:19). Yet faith is difficult to do—"the gate that leads to life is narrow and the road difficult" (Matt 7:14)—because it is a basic act that changes us in every way.

A PASTORAL NEED

For most twenty-first century adults, opportunity for real change is rare. A crisis may precipitate change. Occasionally an adult succeeds in adding flossing or fiber to their routine. Once in a while someone lets something or someone go. But lasting change is hard to come by. For many, personal transformation is a one step forward / two steps back struggle. The weight, the cholesterol, and the credit card debt are stubborn, and their spiritual counterparts all the more so.

While this is true particularly in regard to the life changes we will ourselves to make, it applies also to the ones that roll over us. We would like to live hopeful lives. We would like to be reckoned as righteous in God's sight. We would love to find the spiritual channel or current that would carry us through a life lived in accordance with God's will. But the world around us roars (Ps 46:6). Disasters sweep everything away "into the center of the sea" (Ps 46:2).

We are powerless to make the big and little changes we'd like to make in our lives, or even to stand up to the changes that wash up against us. The only real change that comes to most of us is the change represented by the move to faith. By the decision to believe. By the placing of hope in the Source of Hope. The Source of Faith. The Source of All Things Right. Fortunately in that change is the seed of every other.

ETHICAL IMPLICATIONS

Taken together, today's texts can be read to make two claims: "the righteous have a good deal of faith" and "faith produces righteousness." The first is easy to see. Examples from scripture and beyond come quickly to mind. However the second is not so obvious. Is it true that faith produces obedience?

Few people like to contemplate *obedience*, and to contemporary ears *righteousness* is an odd-sounding word. But in our culture we are all quite interested in "self-discipline." Diet, fitness, and personal grooming are the most obvious examples. We believe in willpower; we just wished it worked faster and . . . better. We would like to achieve what today's texts call *obedience*, but spiritual fitness has proven to be as difficult to achieve as strong abdominal muscles. We want to line ourselves up with God's will for the world, but we somehow end up sleeping in. And if we find it difficult to use willpower for our own good, active obedience or obedient doing that improves the lots of others comes a distant second.

The good we are not able to do under the steam of our own willpower, we are often able to do through the power of God. Fueled by love, on the strength of faith or by dint of hope, much has been accomplished. Over and over again the people of God have been amazed to find that causes that once seemed removed and abstract—environmentalism, global hunger, and homelessness, for example—can become compelling. The tedious—recycling, remembering to take canned peaches to church, organizing shelter—can be so satisfying. It turns out that when bending ourselves to care for others is the product of God's work in our lives, it produces not just obedience, righteousness, and good works but also joy.

GOSPEL IMPLICATIONS

For preachers and congregations alike it is tempting to psychologize faith and romanticize faithfulness. In fact it is hard not to. It is difficult for us to imagine a "faith" that is something more than brand loyalty. "Faithfulness" makes us think of the piety of our grandparents and the loyalty of four-footed friends. We are confused on both fronts. And we are not the only ones. The following conversation could be overheard almost anywhere strangers are standing in close proximity and have a lot of time to kill. "I was raised in a very religious home, but I don't go to church anymore." "Oh well it doesn't really matter, does it?" "No, I don't think so."

There are a lot of different religions after all." "Yeah, who's to say which is right?" "I've always said it doesn't matter what you believe as long as you believe something."

In our culture, holding an opinion or worldview, magical thinking, and cognitive restructuring all count as "faith." But in Christianity, faith and faithful obedience are exemplified in the life and death of Jesus. They are rewarded in Christ's resurrection. Most of all they are celebrated in the way God shares the benefits with us, even those of us who thoughtlessly chew the fat in grocery store checkout lines and in the aisles of de-boarding 747s.

JANA CHILDERS

GREGORY ANDERSON LOVE

PROPER 5 [10]

THE LESSONS IN PRÉCIS
Faith is reckoned as righteousness.

> *Genesis 12:1-9.* God commands Abram to leave home for "the land that I will show you" (v. 1). Unhesitating, Abram packs up the household and sets off, following God one step at a time.

> *Psalm 33:1-12.* All God's works are "done in good faith" (v. 4). The earth and all its inhabitants fear the Lord "because when [God] spoke, it happened!" (v. 9).

> *Romans 4:13-25.* God's promise comes to Abraham "through the righteousness that comes from faith" (v. 13). As Abraham's faith in God was "credited to him as righteousness" (v. 22), so is ours. "It will be credited to those of us who have faith in the one who raised Jesus our Lord from the dead" (v. 24).

> *Matthew 9:9-13, 18-26.* Matthew, like Abraham, responds to Jesus' call with instant obedience. "I didn't come to call righteous people, but sinners" (v. 13). Jesus says and responds to the faith of a civil administrator and a hemorrhaging woman with healing.

THEME SENTENCE
God looks upon faith with favor. Three of the four texts celebrate faithful people, and the psalm celebrates a faithful God. Genesis and Romans describe the evidence of Abraham's faith and connect it to God's fulfillment of the promise. Matthew gives three examples of people who act on faith.

A KEY THEOLOGICAL QUESTION

The Faith That Saves Us. In Romans, Paul is clear that we are not saved by following the Torah. Are we then saved by our own act of faith? The paradoxical answer found in all four texts is that we are saved through faith alone. Yet faith is not a righteousness-gaining work but an existential orientation in which we cease to rely on our own efforts to secure the meaning of our existence.

The faith that God "credited" to Abraham "as righteousness" (Rom 4:22) was faith with a particular shape. Abraham did not have a mere general trust in God. Rather, Abraham trusted that God would fulfill God's promise in relation to his and the world's future. When God promised to give him many descendants and to bless the world through him, Abraham believed God. Told to leave his home—the basis for his present and future life—and go to a land that God would show him, "Abram left" (Gen 12:4).

Doing this act meant that Abraham trusted in the character and intention of God toward him, that God is the giver of life (Rom 4:17). This trust simultaneously shaped God's life, for God's future and redemptive plan were now linked to the future of the one who had responded with trust (see Gen 22:16-18; 26:4-5, 24; Gal 3:8; Heb 11:8-16). Paul's interpretation of faith as persevering in hope when all reasonable expectation would have urged a promise's impossibility— "[Abraham] had faith in the hope"—was unseen in previous Jewish explanations of Abraham's faithful role (Rom 4:16-22).

In believing that though one is "as good as dead" (Rom 4:19), God will bring life, Abraham is also the prototype of one who is truly human. As the psalmist likewise demonstrates, to be truly human is to have absolute trust in and loyalty to God as the center of one's existence, believing that God is powerful and loving enough to secure the meaning of one's existence.

Christian faith combines the existential trust of the psalmist with (Abraham's) "faith in the hope" (Rom 4:18) in very specific, divine promises of redemption. Christians believe that their future redemption is already guaranteed in what God has done in Christ. They believe that God raised Jesus from the dead, that he is the first of the general resurrection of the dead, that he overturns evil and restores justice (Rom 4:23-25; see 8:11). They believe that Jesus wields the power of life over death. Such resurrection faith is exemplified in both the synagogue leader, who trusted Jesus to have power sufficient to raise his dead daughter (Matt 9:18-19, 23-26), and the hemorrhaging woman, who believed Jesus' touch alone would give her life (Matt 9:20-22).

Abraham hoped for the fulfillment of these promises. Christians experience them as fulfilled in Jesus the Messiah, Lord of the world (and thus its hope). Sharing the same faith, Abraham and Christians are part of one Jew-plus-Gentile family that trusts the same God (Rom 4:18-25; 10:6-13).

How is one included in the promises given to Abraham and fulfilled in Jesus? Inclusion is not gained by keeping the Mosaic Torah and practicing circumcision and purity regulations. Such rituals of identity are excluded because they do not work to effect righteousness; more importantly, they are used to divide Jew and Gentile, rather than bring them together (see Rom 2; 3:21; 4:13-15).

Yet works of the law are not replaced by the work of faith. The inclusion of humanity into the promised fulfillment of all things is not by human effort at all. It is, rather, by grace alone, a free gift, and thus guaranteed to those who cling to grace (Rom 4:16). People do not volunteer to follow him; he calls them (Matt 8:18-22). And he calls not the righteous but the rejected—precisely those who bring no worthy efforts at all (Matt 9:9-13). Through the mediatory efforts of Christ and the Spirit, those who are called are led through the wilderness to the new creation (see Rom 5–8); they are not led by the identity markers in the Torah or by their own self-efforts at drumming up faith.

Yet, though saved by divine grace alone, the human role in salvation is faith. Faith, however, is not an act which merits inclusion in the promise. Rather, the promise envelopes us, and in faith we do not run away. We yield to the promise of redemption, to the good that God would do for us. Like Abraham and the psalmist, like the synagogue leader and the hemorrhaging woman, like Matthew the tax collector and Paul himself, when the sphere of grace surrounds us, we let it be our context. We let God be the God of life, who opposes death. This trust-filled yielding is "credited as righteousness" (Rom 4:3, 22; Gal 3:6) not because it earns something but because through it, we stop pushing God away. We become hospitable. Baptism (not circumcision) becomes the sign of that yielding.

That we are saved by grace through faith alone, not by possession and adherence to identity markers in the Torah, Paul and Matthew consider good news, for human mistrust and cycles of violence are all overcome in the new community rooted in equality and reciprocity. Instead of ethnic divisions, there is one Abrahamic family forged apart from ethnic ancestry. Jewish and Gentile believers all share the same Lord, the same Spirit, the same faith, the same baptism (Rom 3:27-30; 4:13-17, 23-25; 10:11-13; 1 Cor 1:10-17; 12:4-5, 11-13; Gal 3:2, 23-29; 5). God's blessing is accessible to all.

Such a family is rooted not in behaviors or ethnic legacies but in a singular gift, in grace: the free forgiveness and mercy of God (see Matt 9:2, 10-13).

A PASTORAL NEED

Some people charge through life, but most of us have occasional patches of *acedia*—the inability to care that we don't care. The pertness of Abraham's response to God is unimaginable during such a time. Matthew's jump-up-and-go answer to Jesus' invitation is mystifying. It's hard to identify even with the hemorrhaging woman; after all she had the wherewithal to lift her arm and stretch it out in the general direction of Jesus' hem.

Acedia is a spiritual foe. Whether the bout is short or long, weak or intense, it has a way of numbing and lulling a person. God seems remote. Our confidence or sense of faith fades. Inertia, cocooning, and following the path-of-least-resistance set in. We struggle to get out of bed spiritually, and sometimes literally.

The effects of acedia are not limited to those who struggle with doubt or depression. Even high fliers and hard chargers suffer from it. The need for an extra glass of wine or mindless sex can signal its presence. Credit card debt or an addiction to trash TV can point to the desperate need to numb-out. It can be tempting to see the problem as innocuous, to pass it off as a symptom of the "stress" that pervades twenty-first century life. However, in reality acedia is a serious spiritual disease. In keeping us from acting on our faith, it has the power to wither both faith and spirit.

ETHICAL IMPLICATIONS

Dorotheos of Gaza was a sixth century abbot who knew a good deal about struggling with faith and the problems such struggles can cause in community. He taught the young monks in his charge to imagine a wheel with many spokes. Each monk should then imagine himself as a point on the rim of the wheel at the outer end of one of the spokes and imagine his brother monks as similar points. Dorotheos instructed them to think of the world as a circle with God as the center, and each radius is a single human life. (His image is rather like a wheel where all the spokes meet at the hub.) Dorotheos then drew the obvious conclusion: if each of you takes a step closer to God at the center, you will also be taking a step closer to each other. But the converse is also true, he said. The steps you take that carry you closer to another person lead you deeper into faith and communion with God.

Every casserole, every encouraging phone call, every night spent at a shelter, even every bottle you recycle, can lead you farther out of doubt and inertia, into a larger faith. Steps-in-faith may be literal. They may carry you through your own front door and out to serve God in a larger world, as they did for Abram and Matthew. Or the movement they represent may be figurative. They may cause you to extend yourself for the healing of others, as the civil administrator did in Matthew's story. They may carry you across the lines of "decency" or "proper behavior," as they did for the hemorrhaging woman. But whenever you put your faith into action on behalf of others, you can be sure it will not only carry you out of yourself but into a bigger world. Even, perhaps, into the heart of God.

GOSPEL IMPLICATIONS

Struggle and doubt are part and parcel of faith. Most everyone knows times of doubt, and many know well the inertia it can bring. God, on the other hand, is faithful, constant. "Summer and winter and spring time and harvest" as the hymn says. There are no lags or lacunae in God's "faith" or faithfulness. God is always acting in faithfulness for our benefit. Active faithfulness is a hard-core, bottom line element of who God is.

When the scriptures claim that God looks upon faith with favor, they may mean something like this. Whenever we put our faith into action, we come closer to God. Acting in faith we take a step toward or even into God. Our lives parallel or resonate with God's way of being. We are drawn farther into communion with God, conformed a bit more closely to Christ's image.

Perhaps this is why when we act in faith our faith seems to enlarge. Faith is not a static thing. It is something that catches us up into the largeness of God's life. It draws us off our spiritual couches and into something much larger than our own fears, psyches, and egos.

Whether our faith seems weak or strong, we remember that Jesus is the "perfecter" of faith (Heb 12:2), and through faith, by grace we are counted as righteous (Rom 3:28).

———————

JANA CHILDERS

GREGORY ANDERSON LOVE

PROPER 6 [11]

THE LESSONS IN PRÉCIS
Our God is a God you can put your hope in.

> *Genesis 18:1-15, (21:1-7).* God promises a son to the elderly Sarah and Abraham. Sarah laughs, but God reiterates the promise. "Is anything too difficult for the LORD? When I return to you about this time next year, Sarah will have a son" (18:14).

> *Psalm 116: 1-2, 12-19.* "I love the LORD because he hears my requests . . ." (v. 1). The poet offers thanksgiving because God has responded to his cries for help.

> *Romans 5:1-8.* "Hope doesn't put us to shame . . ." (v. 5). God's prevenient grace shown in Christ provides the basis for our hope and "shows [God's] love for us" (v. 8).

> *Matthew 9:35-10:8, (9-23).* Jesus has compassion on a needy crowd, who were "troubled and helpless, like sheep without a shepherd" (9:36). He preaches and performs many healings, sending the disciples out to do the same.

THEME SENTENCE
God makes good on God's promises. Our hope in God is never misplaced, as all four of the lessons proclaim. They picture a God moved by and providing for human need, not because help is deserved or earned but because of the "grace in which we stand" (Rom 5:2).

A KEY THEOLOGICAL QUESTION

Perseverance in Hope. Paul celebrates God's goodness or "righteous-ness"—the fulfillment of God's covenant purposes to Abraham and the created order through Jesus the Messiah (Rom 3:21-22). Paul declares our justification and reconciliation with God, also through Christ (3:24-26; 5:6-11). And in Romans 5, he notes that Christians "boast in the hope of God's glory" (5:2b).

What is the basis of this hope? All four texts are clear. The basis for hope is not found in some type of worldly success, for the disciples will suffer just as Jesus did (see Matt 10:16-25; Rom 5:3-5). The hope of restoration—of personal sanctification and glorification, and of a renewed created order—is externally centered in the persons and actions of the Triune God, who brings the new creation from the future into the present reality.

The basis of hope for sanctification is not found in our abilities; it is found in the character and intention of God. Our hope is in the love of a God who died for us not while we were strong and righteous, but while we were powerless and ungodly (Rom 5:6-8). Through the work of Christ, we already live within the free space of God's grace (5:1-2a). This God is compassionate toward us in our weakness (see Matt 9:35-38).

Further, our hope is not in our perseverance, but in God's. Our behavior may shame our faith (see 1 Cor). Yet God justifies the ungodly for the purpose of allowing the divine love to transform the person back into a truly human being. Those whom God justifies, God also glorifies (Rom 5:8-10; 8:30).

Our hope is in the power of God, who has the ability and intent to fulfill God's promises of restoration, as God demonstrated to Abraham and Sarah (Gen 18:13-14; 21:1-7) and to the psalmist.

Beyond the character of God, hope is based in the new form of humanity already made real in Christ. The ability to embody the loving fidelity of God, which humans lost in the fall (Rom 3:21), is restored to humanity in Jesus (5:12-21; 8:29-30). Humanity is restored to its beauty. Further, the powers of the new creation are present in the new human being, restoring humans to their role as co-regents over creation (Rom 8:18-25). Our glorification is thus already present "in Christ," and secure for us as we cling to him, and as he dwells within us with the new life (Col 1:27-28). In this sense, we are "saved by his life" (Rom 5:10b).

Finally, hope is secured by the indwelling presence and power of the Holy Spirit. The Holy Spirit guarantees the future fulfillment, for the Spirit is the Spirit of the new creation, present now in our reality. Our texts suggest two first fruits of the Spirit's power. The Spirit, whom God pours into our hearts, allows us to hear the gospel of God's overcoming of sin and evil and God's restoration of humanity. This Spirit enables our response of love for and hope in God, which fulfills the central command of the Law (Rom 5:5; 8:9-17, 23-27; 2 Cor 1:22).

A further sign of the Spirit's power is seen in the fact that the Triune God delegates the continuation of Jesus' Messianic mission to his followers. Jesus passes on the same eschatological Spirit who was in him to the disciples (Matt 3:11; 10:20). The disciples thus wield the same powers of the new creation first demonstrated in Jesus. They go to the same lost sheep of Israel as Jesus did. They proclaim the same message; they perform the same healings, exorcisms, and raisings of the dead (Matt 10:1, 6-8a, 27).

God will bring believers into the new humanity for which God made them. But this new humanity is impossible without a new human social order, and a restored natural world. Humans are not the only ones who groan with labor pains; so also does creation (Rom 8:19-23). As with individual glorification, so with corporate restoration, hope is based on the compassion, perseverance, and sovereign power of God; on the resurrected, indestructible life of Christ, the new being; and on the sanctifying power of the Holy Spirit.

A key point, however, also comes in our Romans text. As Paul revealed, idolatry leads to tribalism, the division of humanity into separate groups, and the restriction of access to mercy, human and divine, based upon those distinctions. Yet on the cross, all such distinctions came to an end. There is no longer any separation between the godly and the ungodly, between a superior and an inferior class of persons, between the weak and the powerful, between sinners and the righteous and the good (5:6-8). "There's no distinction," Paul writes (3:22). "While we were still weak, . . . Christ died for ungodly people" (5:6).

Writes Fleming Rutledge: "That's the heart of the gospel, right there. It's the most radical utterance uttered, because it does away with religious attainment altogether . . . . [Christ] died for those on the wrong side of the rope, the wrong end of the temple, the wrong side of the tracks. No wonder Paul could write, 'There is neither Jew nor Greek, there is neither slave nor free, there is neither male nor female; all are one in Christ Jesus' (Galatians 3:28)" (Rutledge, 2002, 185-86).

The mercy of God is open to all human beings, as is their glorification. This fact is revolutionary, for it creates a community that is not based upon super- and subordination. As Paul has said, God's righteousness, the fulfillment of God's plan, is that God has created such a community. And it will spread. That is the basis for hope.

A PASTORAL NEED

"If you didn't laugh, you'd cry," is often spoken in the midst of seemingly hopeless circumstances. Sometimes hopelessness seems so pervasive that it is absurd. We work to keep our kids healthy and safe only to learn of their reckless teenage behavior. We string pearls of sobriety one day at a time until a party threatens to snap the fragile filament. Who can give us hope that lasts and doesn't ultimately disappoint us?

We cynics who laugh at the prospect of such a hope are in good company. What can Sarah do but double over at the idea of her geriatric pregnancy (Gen 18:12)? It is not ridiculous that Christ loves us up to the point of his own death and beyond, even while knowing that we are as ungodly as they come (Rom 5:5-8)? Yeah, right. It is hard not to respond with incredulous laughter.

Another kind of laughter rings from these lessons as an antidote to hopelessness. And people long to hear it. We do well not to overestimate our listeners' cynicism. They (and we) want very much to hear how God is active and making good on promises to those who have no hope. We find hope in Jesus Christ, who hears our voice and our supplication (Ps 116:1), who shows the love of God. Can we name the actions of a hopeful God into the seemingly hopeless situations in our own day? The listeners will strain to hear that message. They long to chortle with delight more than they want to snicker with skepticism.

ETHICAL IMPLICATIONS

God sees and is moved by human need. God meets Israel's need through Abraham and Sarah. The psalmist jubilantly sings of a God who loosens tight bonds. Paul preaches a God who extends salvation toward us when we are too weak to reach for it ourselves. Jesus sees the shepherdless sheep and cures their every disease. God sees and moves to heal first. But in each case, God involves humanity in this hopeful work. God empowers humans to see and to heal as well, even in the face of laughable odds.

In 2004, Jorge Muñoz was driving a school bus by the corner of Roosevelt Avenue and 73rd Street in Queens, NY, under the shadow of the elevated train. The underpass was populated with scores of hungry folks, looking for work, mostly immigrants to the U.S. like himself. When he saw them, he remembered some of his friends in the food service industry telling him about all of the food wasted each day that they could not use or sell. Jorge saw both the hunger and the food. Connecting the two became his passion. Starting a few days a week with bag lunches, he began serving hot meals, made after work in his home kitchen, from the back of a truck to everyone who wanted one. At this writing, he has served over 100,000 meals for no compensation. "I know these people are waiting for me. . . . You have to see their smile, man. That's the way I get paid." Eduardo, one of the regulars, can see right through Jorge: "I thank God for touching that man's heart." The Holy Spirit is still seeking her harassed, helpless sheep through contemporary disciples. May we wield the powers of God's new creation with loving compassion toward all whom we are made, by grace, to see!

GOSPEL IMPLICATIONS

Confronted by the claim that the world's hope is an executed, first-century, Jewish criminal, we might find it difficult not to roll our eyes or nervously giggle over such a preposterous claim. The alternative, however, is to try to find the fulfillment of God's promises in our own ingenuity and effort. Not that human effort isn't awesome. People *do* co-operate with God's work in human life to fund hope. But any notion of consistent, ethical human progress becomes laughable in the face of the many intractable problems so well told in our histories.

Faith in the resurrection of Jesus creates hope beyond the limits of logic or effort. The resurrection breaks open the whole story of Jesus and reveals how it all makes good on God's promises. Through the lens of the resurrection, even the cross may be understood as a path made by a tenacious sort of love that can bear us through suffering even to hope itself. And in those lives where suffering and death do not relent and swallow hope behind mocking laughter, we trust that God-in-Christ is there to receive our sisters and brothers. We trust that God is restoring to them a warm meal; a place to belong; and hearty, hopeful laughter.

Notes

Fleming Rutledge, *The Undoing of Death*, 2002.

Adam Ellick, "The Chicken and Rice Man," *The New York Times*, November 25, 2007.

SAM PERSONS PARKES

GREGORY ANDERSON LOVE

PROPER 7 [12]

THE LESSONS IN PRÉCIS
God's support against enemies.

> *Genesis 21:8-21.* After Isaac's birth, Sarah tells Abraham to send Hagar and Ishmael away. God sanctions the plan, and Abraham takes the mother and child into the wilderness where he leaves them to die of thirst. But God provides a well and a way for Hagar to raise her child.

> *Psalm 86:1-10, 16-17.* The prayer offers supplication for help with "those who hate me" (v. 17). The phrase "save this child of your servant" (v. 16) may remind the reader of Ishmael and his ordeal.

> *Romans 6:1b-11.* "But if we died with Christ, we have faith that we will also live with him" (v. 8).

> *Matthew 10:24-39.* Jesus warns the disciples to expect persecution and reassures them of God's care for them ("even the hairs of your head are all counted" [v. 30]). He reminds them that though following him may involve them in conflict, "those who lose their lives because of me will find them" (v. 39).

THEME SENTENCE
God bears us through the worst. God's trustworthiness is celebrated in all four texts. Genesis, the psalm, and Matthew speak of divine support in situations of danger and especially against enemies. Romans offers reassurance that both in and beyond this mortal life God has provided for us.

A KEY THEOLOGICAL QUESTION

The Christian Life as Resistance to the Lordless Powers. In the Christian communities Paul and Matthew addressed, many believers must have misunderstood the implications of the gospel—and thus also the gospel's meaning. Both authors respond strongly.

Some in Matthew's community must have thought they could give absolute trust in and loyalty to the God revealed in Jesus Christ, yet withhold a radical commitment to living out the ethics of the new community Jesus revealed in the Sermon on the Mount and the love commandment. Certainly they could follow Christ and not go so far as to "lose their lives" (Matt 10:39)? Certainly old loyalties could remain intact? Do not compassion and mercy predominate in the way of both God and Jesus toward us (Matt 9)?

Similarly, some in the communities begun by Paul must have concluded that since sin is universal (Rom 5:12), and since "Christ died for ungodly people" (5:6), then there is no point in worrying about how much one sins. Believers may "continue sinning so grace will multiply" (6:1; see 6:12), a type of revelry in anarchy.

Members in both communities presume that grace makes no demands upon those who receive it. That it is, as Bonhoeffer said, "cheap."

"Absolutely not!" (6:2) Paul responds. And Matthew's Jesus says: "Don't think that I've come to bring peace to the earth. I haven't come to bring peace, but a sword," and then to clarify the point, "Those who don't pick up their crosses and follow me aren't worthy of me" (Matt 10:34, 38).

For both Paul and Matthew, the Christian life is one of resistance against what Karl Barth called "the lordless powers," fought in the light of ultimate victory (Barth, 1981, 205-33). This battle happens both within the self and in the social world.

Sin is a difficult power, even for the Christian. For Paul, sin and death are like a dark ruling power, a field of force with attractive and destructive effects. Many believe the Christian still has a portion of the self under the dominion of this dark, centripetal force.

Paul forcefully disagrees. By our union with Christ through faith, we have been freed from the tyranny of this dark force (Rom 6:6-7). The statement is absolute and in the past tense, just as his claim that we are glorified is absolute and in the past tense (8:30). We can resist sin and evil because we have been transferred out of the dark force field of sin, and into the inbreaking force field of the resurrection and its power of the new creation.

Paul is a realist. He knows that sin remains attractive to Christians. (See 1 Cor 9:24-27; and Rom 7:14-25, which seems to run counter to the "past tense" status of sin's dominion in Rom 6). And physical death remains. Yet we face these enemies from the force field of the resurrection. For Christ's history includes within it our history. We were "baptized into his death," "buried together with him," "united together," and "crucified with him in order to get rid of the corpse that had been controlled by sin," left in the tomb of Holy Saturday (see 6:3-6). The whole, entire old self is gone (6:6-7).

Our history is taken up into his redemptive history as well. We are "united together in a resurrection like his," "raised from the dead," alive now "with him," and thus also with him, walking "in newness of life" (see vv. 5, 4, 8b, and 4 respectively). As we live in mutual indwelling with this Christ who has overcome sin (see Gal 2:19-21), and as the Spirit of the resurrection also dwells within us (Rom 8:11), we have the power to resist sin (6:11).

In the public sphere, believers also find themselves in a battle, this time with the principalities and powers. Like Jesus, they will be persecuted by the opposition, and identified with the devil (see Matt 9:34; 10:24-25; 12:22-37). Persecution could come from within their families. Yet Jesus insists they must love him more than their most intimate relations, and pick up the cross he picked up, even at the cost of his life (Matt. 10:34-39). They must denounce the lordless powers and announce that the new reign of God's justice is breaking in even now. They must give non-violent resistance to violence, serve the new creation, let go of material possessions (10:8-10) and fear (see 10:26-31). This is Jesus' call for all followers, not just an elite force like "the twelve."

Such public resistance is possible for two reasons. The defeat of the principalities and powers is a done deal. The end of the history of the world is determined in the cross, and in the resurrection of Christ as first fruit of the general resurrection of the dead. So Christians fight on the winning side (though it may not seem like it).

Further, in the midst of battle, the improvisational agency of God goes with us. God cares for all those whom God has made (Matt 6:25-34; 10:29-31) and does what God can to protect them. God works with imperfect people, in complex situations. While Sarah's strategy for forcing Abraham to focus the covenant line on Isaac may have seemed unduly harsh even to God, God chose not to interfere with it. Yet God also acted to protect Hagar and Ishmael (Gen 21:8-21). As the psalmist recognizes, alongside Hagar, Matthew, and Paul, this God of mercy, forgiveness, and faithful love has the power to save. This God is able to do impossible things (Ps 86:8-10, 16).

Even in the disorientation of the battle without or the battle within, this God is with us, for good.

A PASTORAL NEED

There is a difference between a chef and a cook. A chef crafts a meal from the finest ingredients and presents them as edible art in the controlled environment of a restaurant. A good cook takes what is at hand in the home and cobbles together a meal to sustain bodies and souls until the next meal comes along. With six children in the 1930s Depression, my maternal grandmother could make a meal out of almost nothing, salvaging every conceivable part of the pig or chicken, bits of leftover vegetables, and cornmeal. These, along with some molasses, could "tide you over," even abundantly so. A cook improvises a meal from what is at hand in a house with six kids.

When God saves, God is a cook, working with imperfect people, in complex situations. Sometimes we feel uncertain that God can use our imperfections and complexities or believe that God wants us to provide ingredients that are, well, less spoiled. God seems quite content, though, to whip up a future for Hagar and her child in the desert after she has been unjustly run out of the kitchen. Jesus numbers all of our hairs and knows that most of them have stood on end at the prospect of having our families divided by our professions of faith in him. God knows the smell of sin emanating from some dark recess of the fridge. No worries. God is willing to come into our life-kitchens, work with what we have and move us forward for one more meal, even abundantly so.

ETHICAL IMPLICATIONS

Nine-year-old Serena's family has a decision to make. Her hockey league has elected to play games on Sundays during the hour that the family would normally be attending church. Her friends are playing, and she is beginning to beg. What to do!

According to a recent study, the average U.S. low-income household spends about 9 percent of all income on lottery tickets, even considering the terrible odds of winning. Say you're standing on a football field, blindfolded and holding a pin. An ant is released on the field. Your chance of piercing that ant with your pin is about the same as winning a Lotto 6/49 jackpot in Ontario, states the Canadian Broadcasting Corporation. The promise of wealth is alluring to poor families who are disproportionately affected by gambling. The truth is that poor children are the ones who are most deprived of the dollars that could supply more food, secure shelter, and provide appropriate clothing. What to do!

"Resistance is futile," opine the Borg, a cybernetic super-race depicted in Star Trek. The Borg use assimilation to a single opinion to achieve "perfection." But resistance is not only *not* futile, it is also *essential* to the daily walk with the cross that Christians bear. However, we do not bear crosses alone. Matthew reminds us of the high costs of resistance to the culture that constantly pressures modern families. Genesis reminds us of God's loving provision for us in the wildernesses where we find ourselves driven. We are not alone there. God bears with us through the worst and connects us into a church that is never far removed from the sting of death, yet amazingly walks "in newness of life" (Rom 6:4).

GOSPEL IMPLICATIONS

Theodore Runyon, emeritus professor at Emory University, used to say that Christian baptism is more than mere symbolism; it isn't magic, but, *something really happens in baptism:* People are initiated into the only community that God has provided whereby we can learn of and experience the saving acts of God in Jesus Christ.

In Paul's description of our baptism, the church perpetually dwells in Holy Saturday. We *have been* crucified with Christ, and we *will be* resurrected with him (Rom 6:5). Our baptism is the seal on this promise for the future. But Jesus' baptism and our baptism pour real courage into us *today* so that we may face whatever death-dealing thing to which our sin-sick souls are addicted. Through baptism we may face whatever hell is being stoked by the sin-sick systems of the world. How? In baptism, the Holy Spirit gives us to each other. In baptism, the Spirit inaugurates a new order in which God empowers us to bear each others' crosses when the old order deems it necessary to hand them out.

We might want God to fix our brokenness without and within. Instead of magic, we get baptism: The new creation of Jesus' family that, together, faces up to the old creation, trusting in God's promise to finish.

Notes

Karl Barth, *The Christian Life*, 2002.

"Buying the Dream: Mega Millions Frenzy Escalates as Jackpot Swells," *PBS Newshour*, Canadian Broadcasting Corporation, March 30, 2012.

SAM PERSONS PARKES

GREGORY ANDERSON LOVE

PROPER 8 [13]

THE LESSONS IN PRÉCIS

Genesis 22:1-14. God challenges Abraham's faith by asking him to sacrifice the son through whom the covenant that God has established with Abraham will be fulfilled. Both Abraham's obedience to this unfathomable command and God's on-time intervention demonstrate faithfulness to the divine/human covenant.

Psalm 13. The plaintive cry "How long?" (v. 1) begins the psalmist's lament as he seeks God's intercession and looks to God for deliverance in a time of trouble. In a final moment of faith, the psalmist remembers and celebrates the saving love of God to the faithful.

Romans 6:12-23. Paul offers both a reminder and a word of assurance to Christians about their salvation through Christ. The reward of their discipleship is the promise of eternal life and freedom from sin.

Matthew 10:40-42. Jesus continues his teaching on the characteristics and reward of discipleship. His words offer assurance of God's faithfulness to those who carry out Christ's mission in the world.

THEME SENTENCE

God rewards our faithful obedience. Faithfulness, both human and divine, is the overarching theme throughout these texts. Obedience to God is an affirmation of faith that recognizes the covenantal love and saving presence of God in the lives of those who live righteous lives according to the will of God.

A KEY THEOLOGICAL QUESTION

A challenge that has always presented itself to those of the Christian faith who experience lethal oppression and marginalization is the cost of discipleship. Put another way, how does a person, or a people, discern when the cost of discipleship and faithfulness to God require the sacrifice of one's self, one's child, or children? Here I am not raising the question of those who take upon themselves material deprivation as a way to express their faithfulness. Nor am I raising the issue of those who are mentally deranged and kill their own children. Rather, I raise the matter of those whose suffering is anything but self-imposed and who must routinely measure and weigh the costs their children will bear in the hope of a brighter future. These are the ones Howard Thurman (1996) refers to as those "with their backs against the wall." The texts for today can be read largely as grappling with this dilemma.

Before going on, it is important to recall that this question of child sacrifice, while extreme and tragic, is not simply rhetorical. History has demonstrated over and over again that communities that are lethally oppressed will at some point in their history, willingly or unwillingly, usher their children to pyres of sacrifice—figuratively and often literally (Thurman, 1996, p. 54; Eisenberg, 1981, chap 14) The certainty of this eventual "Abrahamic" dilemma, as amply demonstrated throughout history, is what ultimately creates the condition that makes this a theological matter. So, then, how might the texts before us provide ways of faithfully responding to these situations? Note, I am not seeking an answer to the dilemma; it is my sense that only those faced with such sacrifice can give witness to the answer. For the rest of us, we must ask, at least until it is our turn before the pyre, how these texts give guidance that will engender empathy and solidarity.

The test that Abraham faced has traditionally been framed as a matter of trust that God will provide and ensure the future of the promise. Faith has then been made synonymous with trust. The psalmist raises the poignant question of what do we make of the matter when, seemingly, that trust is ill-placed. What do we make of faithfulness or trust when it is not demonstrable that faithfulness is rewarded by God, at least as a historical matter? I do not mean to raise the question of theodicy, which in my estimation is finally a pointless endeavor. Rather, what I am getting at is the deeper question of what we make of faith when it seems unrequited. By asking the question in this way, I question an economy of faith in which God's blessings are reduced to the category of earnings. Are God's blessings bestowed based upon God's pleasure with our deeds, or the inclination of our hearts? While certainly a strong thread in the historical development of the Christian faith and its contemporary being, this particular economy of grace can make no sense of those times when God is silent in the face of the destruction of the faithful; particularly, the annihilation of their hope through the death of their children; or when the wicked seemingly prosper beyond all measures of justice.

The tradition has sought to answer in two ways this matter of God's *seeming* abandonment of the faithful, making foolishness of their trust. The first has been eschatological: we cannot know whether God has been unfaithful until the end of things; the suffering of the faithful and concomitant prosperity of the unrighteous can only be made sense of in light of God's final judgment. A second way is by observing that even in the midst of suffering, life is being sustained by God, if not for all, for most of creation. Thus while many millions of Jews have died, many have lived; while many millions of Africans perished in the middle passage and many more endured the dark night of slavery, not all have perished. God's creative work is to be found throughout creation, no matter the depth of the suffering of creation. The continuing creativity of God means that evil will never finally have the last word, and this recognition is then worthy of faith and trust. Neither of these approaches to the dilemma proves particularly satisfactory. For, in the end, the words of Shadrach, Meshach, and Abednego to the king still hang in the air: "Whether our God will save us, or not, we do not know." So, then, is this the final word about God's faithfulness? We may not know.

What I want to suggest is that the answer to this dilemma is found in the witness of those who suffer. Paul is one person who suffered and whose faith did not waiver. If our response to suffering is empathy for and solidarity with the "little ones" as they stand before the pyre, then perhaps God's response to their faithfulness may be revealed through us to eyes glazed over by privilege and complicity. In so "seeing," perhaps our bondage to the sin that builds the pyre in the first place might be exposed and we might live in ways in which our members serve God's mercy and not the flames of lethal oppression.

A PASTORAL NEED

The idea of God providing largesse to individuals because of their faithful response to God's commands seems to border on the issue, hotly debated in some circles, of preaching a prosperity gospel. The belief that what one does as an act of faithful living is the reason that one prospers in life leads as directly and arbitrarily to disappointment as it does to celebration. Christians who believe that they have faithfully followed God's commandments and lived within the bounds of love of God and neighbor, who yet fall victim to devastating illness or other loss, may rail at the circumstances of life and cry out for divine justice.

The desire to be rewarded for the good that one does is part of the human psyche, whether it is simple recognition, monetary gain, or other tangible rewards. And when the accomplishments of which we are most proud—that reflect our success in life or even our faithfulness to God—go unrecognized by human beings, it seems natural to turn to God for the reward that the deed requires.

The Christian experience is notable not because of the accomplishments that bring recognition but by the knowledge of God's active presence in one's life. In preaching these texts, it is important to acknowledge God's presence as the ultimate reward of our faithfulness. Christian community, the gathering of the faithful in obedience to the will of God, offers witness to the reign of God on earth, and ultimately to God's unfailing, rewarding presence.

ETHICAL IMPLICATIONS

That God would ask anyone to murder their child challenges us in the deepest places of our hearts. Beyond the obvious ethical dilemma of killing an innocent person, there are the challenges to the human spirit of most people, who believe that children are to be protected from the evils of the world. Apart from the issue of human sacrifice that is anathema to our civilized Western, postmodern minds, there is also the unfathomable nature of the command given by the same God who later outlaws murder as contrary to the nature of community.

Following World War II, many participants were convicted for their obedience to commands that resulted in the murder of innocent people, so the dilemma of being obedient to unavoidable but unjust commands deserves deep consideration from both an ethical and a Christian perspective. That God rewarded Abraham's faithfulness in following the divine command, and thereby prevented Isaac from being a victim of his father's obedience to God, does not answer the ethical question embedded in this story.

At the same time, Paul's language of slavery to God, applied to the historical backdrop of American slavery is difficult to hear as one considers the evils perpetrated by professed Christians who benefitted from that hegemonic institution. Additionally, there are many leaders who have proclaimed themselves as God's mouthpiece, who have destroyed the lives of their adherents through the obedience they demanded personally as proof of faithfulness to God. This speaks of the inadequate or inappropriate interpretation that has surrounded that tenet of Christian faith. Ultimately, Christianity points to God, the creator, redeemer, and sustainer of human life. The response of faithful obedience as a guiding principle of our faith must point only to God, who keeps covenant with humanity, sustaining us through life's challenges.

GOSPEL IMPLICATIONS

The promise of reward in the texts may be seductive for those who apply the world's standards to Christian discipleship. Obey God and deliverance will come, promises Abraham's story. Follow the dictates of Christ slavishly and you will receive the eternal reward, says Paul. And Matthew's rendition of Jesus' message directs us to provide for the needy as a sign of righteous living, and divine reward is guaranteed.

The divine response to faithful Christian discipleship is God's presence that enables us to trust God in the face of life's unexpected and often unexplainable circumstances. As Christians living in a world that works diligently to focus our attention on visible success and tangible rewards, a gospel message that promises divine grace, an often unseen and unrecognizable reality is difficult to receive. Yet that is the good news—peace and joy are the rewards of Christ's presence—as Paul said, "nothing can separate us from God's love in Christ Jesus our Lord" (Rom 8:38). Faithful obedience is the response and reward of discipleship. Christ's presence is the assurance of God's grace. Both must be clearly articulated in the context of the hearers' lives in order to move the hearers to a life of faith that remains steadfast, even without the benefit of tangible rewards.

Notes

Howard Thurman, *Jesus and the Disinherited*, 1996.

Azriel Eisenberg, *Witness to the Holocaust*, 1981.

———————————————

GENNIFER BENJAMIN BROOKS

STEPHEN RAY

PROPER 9 [14]

THE LESSONS IN PRÉCIS

Genesis 24:34-38, 42-49, 58-67. With God's guidance, Abraham's servant succeeds in carrying out his master's death-bed instructions. He finds a welcome and a bride for Isaac among Abraham's kinsfolk. Rebekah joyfully leaves her father's home to begin a new life not as stranger but as Isaac's beloved wife.

Psalm 45:10-17. This wedding song reprises the theme of newness and celebration for the family and the community. A royal wedding offers the promise of a rich, new life.

Romans 7:15-25a. Paul writes of the dilemma that confronts him and all those who seek to do the will of God. He laments the fact that sin has made him a stranger to himself and subverts his desire to do good, but ultimately he celebrates the newness Christ offers.

Matthew 11:16-19, 25-30. Jesus' parable of the children in the marketplace juxtaposes his ministry with that of John the Baptist and the response each received. His call is to newness of heart and life.

THEME SENTENCE

God enables us to welcome and celebrate newness of life. Rebekah and Isaac celebrate new life together. The king and princess welcome a new marriage. Paul celebrates new life in Christ. And Jesus Christ calls his followers to a new way of being. In God, newness and celebration are intertwined and welcomed.

A KEY THEOLOGICAL QUESTION

The texts of this lection raise in subtle ways the question of what to make both of the stranger in our midst and of the seeming call of God to become strangers to ourselves by dismissing our old lives. As with other texts, the theological issue that emerges from these texts is very much contextualized by contemporary and historical realities. In each of the texts, whether it be a bride called away from her home to fulfill the request of a patriarch, the psalmist calling the new bride away to gladly join a new life with her king, Paul calling the faithful to begin "new" lives away from the bondage to sin, or Jesus giving thanks for those drawn from the world unto him, a common thread is that the new life means becoming a stranger to one's former life and world. While all of these texts are woven into larger narratives, this focus on becoming a stranger to one's former life and welcoming that newness is central. The two dimensions of this theme on which I focus are the seemingly privileged place that is given to the stranger and the way that this contests familial ideas about both the transmission of the faith and communities that are formed around it.

These are significant points for several reasons. First and perhaps most important, we live in an age when xenophobia has reached such proportions that strangers of differing faiths are legally challenged from worshipping in their own way, or met with such venomous public outrage that their physical safety seems in danger when they choose to do so. As well, the demonization of migrant workers, undocumented and otherwise, has reached such a fever pitch that entire communities are destroyed by xenophobia. These behaviors are nothing new, of course, but not since the pogroms of previous centuries has the Christian faith played such a central role in both creating and sustaining these hellish dispositions towards strangers. Given what we know of the inexorable conclusion to such demonization of "the stranger" (e.g., the Shoah) how do we make sense of the seeming ease with which many in the church embrace it? This posture raises questions precisely because, as demonstrated by our texts for today and others, the welcome of strangers seems important to God—so important, in fact, that fundamental to the very identity of God's people is an understanding that they become strangers to former things and celebrate that newness. The theological question becomes for us, then, how do a people who are called to be "strangers and sojourners down here" become the arch persecutors of strangers in their midst? This is not simply an ethical question, for it cuts to the very heart of how we understand ecclesiology and vocation.

Central to ecclesial understandings in our contemporary context is a reigning metaphor about "church" is family, on both the level of local congregations and larger national bodies. This trend began in the nineteenth century and gained normative status in the twentieth. It is no accident that so many "Christian" organizations have family in their name (e.g., Focus on the Family or the American Family Association). While there are many reasons for use of the metaphor, many good ones, time and again we have seen the bonds of kinship and family spiral into racial supremacy and ethnocentrism, which are sometimes lethal. Precisely because human beings are instinctively protective of the bonds of family, when it becomes the central understanding of communal affiliation, the tendencies toward exclusion and rejection increase.

This situation becomes worse in situations like our own, in which religious identity becomes fused with national and ethnic identity. This is undeniably the case for much of the populace of my nation in which American and Christian function as interchangeable terms. This fusion of ecclesial and national identity is the seedbed of lethal xenophobia, as has been demonstrated throughout the history of the church. The theological challenge is, then, how do we disentangle this heretical notion of Christian identity, rooted in exclusive notions of family, from inclusive positive notions of God's family as universal and inclusive? How do we prevent racial, ethnic, and national xenophobia from being baptized by the Christian faith? Normative ways of being faithful can be to reclaim the true nature of Christian identity, welcoming and celebrating strangers and newness. This is the issue of vocation.

Today's texts come into focus: the calling and empowerment of the faith is precisely away from those bonds in which ethnocentrism and nationalist xenophobia are rooted! Perhaps the insight is that in rooting and grounding one's identity only in God, there is generosity to self and others that comes only with vulnerability. For when one's security is rooted in the power of national arms, be they chariots or tanks, what need is there for God? The theological challenge, then, is framing an adequate ecclesial understanding of Christian vocation and identity. It will resist the very persistent call to exclude and oppress the stranger. Perhaps the first step is becoming in Christ a stranger to our old selves, and celebrating that with praise and thanksgiving to God.

A PASTORAL NEED

The motif of celebration that runs through these texts is intertwined with the theme of newness. We celebrate the community that develops when new people become part of the family, through marriage or otherwise, and as Christians we celebrate new life through Christ. Such celebrations are spawned from the welcome we offer to the newness that changes and hopefully enriches our lives. Expressions of celebration may be different, but every individual needs those celebrative moments that help to lighten the load or dispel the darkness that may overshadow their lives. However, there are many persons and life situations where an anticipated celebration is overtaken by grief or loss, and both welcome and celebration are not possible.

The would-be mother who is unable to conceive or carry a child full-term neither welcomes nor celebrates her situation; the individual whose every personal relationship results in disappointment, or the couple whose marriage disintegrates, all find themselves in new but unwelcome places; the teenager in a new school who becomes the object of ridicule or bullying; and the immigrant victimized by xenophobic laws and restrictive structures in church and society all experience similar feelings in which celebration and praise are unimaginable. Christ in us makes us strangers to ourselves and calls us to welcome the new in ourselves and in our midst. Only through Christ can we leave behind our old lives, opening ourselves and being opened by the Spirit to receive strangers as family and to welcome and celebrate newness of life.

ETHICAL IMPLICATIONS

Paul writes of an ethical dilemma that is faced by Christians, a problem that we encounter as we interact with each other individually or in community. It arises from our inherently sinful nature as we desire to live faithfully within Christ's law of love. If, as Paul says, we are not fully in control of our actions and are victims of the sin within us, we still cannot simply absolve ourselves from responsibility for our sinful actions.

Abraham's servant follows his master's directive requiring Rebekah to leave the familiar and become a stranger. Both his welcome into Rebekah's community and hers into Isaac's family remind us of our responsibility for those whom God sends into our midst, of the need to find appropriate ways to receive and welcome new persons into the community.

Jesus wonders at his hearers' lack of response to the newness of life he offers. The challenge of newness is that it calls us to become strangers to our old selves in order to welcome and celebrate the new. So if we cannot meet that challenge, it is no wonder that we find it nearly impossible to open our hearts and our communities to the strangers that come among us. And yet that call is the substance of our Christian discipleship. We are called and empowered to receive strangers in Christ's name, to welcome them as friends, and celebrate their inclusion in the community. So what will it take for us to reach and welcome the new—new persons and new life? Both our Christian identity and the Spirit shape us to welcome the stranger and become family, the beloved community for new persons.

GOSPEL IMPLICATIONS

The celebration that accompanies our baptism in Christ has much in common with the wedding celebrations in our texts. Both speak of new life, of leaving the familiar and welcoming the new. Both are family celebrations, but they also represent the uncertainty that comes with newness. Isaac and Rebekah must face it, and so must the royal couple, but in each case there is a bond of love that facilitates celebration. In a similar way, God's love enables us to reject the power that sin has over our lives and to accept Christ's offer of new life.

We Christians generally acknowledge God's presence in the successes and celebrations of our lives. But in the ordinary, everyday tasks of living, including welcoming the stranger, we may not listen closely enough for God, who is always present leading, guiding, and enabling us to welcome and celebrate newness in our lives.

God's saving love in Jesus Christ, that makes us new and overcomes our unwillingness or our inability to accept newness and change, enables us to welcome and celebrate the stranger in us and the strangers that we meet so that together we can live as the family of God.

GENNIFER BENJAMIN BROOKS

STEPHEN RAY

PROPER 10 [15]

THE LESSONS IN PRÉCIS

Genesis 25:19-34. The Abrahamic saga continues with the opening act of Jacob's story. As the one through whom the divine covenant will be continued, this story offers justification for Jacob's usurpation of his brother's birthright. The choices made by both brothers impact the heritage of the Christian faith.

Psalm 119:105-112. This section of the psalm holds in tandem the benefit of right living and the challenge of keeping the law as an act of faith in God.

Romans 8:1-11. Paul juxtaposes life in the flesh, lived according to the law, which is death; with life in the spirit, directed by the indwelling of Christ, which gives hope of eternal life.

Matthew 13:1-9, 18-23. The parable of the sower uses common agricultural activity to instruct the church on the expectation of missionary activity. For Matthew, the main focus of such ministry is the message—the word of God—and how hearers receive it and allow it to impact their lives.

THEME SENTENCE

God guides us to make right choices. Human beings are required to make choices at almost every moment of life and ultimately to live with the results of those choices. Regardless of the specifics of the situation, our choices reflect our response to God's guiding presence.

A KEY THEOLOGICAL QUESTION

A significant theological issue from the birth of the church until the contemporary era concerns the question: Who may claim the tradition (in the sense of having "authentic" faith), and who is claimed by the tradition (in the sense of being subservient, still learning)? In the context of many readers of this commentary, the question is largely framed in terms of the Western church and those parts of the church that were born from its missionary activity, directly and indirectly. In asking this question we plumb the larger matter of the status of varying "traditions" of the faith, the discernment of authority within, and adjudication between them. Beyond the obvious historical dimensions of this question, the larger question that has beset the church since Paul's missionary activity is whether the inheritance of the faith is genealogical, or whether it is more properly understood pneumatologically. Does authority, within the broad tradition of the faith, pass culturally through the bloodlines of the faith, or should we look to the work of the Spirit in each generation to discern the form of faithfulness, or is there some blending of the two that is necessary?

Consider what occasions these questions and what is at stake in our grappling with them. The forms the church took/takes in the modern era deeply affected and were affected by the social development and cultures of Western Europe and their scions in the Western Hemisphere (North, Central, and South America). During the period in which much of the world was colonized by nations of Western Europe, the Christian faith went with the colonizers in their missionary activities. The faith of the colonizers was understood to be the authentic tradition of Christianity, and that of the colonized to be derivative at best. In the language of scripture, the colonizers were heirs of the "promises" of God in a way exemplary to that of the latecomers. Precisely because of the type of mutuality that existed between the colonizing powers and the church, this framing of matters extended to the material goods of creation. Thus, this grounded in ecclesial and theological conviction a situation in which the material privileging of some caused the disadvantage of others. This material distortion of the enjoyment of the goods of creation is an unfortunate consequence of the particular intertwining of the Christian faith and the culture just described.

Certainly, there are ethical issues the way that the faith is/was used to authorize the mal-distribution of the goods of creation and the canonization of a particular set of nations and cultures. This collusion distorts both the conceptualization of tradition and its transmission. Put plainly, by reading the tradition along cultural bloodlines, it becomes a matter of ownership, and the "promises" of the faith cease to belong to the work of the Spirit, and instead become the property of some people over others. Without going into a full exegesis, this is the dynamic we see going on between Jacob and Esau in the Genesis text. The promise here becomes a zero sum matter of who receives the inheritance and who does not. It should be noticed that the descendants of Esau are written out of the promise at this point. As an aside, we are left to wonder what the relation of the Abrahamic faiths might be today if Jacob had said to Esau, "Share with me," instead of, "Give me your inheritance." This may be the point Paul wants to make in this text and more generally in Romans—that promise is the work of God in the Spirit, and thus not "owned" by anyone but, rather, shared by all whom God sees fit to call. The promise, its inhabitation, and its exemplification then become matters of the response of the faith to the prior and continuing work of God, not who in this generation holds a particular title.

Here, again, we come to the ethical implications of how we frame authority within and about tradition. If tradition is understood to be primarily the response of the faithful to the prior and continuing work of God in the Spirit then tradition is not an ethnic, cultural or racial inheritance. If true, it might be that the "goods" of creation, broadly understood as the fruit of the promises of God, might also to be the gift of God to all. Beyond ethics, the issue is whether persons and communities orient themselves to it such that they are capable of receiving correction and illumination from God in the Spirit. If one's orientation is that one and/or one's community has all that is necessary to rightly understand and plumb the tradition (e.g., race or ethnicity), then what room is there for the work of the Spirit? Isn't this in the end precisely what Augustine meant when he talked about pride that re-enacts the fall? Has history not taught us that these expressions of the faith are precisely the ones that wither in the noonday sun?

A PASTORAL NEED

At times it seems as though our lives are beyond our control, and we are amazed and discomfited by the things we do. As baptized Christians, we make a commitment to follow Christ and to live by the Spirit of Christ, and yet our minds and actions often betray us. In a world that encourages us to do whatever it takes to be successful, following the precepts of Christ requires a level of faith that comes only through the guidance of the Spirit of God.

But great challenges confront us as we are seduced by the promises of the world's lures, and right choice becomes a matter of faith. Faith in God leads or should lead us to make decisions that are in tandem with the will of God, but even the witness of scripture in places may distract us, as it seems to provide evidence of wrong-doers thriving.

Paul's letter seems to offer a simple solution: let the Spirit of God rule in one's heart, and the resultant actions will not only represent right choices but also give evidence of one's faith in God. Faithful living is challenging, even when one has accepted the word of God as the directive for one's life. God gives us free will, and each Christian makes the choices necessary for her or his individual life. When life in the world conflicts with life in the Spirit, only with God's guidance can we be directed to make right choices.

ETHICAL IMPLICATIONS

Scripture condemns Esau for selling his birthright to Jacob for a meal, but the Genesis text not only gives evidence of Jacob's culpability in his brother's eventual loss of his inheritance but also brings into question God's choice of a trickster. There seems obvious bias in the telling of the story because Jacob is the heir through whom the legacy of the divine/human covenant that began with Abraham is continued. That Esau will also become subject to Jacob raises even more ethical questions regarding the criteria by which the promises of God are realized in individuals.

The love of Christ in our hearts should enable us to operate on a higher plain of existence; however as individuals we are still required to choose right or wrong, good or evil. The violence that overshadows too many areas in the United States pushes even Christians to act in ways contrary to their baptismal covenant. In the news, a senior citizen, an active Christian and church worker, shoots the teenagers who have been harassing her; her hunger to be left alone overcomes her scruples and her Christian commitment. What is the divine response to her actions? Is good character necessary for receiving God's approbation? How are the choices we make influenced by divine response?

Faithful living is the expected choice of the whole people of God. But what is God's response when the church, the body of Christ, is subverted from its foundation of faith and becomes part of the death-dealing systems that infect society? The Spirit of God is the substance of life for individuals and for the community, and must be the directing force for all within it. It is the heritage of faith realized through the covenantal love of Jesus Christ.

GOSPEL IMPLICATIONS

God's promised active presence offers assurance as we try to live faithfully. The new birth of our baptism in Christ offers the opportunity for faithful witness to the love of God that is resident and operating in the heart. As inheritors by faith of the Abrahamic covenant and participants in the divine/human covenant through Christ, Christians have the promise of life eternal through the word of God implanted in our hearts. There is good news for every hearer because the divine word, like the Spirit of God, is present and available to all, regardless of their human situation.

This requires that each Christian seek diligently the path of light and life. Through the saving love of Jesus Christ, we have the gift of the Holy Spirit, which can enable us to live within the covenant of our Christian faith. The word of God in our hearts does not absolve us from sin; instead it enriches our spiritual life, empowers us to face life's challenges, guides us for right living, and enables us to give witness to the presence of God in all of life. By faith in the eternal promises of God, we can claim our heritage and live faithfully as heirs of the covenant.

GENNIFER BENJAMIN BROOKS

STEPHEN RAY

PROPER 11 [16]

THE LESSONS IN PRÉCIS

Genesis 28:10-19a. Jacob's angst as he flees his brother's justified vengeance results in a nighttime message of hope that confirms his place in and benefits of the Abrahamic covenant. It is the assurance of divine grace.

Psalm 139:1-12, 23-24. The psalmist articulates his confidence in the omnipresence and grace of God in the midst of life that enables him to open his life freely for God's investigation.

Romans 8:12-25. Paul reminds us that as Christians we are led by the Holy Spirit, and our life in Christ gives us hope and patience to withstand and overcome the suffering that results from the vagaries of life.

Matthew 13:24-30, 36-43. The parable of the weeds and the wheat refutes any claim that human beings can determine who is righteous and who is unrighteous. It is also a word of hope for those who are overcome by the vicissitudes of life.

THEME SENTENCE

God gives us hope through life's challenges. God's presence as a living reality in the midst of life's challenges is the predominant message of these texts. Deserved or not, suffering is difficult to bear. Assurance of divine presence is a source of hope that enables us to persevere with patience.

A KEY THEOLOGICAL QUESTION

Our texts for today do not so much raise a theological question as provoke ways of thinking about a problem that has ever beset those in the church who suffer oppression, lethal and otherwise, especially at the hands of other Christians. The theological question might be stated thus: What do we make of the faith when Christian identity leads to a willful ignorance of the suffering of others in the church, or worse, causes us to further that suffering? What do we say of these things?

While in the history of the Christian church there have been many instances of the faith being either irrelevant or distorted in situations of intra-Christian oppression, one that stands out is the long history of racial oppression in the United States. Here we have a situation in which oppression not only used the faith as an explanation but also used it to further the lethality of the oppression. Through the dark night of slavery, during the violence of the lynching era, and on through the Civil Rights struggle, Christian people and much of the church have used the gospel to further violence and oppression. Whether it was through specious exegesis like Josiah Priest's *Bible Defense of Slavery* or the cultural acceptance of the Ku Klux Klan's use of the cross as a symbol of fear and hatred, they have all exemplified the problem.

It would be simple enough to write this problem off as a manifestation of the church's continuing struggle with heresy and apostasy, with the commitment to white supremacy simply interpreted as a contemporary manifestation of this struggle; or to resort to the argument that it was never the case that most Christians in the United States were slave owners or lynchers, and, therefore, that it overstates the matter to say this is a problem for the church. This last response is perhaps the most common and, in my opinion, the most troublesome. It is troublesome precisely because it fails to recognize that silence in the face of lethal oppression is complicity, and, further, that complicity in the face of lethal oppression is tacit approval. So, while yes, it is the case that most Christians were neither slave owners nor lynchers, it is also true that virtually all of these people were Christian and felt confirmed in their actions by their faith. Instead of asking why the people felt confirmed in their practice of lethal oppression, might we not better ask why those who felt the lash of whip and witnessed their fathers, sons, and brothers hanging in the tree, or burning on the pyre felt confirmed in their faith?

By shifting the focus to those in the church who have suffered lethal oppression at the hands of other Christians, it is possible to come upon several helpful theological insights. First, we have the capacity to ground reliance upon God in times of trouble within the deep structures of human yearning and pathos. It is one thing to counsel trust in God's presence from the seat of relative privilege and power, and quite another to see those passing through the dark night of suffering bear witness to it. What is living under the terror of the constant threat of losing one's family on the auction block, or to the rope and bonfire, if not passing through the depths of Sheol? Second, we come upon the ever-important insight that the Christian faith is always more than its contemporary bearers. This is not a new insight. This was precisely Augustine's argument against the Donatists. To use his framing, it is the faith that is holy and the Spirit that is reliable, not the fallible bearers of the faith, no matter the position and power that they may hold in the church and in society. What is holding on to the promise that God reveals about the future in the face of a reality in which that very legal and cultural institution grants privilege to those who inflict harm and suffering precisely *because* the perpetrators are deemed "good Christians," if not an enactment of Paul's steadfast faith in the face of suffering? Finally, this change of vantage point leads us to the core Augustinian conviction that God will sort things out. It is precisely this eschatological certainty that gives currency to Paul's conviction that while creation may groan in anticipation in the midst of seeming futility, this hope will not be dashed. What then might be learned from those who held on to hope, Christian hope, through the dark night of slavery when fully eighty percent of those who were slaves lived their entire lives as such, with no hope for an end to their bondage at the hands of their Christian brothers and sisters?

In the preceding, I have hoped to suggest an orientation for how we may find hope in difficult times, particularly when it seems that everything, including others in the faith, are conspiring to further our suffering. This is a word that is of particular resonance when so many are suffering because of the workings of an economic system that many in the church believe has been ordained by God.

A PASTORAL NEED

History reminds us that others have had experiences similar to, or worse than, those that we are experiencing, and that they have persevered and overcome. However, that does little to alleviate or accommodate the suffering of the present. The most recent economic downturns that have plagued societies and nations across the globe have left individuals and families, Christians or otherwise, struggling to live and hold on to hope.

Health crises caused by the many diseases of the age have also resulted in high levels of anxiety, stress, and suffering for individuals, family groups, and communities.

Christians caught in such situations are as much in need of hope as every other person. Many have the feeling that God has left them. Some may even believe that they have sinned in some way and brought their troubles upon themselves, thinking that they deserve God's absence as punishment for their wrongs. Christians need the assurance that God is present with them in all of life and certainly in the midst of life's challenges, but care must be taken not to use the texts wrongly lest they support the mistaken belief that sinfulness is the cause of God's absence.

There is an overarching need in all Christians to experience the loving grace of God in all their encounters with life. In the midst of pain and suffering, we all need the assurance of God's presence that offers both hope and strength to persevere.

ETHICAL IMPLICATIONS

The parable of the weeds and the wheat exacerbates the ethical dilemma the church faces as it confronts social issues. The church's complicity in the evils of slavery should be a timely reminder as the church is confronted today with similar challenges on the issue of homosexuality. As it did with slavery, the Christian church in many places has resorted to a surface and largely erroneous reading of scripture that supports discriminatory practices against non-heterosexuals and causes deep suffering for many Christians because of their sexual identity. In the same way that racial discrimination named persons of different races as deficient, so too sexual discrimination names persons of different sexual identities as deficient, based on some arbitrary norm that has been proof-texted to oppressive meaning and application.

God is as present with every one of us, regardless of color, racial origin, sexual identity or any other element of personhood, and the hope that Christ offers is the same for all who profess Christ. The love of Christ is the same for all people. And, since God is the one who determines the rightness of our identity and the love of Christ that bought our salvation is the same for all people and all are accepted by Christ, we are called to receive all persons equally in the name of Christ. The dilemma of our faith is that we are also called to stand against the evils of our world while receiving all persons without discriminating against them for who they are. It means that we must separate personal identity from individual action, so that we do not brand people as righteous or unrighteous because of their God-given identity.

GOSPEL IMPLICATIONS

The gospel message of God's enduring presence and enabling power through Christ and the Holy Spirit is a source of great hope. This is not always easy for persons to hear when they are suffering, whether from their own actions or the actions of others. Jacob's dream sequence offers reassurance that even with a traitorous past and on the run from home and from well-deserved retribution, he was still worthy of God's consideration.

Paul's message offered the Roman church assurance that their troubles were not sufficient for them to lose confidence in God's presence. Their suffering might continue, but God would give them the strength to persevere and would keep hope alive within them. It is a message that has travelled through the ages to individuals and communities beleaguered by acts of violence, pain, and suffering to body or spirit.

The good news of God's enabling presence does not deny the reality that there is trouble in the world, but it does offer Christians the reassurance that through Christ we have an advocate who will stand beside us in the midst of trouble. Confidence in God's presence is a source of hope, regardless of the circumstances of our lives.

Notes

Augustine, *A Treatise Concerning the Correction of the Donatists.*

Augustine, *The City of God.*

James H. Cone, *The Cross and the Lyncher's Tree*, 2011.

GENNIFER BENJAMIN BROOKS

STEPHEN RAY

PROPER 12 [17]

THE LESSONS IN PRÉCIS

Genesis 29:15-28. Deception is the order of the day as Jacob, who covenants with and works for Laban for seven years as the bride price for Rachel, Laban's second daughter, is given the first daughter, Leah, as his bride. It is a betrayal of the covenant between Jacob and Laban.

Psalm 105:1-11, 45b. This festal psalm calls the people to offer their praises to God because of who God is and particularly what God has done as part of the covenant between God and the people.

Romans 8:26-39. To the church in Rome that is suffering persecution as followers try to live out their faith, Paul offers a much-needed reminder of the promises inherent in trusting Christ. It is the enabling presence of Christ that will support the community through its trials.

Matthew 13:31-33, 44-52. Matthew presents five parables whose imagery connects metaphorically the old and new covenants, and reframes the picture of the kingdom of heaven.

THEME SENTENCE

God covenants with the community. Living as covenant community is a predominant theme of these texts. For Laban, community practice overrides personal desires. The psalm calls to remembrance Israel's covenant. Paul claims community as a word of assurance to suffering people. Matthew's parables address the ultimate community, the kindom of God.

A KEY THEOLOGICAL QUESTION

In the midst of trial and the seeming litany of suffering that plagues so many of the faithful, it sometimes seems that deception and illusion has hidden the kin-dom of God. The path and the way of fulfillment of God's promise are neither clear, nor without difficulty. The question that this raises is simply, why? Why is it a challenge for those whom God has, at least according to Christian scripture, chosen for eternal fellowship with God and the church triumphant? Why is it a challenge and not simply in the order of things? More than not in the natural order of things it seems quite the opposite; it often seems that creation and the things of it conspire to impede those chosen by God. Moreover, it sometimes seems that God chooses ways to bring about the promise that mean more "work" for the faithful. Here I am not contemplating the simple and not uncommon experience of the trials and tribulations that attend life in a late modern, over-consumptive society (e.g. debt, obesity-related illness, fractured families, etc.). While certainly these are very real matters that demand both ecclesial and pastoral response, the implication of divine handiwork to them serves only to mask the way that systems coalesce to bring about particular suffering; frequently, undeserved suffering. It is this second sort of trial and tribulation that I think raises the theological question for us, precisely because it is this type of suffering that emerges from the bending of creation such that it seemingly becomes the natural order of things. It is this, the hurdles of this sort that raise the question, as intoned by Anthony Pinn (1996), "Why, Lord?"

One way of making sense of this question is by resorting to the Christian doctrine of the fall. This doctrine holds that creation as we inhabit and experience it, is exactly *not* what God created things to be. It is important to note before going on that this is a Christian doctrine, meaning that it does not inherently emerge from the Genesis text. Having said that, let us notice that this doctrine holds that the actions of Adam, Eve, and the serpent brought creation under the sway of sin and death. This provides a framework for understanding the trials and tribulations of the faithful.

At a basic level, resorting to the Christian doctrine of the fall does provide a riposte to the quandary of the many hurdles faced by the faithful on their journeys. The appropriation of this doctrine has, however, not been without problems in the tradition. Specifically, it has often facilitated the complicity of Christian communities with the degradation of the planet. Because generations of Christians have devalued the planet as fallen, neither health of the planet nor of those peoples closely identified with it (indigenous and non-Western peoples) have been taken with particular seriousness. Certainly this has begun to change. Theologians such as Sally McFague and Mark Wallace, and movements such as the Evangelical Climate Initiative have called to our remembrance the created goodness of all creation and the need to care for it as stewards. Unfortunately, this is still a minority voice in very many parts of the church. It is my sense that even if it is only as pre-thematic backdrop, the doctrine of the fall still leads to a generally untoward posture toward creation by many in the faith.

So, then, if resorting to the doctrine of the fall provides only a preliminary, and in some ways unsatisfactory, way to account for the trials and tribulations of the faithful in God's good creation, where might we next turn? My sense is that the question is open and that perhaps there is no adequate answer. It may well be that what we run up against here is the impenetrable veil of finitude. It may be one of matters of existence that is simply a thing of faith. This does not mean, of course, that we overlook the witness of the faithful, who through time have found comfort and an answer satisfactory to their own needs. To do so would be to look away from a great treasure entrusted to us. I do, though, want to resist saying that this witness gives a definitive and generally applicable answer. Any attempt at a comprehensive explanation of why it seems that trials and tribulations beset us makes a mockery of the suffering of those who have faced annihilation in wonder and anguish as the "skies remained silent" (Wiesel, 2006, 69). So, we may say, provisionally, that while there may yet be found testimonies of personal peace in the face of it, the question still remains, "Why, God?" I say *provisionally* because it may well be that faith points us only to a posture toward the question; not an answer. That posture is one that simply trusts in the face of the inscrutable.

A PASTORAL NEED

There is a covenant, whether implied or explicit, that holds a community together. For Christians in this postmodern, Internet age, living into that covenant holds serious challenges. In fact, how does one even create community when individuals are physically distant from one another? Social networks have become the starting point for intimate relationships, and many Christians reject the need to gather together as a requirement of congregational membership.

At its foundation, community addresses the need to be loved and connected to others, physically, emotionally, even spiritually. Additionally, Christian community connects us with God through the divine/human covenant that provides direction and support in the midst of life's trials and attendant suffering. Thus for Christians, the church community is important for living out that covenant. At its best it transcends the differences that make us strangers and guarantees recognition of our individuality as members, even as it celebrates our commonalities for the same reason.

The covenantal love of Christ brings individuals together and enables the church, at its best, to become the beloved community. As the beloved community, Christians live within the covenant of love proclaimed in their baptism. Each member is privy to divine love that provides strength for life's journey. Members of the beloved community give and receive love that originates from Christ, provide support to each other in times of trial, and welcome others in the hope of expanding the community to the whole world, thus ushering in the kin-dom of God.

ETHICAL IMPLICATIONS

"Turnabout is fair play." Perhaps one might be forgiven for having this response to Jacob's situation, as he is the victim of Laban's trickery. Jacob had tricked his brother into giving up his birthright, so having his uncle switch brides on him seems like appropriate payback. Yet Jacob's anger seems justified when he accuses Laban of breaking his word. Laban's response, that community norm takes precedence, is unsatisfactory on many counts. It is Laban's community, so Jacob can have no expectation of support for his rightful claim.

On the other hand, Paul is writing to a community that exists under the Lordship of Christ, so there is expectation of support in their time of trial. That is the assurance Paul intends his letter to deliver, but in the face of persecution is it sufficient to meet their needs? Being part of a community, whether family, church, or any other group, requires that members commit to a covenant that guides their life together. Church systems are complicated because, unlike family systems where choice is not always a factor, Christians become members by choosing to follow Christ.

The Christian covenant that binds the community is intended to offer spiritual strength through Christ's indwelling presence. Just as the Roman church needed it, so too does the twenty-first century church need the covenantal assurance of Christ's presence as it strives to exist in the midst of destructive world systems. As head of the church, Christ is the fulfillment of the divine covenant. The love of Christ is assured not only for individuals but also for the whole community. That love is the guiding principle on which the church is built. It is the glue that must hold the community together, in order for the church to be the beloved community, the kin-dom of God on earth.

GOSPEL IMPLICATIONS

The church as the body of Christ takes its direction from Christ its head, and the community under the Lordship of Christ calls into living reality the family of God, ruled and guided by Christ's law of love. Jesus named the great commandments as love of God and love of neighbor, and the church family operates within a circle of love. Christ not only loves us individually and as the church, but the love of Christ in our hearts enables us to be people of love, members of the beloved community. That is the nature and the substance of the new covenant.

Maintaining relationships in any community, especially in the midst of trials requires more than strength of will. As Christians, it is covenantal love that directs us for faithful living as individual members and corporately as the body of Christ. It is the love of Christ and not simply our membership in the church that enables us to be a community of love in the midst of a world that is often unlovely. The eternal love of God gave Jesus Christ to the world so that all may live as one community within God's covenant of unending love.

Notes

Anthony Pinn, *Why Lord? Suffering and Evil in Black Theology*, 1999.

Elie Wiesel, *Night*, 2006.

Sallie McFague, *The Body of God: An Ecological Theology*, 1993.

Mark I. Wallace, *Green Christianity: Five Ways to a Sustainable Future*, 2010.

www.christiansandclimate.org

GENNIFER BENJAMIN BROOKS

STEPHEN RAY

PROPER 13 [18]

THE LESSONS IN PRÉCIS

Genesis 32:22-31. Jacob wrestles with the angel of God by night and prevails. His persistence is rewarded with a blessing, a new name, and a new mission that ratifies the divine/human covenant that is his legacy and his future.

Psalm 17:1-7, 15. The psalmist professes faithful obedience and constancy to the dictates of the law, even as he pleads for vindication from God against unjust accusations.

Romans 9:1-5. Paul is troubled on account of the situation of the people of Israel. A Jew by birth, he is deeply distressed that despite many time-honored proofs, they have not honored their place in the covenant, nor have they acknowledged Jesus Christ as the fulfillment of the messianic promise.

Matthew 14:13-21. The crowds persist in reaching Jesus, seeking his help and healing. Jesus responds with compassion and models for the disciples and for the church their responsibility to care for both the physical and the spiritual needs of the people.

THEME SENTENCE
God's presence enables us to persevere through life's challenges. Whether wrestling with angels or confronted by the inconsistencies of life, human ability to persevere comes from God. It is an act of faith in the divine/human covenant that gives us the assurance of relief from physical and spiritual ills.

A KEY THEOLOGICAL QUESTION

The theological question emerging from these texts is related to the possibility that the traditional reading that persistence will finally be blessed by God may be not only problematic but also deeply unfaithful. When read in the traditional mode, these texts provide for the care and sustenance of the faithful as they strive to seek the protection and blessings of God as individuals and communities. This reading is, in itself, a faithful witness to deep threads of conviction in the Christian faith since its beginning: namely, that God's mercy and grace are both available and waiting for the persistent believer. It has been both a source of comfort for Christian persons and communities in times of trial and in their regular journeys of faithfulness.

It is not this dimension of the reading that I want to problematize. Rather, it is the fact that we, the readers, are engaging the question of God's provision after the Shoah. This contextual reality places several hermeneutical responsibilities on the contemporary reader. The theological question they raise is: Will God provide? The question is not whether God *can* provide, nor is it an ambivalent conjecture that God *may* provide. This is the question of neither the atheist nor the agnostic but, rather, of the deeply faithful for whom the well of hope and trust in one's fellow human beings and in creation has been exhausted; and it seems that God is the only hope. It is my sense that if we cannot grapple with this question in light of the Shoah in a theologically responsible way, then it might be better to leave it unanswered, and live in that ambiguity.

Throughout the Epistles, Paul struggles with the relationship between the Jewish faith (Israel) and the growing Gentile reality of the church. Recall that Paul and all of the disciples lived and died as Jews who believed in Jesus Christ. In his wrestling, Paul never departs from the conviction that God's covenant with Israel remains intact and that God's fidelity to it is a measure of how God will be faithful in Christ to the church. With this in mind, what do we make of claims of God's faithfulness in the face of the Shoah? This is the first matter to deal with in terms of contextual responsibility. It is simply not the case that we can say God *will* respond to those who seek God's protection and fulfillment of the promises. As a truism, the claim is demonstrably false. While it is true that many of the Jews murdered during the Shoah were not religiously observant, substantial numbers were. We know from the remains of their witness that many, indeed, sought God's protection and the fulfillment of the promise; seemingly for naught. Moreover, given that the Shoah was, as one of my students puts it, a "singularly" Christian event—meaning that, while not the only cause, Christian anti-semitism was indisputably the necessary cause. What do we make of God's faithfulness to the church that wickedness could become so normalized that the Christian faith not only occasioned the Shoah but also gladly promulgated it? So, it seems that, at least in this case, God neither provided for the church nor Israel. It is in the shadow of this reality that we have the first challenge theologically and hermeneutically.

The second hermeneutical challenge emerges from the long tradition of the saints in the midst of persecution that God is present, providing and protecting. The challenge here is one of not breaking faith with those who have gone on before us and through their testimony given witness to the truth of the basic conviction mentioned earlier, namely that God's mercy and grace are available and very present. It is my sense that keeping faith with this tradition appears deceptively simple. This is so because it is often the case that when this witness is read, it is done without adequate attentiveness to the ambiguity and uncertainty that attended the situation in which the witness is born. An example is the testimony that emerged from the community of enslaved African-Americans of the seventeenth to the nineteenth centuries. While their witness is often celebrated by many in the contemporary church as being exemplary of persistent faith in the midst of trials, the reality is that most of these enslaved persons spent their entire lives in bondage. In other words, theirs was a witness in the midst of a time when, at least in terms of material freedom, God's blessings and grace were unapparent. What I want to suggest is that if the material ambiguity of their circumstance—they experienced God's grace but were still in bondage—is not taken seriously, then neither can one fully honor their witness.

Together, the preceding hermeneutical challenges point to the need for any interpretation of these texts to recognize the profound ambiguity of this, and earlier, historical moment(s) in regard to God's blessing in response to faithful persistence. What I am getting at is the need to take seriously that how we talk about God in light of the Shoah, and the cloud of witnesses gone on before, is a substantial mark of responsible theological reflection. It is in light of this responsibility that I say the theological questions from these readings are about whether God will provide protection and blessing to the persistent. How one approaches an answer to this question is then the theological challenge.

A Pastoral Need

The need to feel God's presence in the midst of life is common to all who believe in any iteration of the divine/human relationship. One hopes for God's compassionate intervention when confronted by the challenges of life, whether they are caused by one's less-than-salutary actions, by unjust accusations, by physical or spiritual needs, or by the relationship with one's community. When the challenges engender fear, God's intervention may be the only mitigating force for our salvation. Jacob, the psalmist, Paul, and the crowds seeking Jesus are all influenced by fear, but their actions are empowered by faith. In each case, they face challenges that cannot be overcome on their own initiative, and they must look to God. They appeal to God and persevere in their desire for God's affirming intervention and transformative grace because of faith in God.

Both fear and the desire for God's active presence are often controlling forces in the lives of individuals, families, and communities that direct or influence their actions. In every case where there is fear, it is accompanied by the expectation that God's presence will result in resolution and blessing. When neither timely resolution nor divine blessing occurs, lament to God is often the response. When the lament goes unanswered, it requires faith to persevere, which in turn requires God's empowering presence and grace. Constancy in one's relationship with God is a supreme act of faith, fueled by God's covenantal grace.

Ethical Implications

The psalmist expresses confidence that God will respond to his cry, and in Matthew's Gospel Christ responds with compassion to the needs of the community. Both stories help Christians believe that God will also respond to their needs. And yet that has not been the experience of many devout Christians. Often, silence is the only response to their lament or their situation. So why do good people suffer? Why do Christians fall victim to the troubles of life? The economic meltdown that resulted in collapsed businesses, lost jobs, and foreclosed homes incites fear and raises questions about the divine/human relationship. Many wonder about God's compassion or presence in their lives and slowly or instantly lose faith. Others persevere, trusting completely in God's faithfulness.

But there are other important questions these texts raise. Why do Christians so often respond to others, and even to each other, without compassion? The evidence of Christian collusion with demonic world powers is a historical reality that cannot be dismissed. The evils perpetrated or supported by Christians bring into question the meaning of faithfulness to the Christian covenant. The effort to live as true Christians is a daily struggle that engages the whole being.

How can Christians persevere in their faith so that their actions exemplify the compassionate love of God? Additionally, how can Christians respond compassionately to the magnitude of the world's need? Jesus called on the disciples to use whatever resources they had to feed the crowd, while Paul's response to Israel's situation was prayer. Both actions represent appropriate Christian responses to the magnitude of societal and ecclesial challenges. In every case, there is the temptation to give up, but through faith in Christ and the empowering grace of God, we can persevere and offer ourselves and our service to God.

GOSPEL IMPLICATIONS

The theme of God's compassionate response to our needs seems to offer nothing but good news for Christians. Christ is fully present to the situation that confronts the disciples and the crowd, and when the disciples are unable to respond to their hunger, Jesus steps in, blesses their offering, and provides food for all people in abundance. This story bears direct correlation to the story of redemption through Christ. God understood the magnitude of human need, and so God's only son, Jesus, was sent to be the atoning sacrifice for human sin. The law and the prophets of Israelite history could not do the work of salvation, only Christ's offering of himself could.

The message of God's love for humanity transcends human sin and our struggle to be faithful, just as Jacob struggled with the angel in his dream. That God responds with love and compassion is indeed good news. The preacher offers this message faithfully only when he or she does so within the reality of unrealized hopes and unanswered prayers, which seem to represent God's absence. The greatest good news is God's eternal love that sustains and enables the faithful to persevere.

GENNIFER BENJAMIN BROOKS

STEPHEN RAY

PROPER 14 [19]

THE LESSONS IN PRÉCIS

Genesis 37:1-4, 12-28. Joseph, the favorite and youngest son of his father, is sent by Jacob to go and see his brothers as they are grazing flocks. When Joseph approaches, they throw him into a cistern and sell him to a band of Ishmaelites journeying to Egypt, thus extending the story of God's redemption in Israel.

Psalm 105:1-6, 16-22, 45b. Praise for and memory of God's actions are connected. The story of Joseph is recalled as affirmation that God persistently acts on behalf of the least.

Romans 10:5-15. Paul asserts, "The word is near you; in your mouth and in your heart" (v. 8). The salvation of God is announced by sent ones who "announce the good news" (v. 15).

Matthew 14:22-33. Jesus walks on the water toward his disciples, who are in a boat. Peter attempts to walk to Jesus but, overcome by his surroundings, sinks in the water. Jesus' rescue is the occasion to call for belief that presses beyond current circumstances.

THEME SENTENCE

God redeems beyond current circumstance. The story of Joseph, which Psalm 105 echoes, asserts that God's redemptive actions in the world, particularly on behalf of the least, are indeed sure. The Joseph narrative, joined by the Gospel lesson, invites the listener to imagine that beyond current circumstances, God's redemptive purposes are mysteriously in motion.

A KEY THEOLOGICAL QUESTION

The nature of Christian hope is such that it defies common sense observation of human circumstances. This is as true in our personal, emotional lives as it is in the witness of this text regarding the (almost literally) incredible redemptive action of God in the narrative of Joseph and his brothers. This theme is echoed in the familiar story of Peter, desiring a faith robust enough to defy the common sense observation of his circumstances, but failing. Certainly, a hope in redemptive, divine action unsupported by any observable evidence in current human reality is, shall we say, a bit crazy. And a stubborn insistence on this particular form of Christian craziness may be just a bit unpersuasive to the more cynical, hardheaded realists among us—or perhaps even the cynical, hardheaded realist within us: that un-still, not-so-small voice that may beleaguer us in the wee hours. How is it that we can legitimately insist that God's redemptive action is present, if in fact we cannot see it? Must Christian hope always remain deferred, and if so, how on earth is it even useful or relevant?

The gift of these lessons to the hearer is both the acknowledgment of this difficult existential reality, and an accompanying assurance that, no matter how dire, God is indeed active in ways that defy common sense observation and hardheaded cynicism. It is a refusal to defer Christian hope to the eschaton, as if God were uninterested in anything prior to that final triumph. But it is a refusal that also avoids the easy platitudes with which we sometimes torture each other. Everything may indeed work for good, here; but the unease, the doubt, the suffering, the contingency of the human experience, that we see near at hand, is not overcome by far-sightedness that views final triumph. The experience of the meantime counts; it is, after all, what defines the content of human living.

The theological issue of "divine action" is a vexed one. It evokes questions of divine character (Why does God act in these ways? Why does God act at these times but not others? Why does God act on behalf of these people? Why doesn't God act on behalf of others?). It also provokes questions of divine prerogative (How does divine action operate within the natural and historical realm?). These sets of questions are intertwined, overlapping in the notion of divine sovereignty. If God is able to act unilaterally for those in need, why is it that so often this action is hidden or delayed? Why must Joseph wait years, suffering both emotionally and physically, for the redemptive action of God to take effect? A truly sovereign God might have whisked him up from the pit his brothers tossed him in, right in front of their eyes, in an immediate vindication of Joseph.

But the witness of the text is simply that God does not operate in this way. As Joseph's brothers debate amongst themselves precisely how violent they wish to be, and what they can get away with and how, God's mysterious and persistent action on Joseph's behalf shows up, not in a spectacular and supernatural intervention but in the words of Reuben: "Let's not take his life . . . don't lay a hand on him" (Gen 37:21-22).

In the Epistle reading, Paul asserts that "the word is near you" (Rom 10:8) and that the salvation of God is announced by those sent to proclaim the good news. Again, the persistent, mysterious, redemptive action of God is not a unilateral show of supernatural power. Rather, there is a witness that the actions of God in the world are undertaken not just on our behalf but with our cooperation. We, bearers of the word and proclaimers of the good news are not just the beneficiaries and recipients of the mysterious redemptive acts of God; we are also the joint enactors of them.

This is true both in an individual and in a collective sense, a matter of personal and ecclesial sanctification. The interplay between these intertwined dimensions of the human spirit is most evident in the Gospel lesson. We often fault Peter for lack of faith, as if somehow he were wrong to notice that he was surrounded by wind and waves, attempting the impossible. But what if his mistake was in aspiring to leave the boat? The boat, a historical symbol of the church, is where the community of disciples has gathered; Jesus' destination is the boat; Jesus' rescue of Peter brings him not to shore but back to the boat.

Why does Peter jump out, leaving his friends behind? Is his mistake mere impetuousness, the impatience we often associate with this disciple? Or is his mistake forgetting that we cannot believe in—much less cooperate in enacting—God's redemption in the world unaided? Without the support of his community, outside the boat, it is no wonder Peter finds himself overwhelmed and sinking. Without the combined witness of the community of God's people, it is too easy to forget that the essence of Christian hope is a faith in the trustworthy nature of God, even when the testimony of our eyes and ears and emotions is one that provides no assurances. There are indeed times when we will find ourselves in our own version of Joseph's pit, in our own version of the wind and the waves beneath our feet. There are indeed times, as these lessons suggest, that God's redemptive action is hidden, delayed, mysterious, and not at all evident in our current circumstances. In those times, the witness of the scriptures and the witness of the church must simultaneously acknowledge this hard truth, even while assuring us that however hidden, God is still at work on our behalf.

A PASTORAL NEED

One does not have to work hard at naming the absence of God. For all the assurance of God's merciful and sovereign reign over all things, we keep bumping up against a world gone wrong. The plates beneath the surface of the earth shift. Gaping fractures open up in the surface of the earth, leaving houses and lives in ruins. Floodwaters rise in New Orleans or Pakistan, choking out life for people for whom the journey is already far too difficult. Mothers, having buried their sons and daughters in the aftermath of war, return home to the gaping hole in their lives that will never quite close. Some benefit from absurd prosperity while others do not have access to the most basic elements to sustain life. In many ways, it is hard to discern the presence of God.

The experience of the absence of God is tangible, and these texts offer us vivid language and imagery for it—a dark pit, wind, waves, water. The chaos still lurks about us. The world still heaves in deep groans. What is it to believe in the reign of God in the experience of its absence? The sermon must name the tension between faith and doubt, between the absence and presence of God, between hope and despair. Only when the sermon invites us into the space of this need can it begin to proclaim a word of good news and discover that God dwells in the hidden places.

ETHICAL IMPLICATIONS

For Luther, the divine nature is first compassion, literally "with-suffering." Mirroring the divine nature, Christian life enters into the suffering world. It is precisely as we enter into the suffering world and the experience of God's absence that we may anticipate the presence of God.

We do not foreclose the experience of God's absence by minimizing suffering or injustice, nor do we easily dismiss the doubts that arise in the face of these things. When God seems absent or silent in the face of such suffering and injustice, we do not need to fill the silence with words. To do so would not account for the breadth of human experience that includes pain and confusion, and often confounds easy explanation. Psychologists might tell us that this form of denial serves only to suppress grief so that deeper healing is never realized. The life of faith does not preclude wrestling with doubt, and the Christian community should be a place in which doubt and uncertainty can be acknowledged in the experience of God's absence.

The presence of God in and with Joseph from the pit to Egypt is indeed hidden through hours and days and weeks and years of deep uncertainty about the purposes of God. Peter's sinking cry "Lord, rescue me!" (Matt 14:30) is a very real cry of desperation in the midst of life-threatening circumstances. Though Jesus is swift to rescue, we need not minimize the experience that births the cry.

We live as those who trust that the promises of God are true, that God will never leave us or forsake us. But such faith is forged in the midst of a broken world and through the experience of God's absence so that we might proclaim with those first disciples, "You must be God's Son!" (Matt 14:33).

GOSPEL IMPLICATIONS

For the sermon to name good news, it must also acknowledge bad news. Adequate time should be spent in the sermon acknowledging the troubling question of God's absence. Surely the story of Joseph or the account of Peter's attempt to walk across the water to Jesus provide ample narrative space to reflect upon our own experience of God's absence.

But the sermon must not remain there if it is to proclaim the gospel. The difficulty is to proclaim the hope of God's future, the promise of God's presence while not trivializing the experience of God's absence. Perhaps the key to this is found in the words of Paul in the Epistle lesson, "The word is near you" (Rom 10:8). The salvation, redemption, and reconciliation of God has been announced in the resurrection of Jesus. Death has not overcome life. Light has overcome darkness. This news "is in your mouth and in your heart" (Rom 10:8). The announcement of this word of good news means that it is already occurring. The sermon proclaims the gospel as it acknowledges God's absence and names with some concreteness the in-breaking of God's life-giving presence.

STEPHEN C. JOHNSON

JENNIFER JEANINE THWEATT-BATES

PROPER 15 [20]

THE LESSONS IN PRÉCIS

Genesis 45:1-15. Joseph, who has ascended to prominence and influence in Egypt, reveals himself to his brothers, telling them that their actions to sell him to Egypt were God's actions. Joseph responds to his brothers with astonishing mercy and great love.

Psalm 133. The psalm declares that unity among "families" (v. 1) is a place where God's life and blessing are bestowed.

Romans 11:1-2a, 29-32. Paul takes up God's work of salvation in the world for Jews and Gentiles alike. He affirms that God has not rejected Israel and that God's purpose is an inclusive reality for all people, Jews and Gentiles alike.

Matthew 15:(10-20), 21-28. A Canaanite woman comes before Jesus and persists in great faith at his feet, pleading for her daughter's healing. In the end, Jesus' response to her presses beyond the differences, whether gender or nationality, that exist in human community.

THEME SENTENCE

God reconciles fractured humanity. The lessons continue themes of God's redemptive and reconciling action in the world, particularly at the point of human relationship. The familial relationship between brothers provides a beginning place to explore this theme but should also include the reconciling work of God across national, racial, cultural and gender fractures in human community.

A KEY THEOLOGICAL QUESTION

"Blood is thicker than water." We often take for granted that the ties of natural kinship and blood relation can be the strongest force defining our lives. Who we are as individuals is bound up in who our parents and grandparents are, who our siblings are. As children, we are so-and-so's son, or so-and-so's little sister, to the point that perhaps we wish for a recognition of our individual identities that doesn't reference these blood relations. But this is who we are, and how we learn who we want to become. Yet as our lessons plainly demonstrate, God invites us to radical inclusion, radical reconciliation.

Joseph might dispute the value of blood kinship. After all, it did not prevent his brothers from selling him out—and this, as a kinder, gentler alternative to outright fratricide. The result of this betrayal is that Joseph's alienated status within his family becomes an explicitly alien status. He becomes a literal alien and stranger, an Egyptian nobleman and potentate that his family encounters as an unknown other. He is not known to his brothers; Joseph's identity is no longer one defined by those ties of natural kinship and blood relation, which were, in any case, inadequate to protect him from his brothers' anger and hatred.

Anonymity could have been an opportunity for revenge, or, more benignly, a protection from these men who had betrayed the natural bonds of kinship and sold him into slavery. Anonymity would have provided an escape, a way of avoiding the dangers of truth and reconciliation. But Joseph chooses to "reveal his identity" (Gen 45:1).

This "terrified" his brothers (Gen 45:3). This powerful stranger, into whose world they have ventured, vulnerable and starving, already held a life-or-death power over them and had no particular reason to help them, except for recognition of their desperate need. And now, revelation of their blood kinship serves not as a reason to help but as the opposite.

So why does Joseph reconcile with his brothers and instruct them to settle in Goshen with their children and children's children and all that they have? Is it because of the impossible and enduring strength of blood relation and natural kinship? Or because Joseph was already prepared to treat these starving, desperate strangers as kin?

Forging, and in Joseph's case re-forging, kinship across the lines of estrangement is not a given, not even where we might presume that natural kinship and familial ties lie under the surface, simply waiting to be discovered. The fractures of humanity along national, racial, cultural, gendered, and ideological lines of estrangement are not healed through the presumption of a natural kinship somehow bridging the divide. Rather, reconciliation takes place when natural kinship is not a prerequisite for understanding, recognition of need, and willingness to connect.

Jesus' encounter with the Canaanite woman underscores the irrelevance of natural belonging for the expression of kinship and reconciliation that Jesus offers. This is a person whose cultural and gender identity makes her doubly inappropriate. Jesus' first response is one that, problematically, reinforces the lines of estrangement between himself and her: "I've been sent only to the lost sheep, the people of Israel" (Matt 15:24), he says. She does not accept the dismissal, and persists—even while accepting the categorization of herself as outside the boundary of Jesus' ministry. Her final reply, "Even the dogs eat the crumbs that fall off their masters' table" (v. 27), receives a commendation, "You have great faith" (v. 28). What is her faith, exactly? It seems clear that she is not a Christ-follower in the same way the disciples are; they see her as an annoyance, and urge Jesus to send her away. She is a Canaanite, not a Jew; her religious convictions are probably highly questionable. So what does Jesus commend her for?

It is her insistence, even in the face of being ignored, grumbled at, rebuked and dismissed twice, that the gospel of Jesus was also for her and her daughter, even if only in the form of crumbs; the recognition that being Canaanite, being female, being inappropriate, is no barrier to receiving the good news, and no barrier to entering the kingdom of God. Jesus requires nothing of the Canaanite woman; no conversion, no go-and-sell-all-you-have, not even a go-and-sin-no-more. The Canaanite woman remains who and what she is, and Jesus vindicates her insistence that she too is "kin," even across the lines of estrangement that separate him from her. This is radical reconciliation that disregards bloodlines.

Paul's letter to the Romans addresses this same issue of fractured humanity, but with regard to the social and ecclesial context rather than the interpersonal contexts of the Old Testament and Gospel readings. The Roman church, at the time of Paul's writing, was facing an identity crisis prompted by the demographic shifts caused by the expulsion of the Jews (including Jewish Christians) under the edict of Claudius (49 CE). The Jewish Christians who returned to Rome after Claudius' death found a church that had shifted from the synagogue-based, mostly culturally and ethnically Jewish church they remembered to a predominantly culturally and ethnically Gentile church. Here, the lines of estrangement run straight through the middle of the church itself.

Paul's argument about reconciliation focuses on the way Christian identity supersedes, without negating, ethnic identity. The differences do not disappear; but neither do they constitute lines of estrangement—instead, they become a symbol of God's inclusive reconciliation. God has not rejected the people of Israel, whom God foreknew, Paul avers; but this does not imply the necessary rejection of the Gentiles or even the necessary conversion of the Gentiles to Judaism. Rather, God's relationship with Israel becomes the very means by which God reaches across the boundaries of a fractured humanity to the Gentiles—a reality of radical inclusive reconciliation that Paul urges his audience to enact within the church.

A PASTORAL NEED

Those who gather around these texts will likely have little difficulty recognizing the division and fragmentation they represent. Beneath a world marked by the increasing polarization of individuals and groups lies the need for healing, wholeness, and reconciliation. The fractures that have historically divided people from one another run deep. What is it that divides "families" (to borrow language from the Genesis text), that divides person from person?

We experience the fragmentation of human community in many ways. While the world's great movements to reconcile persons divided by race or ethnicity, in South Africa, the United States, and most recently in Rwanda, have brought a measure of healing, the deep wounds of racial division still mark the landscape of human experience. We experience the devaluing of human personhood by gender as well. And the current climate of increasing mistrust and hostility between those of differing world religions is yet another way in which the human community increasingly experiences this fragmentation.

The closer the experience of division moves toward us, the more apparent our need for healing and reconciliation. Perhaps this is why a story about a family is so significant in this week's lessons. Family relationships are those that sit closest to the center of our lives. Therefore, they are often the location of our deepest pain and division.

The fragmentation of human relationship, whether in the form of racial, ethnic, gender, religious, or family division, reveals the need for healing and reconciliation.

ETHICAL IMPLICATIONS

God is the primary actor in the healing and reconciliation of fragmented humanity. The radical reconciliation of all things is the eschatological horizon upon which all things move. This vision asserts that God is gathering a kingdom "from every tribe, language, people, and nation" (Rev 5:9) and that at the center of the new creation is a tree whose leaves are for the healing of the nations. This eschatological vision of the fulfillment of God's reign is the center of Christian belief and practice.

Vision of God's healing and reconciling work calls those who belong to him to participate in it. The beginning place for this work is the acknowledgement that human community is indeed fragmented and broken in many ways. Confessing and lamenting the deep divisions that exist between us opens the space for God's healing and reconciling work. From this place, we may begin to speak and act in ways that embrace God's reconciling work in human community. Such work attends not only to reconciliation as a lofty ideal, but grounds this work in attention to the smallest, most ordinary things. But there are also crucial moments in which we might embody the reconciling work of God—Joseph's moment before his brothers, a Canaanite woman's bold persistence, Paul's pastoral and prophetic ministry among Roman Christians. These are critical moments of witness in which something of God's reconciliation is propelled forward by God's servant.

Further, speech and behavior are located in communities that both produce and inform them. We nurture God's reconciling life between us in communities of peace and healing. The church's life is both a sign and foretaste of God's reconciling work. The preacher does well not only to articulate this vision but also to guide the church's practice to concrete expressions of reconciliation in human community.

GOSPEL IMPLICATIONS

The sermon names good news when it points to all those ways the healing, reconciling work of God manifests itself in the world. The preacher can name this good news on a global scale, pointing out those moments when the large structures of our common existence are mended. Sometimes it is easier to name God's work of reconciliation when we have enough experience or historical distance to recognize it. Joseph's interpretation of his brothers' actions was possible because he stood at enough distance to recognize God's presence to heal and restore.

But the sermon will announce good news most profoundly as it moves the expression of God's healing closer to the life of the listening community. This move will require the preacher to be a careful reader of the context. A careful reading will be attentive not only to the obvious expressions of God's reconciling work but also to the small, unnoticed expressions as well.

Finally, the sermon is good news where it names God's reconciling work in the world and invites the listening community to participate in it. The gospel sermon stirs the imagination to conceive of the power of the resurrection in God's radical plans for reconciliation: as Paul says, "God was reconciling the world to himself through Christ, by not counting people's sins against them. He has trusted us with this message of reconciliation" (2 Cor 5:19).

STEPHEN C. JOHNSON

JENNIFER JEANINE THWEATT-BATES

PROPER 16 [21]

THE LESSONS IN PRÉCIS

Exodus 1:8-2:10. The Israelites grow numerous. A new king plans to deal with the increase in population by asking midwives to kill the males at birth. A Hebrew woman gives birth to a baby and hides him in the Nile River. The baby is found by Pharaoh's daughter, who takes the child as her own son and names him Moses, "I pulled him out of the water" (2:10).

Psalm 124. The psalm proclaims the Lord's deliverance of Israel from those who would have devoured her. The water imagery of "torrent" (v. 4) connects this psalm to the name ascribed to Moses.

Romans 12:1-8. In light of God's salvation for both Jews and Gentiles, Paul urges those who are a part of the church to offer themselves as "a living sacrifice" (v. 1). He argues that the giftedness of each is the basis of inclusion and unity in Christian community.

Matthew 16:13-20. Jesus asks his disciples about his identity. Peter answers, "You are the Christ, the Son of the living God" (v. 16). Jesus affirms this response as divinely revealed and the foundation for the life of the church.

THEME SENTENCE

God empowers each of us to live as a transformed "living sacrifice."
Just as Moses, the deliverer, and Jesus, the Messiah and Savior, lived humble lives preceding the recognition of their transformed identities, we too are empowered by the Spirit to recognize that we are to offer our full living identities to the transformative call of God.

A KEY THEOLOGICAL QUESTION

God's call is also God's empowerment. God never asks us to do something without equipping us with the means of doing it.

Moses' back story is every bit as amazing as his future as leader of the Israelite exodus. And yet, as a baby, Moses is a bit player in his own story. The heroes of Moses' backstory are humble midwives, only two of whom are named: Shiprah and Puah. These midwives, who "respected God" (Exod 1:17), defy the direct orders of the Pharaoh, refusing to selectively kill the boys born to laboring Hebrew women. These Hebrew midwives apparently openly defy Pharaoh, for he calls them to account, and they offer a lame excuse for their disobedience. It's not clear what is Pharaoh's response to their disobedience or excuse. What the text does make clear, however, is God's response: God dealt well with the midwives and gave them families of their own. This, of course, does not end the problem of Pharaoh's murderous intent; instead, he leans on his own people, the Egyptians, to carry out his wishes. Again, it is the defiance of women, empowered by God, that saves Moses: his mother, his sister, and a miracle in itself, the Pharaoh's own daughter. Moses grows up in the care of his own mother, claimed as son by the Pharaoh's daughter, eventually to become the leader chosen by God to lead the Israelite people out of exile and slavery.

Moses' life is a study in secrecy and divine protection. Hidden as a baby until the age of three months, he is then rescued by Pharaoh's daughter and grows up, a forbidden Hebrew boy, under her protection and claimed as her son. Still later, Moses flees to the Midian desert to live for years in anonymity, only to be called out of that secret hiding place by God. Moses is hidden in secret, discovered and preserved, but his Hebrew identity (as a Levite!) is submerged under an acculturated Egyptian one, until God calls him forth as a savior to his people. What empowerment did it take for a man raised in secrecy and trained to cloak his Hebrew identity to honor that call?

So, too, does Jesus live "secretly" in a significant sense—a prophet, a teacher, a rabble-rouser, but not "the Christ, the Son of the living God" (Matt 16:16). In the Gospel text, only Simon Peter can make this confession of Jesus' identity. Others confuse him with John the Baptist or name him as the returned spirit of prophets long gone. Jesus' true identity becomes evident only when God calls him to present himself as the one, final "living sacrifice." It is often difficult to consider the struggles and temptations of Jesus, to consider his humanity separate from his divinity. We often presume a divinely gifted serenity to Jesus' inexorable progress toward his death in Jerusalem. In doing so, our knowledge of Jesus' unique identity as Messiah and Son of God gets in the way of our comprehension of his sacrifice. What did it take to give up the security of his humble identity as prophet, teacher, and rabble-rouser and proclaim himself as Messiah? Was it this that prompted him to "order" (Matt 16:20) his disciples not to tell anyone that he was the Messiah?

In these narratives, we see that the answer of God's call upon the lives of his followers requires the sacrifice of former identities, the willingness to give up one's life as it is in exchange for the empowered and transformed life of God's will. God's call plucked Moses out of secrecy and security, just as God's call placed Jesus on a path out of anonymity to notoriety and death. Their lives became "living sacrifices," total offerings on the altar of God's will.

When we read Paul's exhortation to the Roman Christians to "present [their] bodies as a living sacrifice that is holy and pleasing to God" (Rom 12:1) we often interpret these words as an admonition about purity, sexual or moral. But this reduces the significance of the Christian life as "a living sacrifice"—as if bodies were simply a tool we should keep clean and in good condition—while the rest of who we are escapes the sacrificial mandate. To be a living sacrifice is a total condition, an offering of self that leaves nothing out. It is no surprise, then, that Paul's next words instruct us as to the empowerment we receive, "be transformed by the renewing of your *minds*," for without such empowerment and transformation, how could we present our bodies as living sacrifices, holy and acceptable to God? There is no mind/body split here. Instead, there is a recognition that our identities as human beings are a whole, and an exhortation to present our whole identities and whole selves to God.

Perhaps it is hard to think of ourselves as under the same necessity, and subject to the same call as Jesus or Moses. These were, after all, extraordinary men of God—and more. So consider, again, the plight of the Hebrew women and midwives. For them, the safe choice was to obey the one who literally held the power of life and death in his hands. What did it take for them to openly defy orders and honor the call of God to preserve and nurture life? It took no less than the willingness to be "living sacrifices," placing their lives and selves on the line for the sake of others, trusting in the power of God. They offered and risked no less than Moses or Jesus would; they offered and risked their lives in submitting them to the will of God. These Hebrew women, ordinary women, are no less extraordinary than Moses himself; and they provide for us, ordinary people, an example of living sacrifices perhaps more obviously within our grasp than Jesus' death on the cross. God empowers us to meet our calling.

A Pastoral Need

These texts, as we read them together here, point to the need and privilege of transformed identity. The transformation of one's identity is often the recovery of one's true, God-given identity or one's true self in the face of the false selves we have received. Among the false selves constructed for us are those that say:

- Your beauty is determined by conforming your body image to some cultural standard;

- Your worth is determined by your ability to produce goods and services;

- Your value in society is determined by the amount of goods and services you can consume;

- Your position in society is determined by the color of your skin;

- Your value in culture is directly related to your gender.

In many ways, we receive messages that construct a false self and form a distorted sense of identity. The false identities we receive do not give life. Over time, if we live with our false selves long enough, our lives are drawn into painful conflict. We have become something other than God has created us to be.

The careful articulation of the need for the true self, then, is the condition of proclaiming God's transforming work to restore our identity in God's image. The preacher's work is to inhabit the biblical text, its language and imagery, in such a way that it names the deep need for the transformed self.

ETHICAL IMPLICATIONS

God's work to transform lives and identities can first be embraced in the space of our own lives as we receive the gracious gift of God's empowering work in us. As recipients of this work, we confess our need for God's transforming presence and our resistance to receive it. We live out of a confessional awareness of the way in which false identities have been constructed for us. We acknowledge the wounds inflicted on us by our false selves and courageously turn our face toward God.

As we receive God's transforming work in us, we live in ways that extend God's transforming work to others. In many ways, we may find that living a new, God-given identity means that our lives function prophetically over-against the dominant assumptions about human value and worth as they influence the identity of others. Because we understand our identity in the self-giving life and purpose of God, we make choices about how we interact with others and participate in the social and economic structures of the world that draw attention to the prevailing assumptions about human identity, value, and worth.

Because God is renewing and transforming all things and all people, those who find their identity in the life of God advocate for those who are yet held in the grip of a false sense of self. Sometimes this requires divine empowerment and willingness to speak words of judgment to the power structures that reinforce destructive and oppressive systems of self-understanding. Other times it may mean working overtime with the Spirit, carefully and systematically, to birth life-giving movements that create the space for God's transforming work in the lives of others.

We become participants in God's renewing and restoring work in the lives of others by living our true, God-given identities as prophetic witness and advocate.

GOSPEL IMPLICATIONS

The narrative arc of the story of the Bible declares the good news that God is indeed making all things new. Within the space of individual lives and events, God transforms the world and calls and empowers all who inhabit it. The story of God's deliverance of a people from Egypt gathers this good news in a single instance. The story of the oppression of one people by another is surely a telling of the false construal of humanity and human identity. Over against the false construal of humanity by empire, God's transforming work ensues not only for the oppressed Hebrews but also for the sake of the whole world. Within the context of this story, the character of Moses represents both the complexity and certainty of God's work to transform human identity in a way that reflects life, wholeness, and flourishing.

The conversation between Jesus and his disciples about his identity as God's Messiah participates in the narrative trajectory of the Exodus story and its announcement of good news. As God's Messiah, Jesus embodies what is truly human. He will not only bear the name "Messiah" or "Christ" but will also embody self-giving for the sake of human wholeness and flourishing. In our baptism, and in our receipt of the Holy Spirit, we find our calling and the empowerment to fulfill it.

———————————

STEPHEN C. JOHNSON

JENNIFER JEANINE THWEATT-BATES

PROPER 17 [22]

THE LESSONS IN PRÉCIS

Exodus 3:1-15. God calls to Moses from a burning bush. God has heard the cry of God's people and will deliver them from the hand of the Egyptians. Moses resists God's call but is assured of God's presence and authority.

Psalm 105:1-6, 23-26, 45b. The psalm connects the story of the oppression of the Israelites in Egypt and the sending of Moses to the action of God. Recalling this, God's people are to "seek his face always" (v. 4).

Romans 12:9-21. Paul exhorts an ethic of genuine love that is patient in suffering. He instructs Christians to "bless people who harass you" (v. 14) to "consider everyone as equal" (v. 16) and not to "payback anyone for their evil actions with evil actions" (v. 17).

Matthew 16:21-28. After Peter confesses Jesus as Messiah, Jesus foretells his own suffering, death, and resurrection. Peter rebukes Jesus, insisting this will never happen. Jesus calls his followers to join him in the way of the cross.

THEME SENTENCE

God enters into the suffering of God's world. Jesus' words about his suffering are heard alongside God's declaration that he has indeed seen the misery of his people in Egypt. The lessons connect the nature of the suffering of God to the call of disciples who are to enter into the suffering of the world as a means of bringing God's peace.

A KEY THEOLOGICAL QUESTION

Many of us at times might choose the ways of vengeance, violence and retribution, but God's way is to enter the places of human suffering. "Beloved," Paul writes to the Christians in Rome, "Never avenge yourselves, but leave room for God's action in the world" (Rom 12:19). This may be the most counter-intuitive, un-human ethical advice ever given. Don't hit back. No more tit-for-tat.

In game theory terms, tit-for-tat is an "evolutionarily stable strategy." In other words, it works—it ensures the survival of the individual under uncertain circumstances, when others may be either friend or foe, or turn suddenly from friend to foe without warning. In game theory, tit-for-tat is a strategy that communicates, "I'm willing to help you, but I'm no sucker, and I'll hit back when betrayed."

And yet, tit-for-tat is not optimal. It can quickly degenerate into a "death spiral" in which both sides see themselves bound to punish the other in self-defense, never again achieving the cooperation and understanding that would be mutually beneficial. One way out of this degenerative spiral is simply for one side to arbitrarily refrain from punishment for one round; tit-for-tat-with-forgiveness, the presentation of an opportunity for re-establishing cooperation and reciprocity. It's a counter-intuitive risk that offers a way out of the escalating cycle of violence.

When God calls Moses from the burning bush and announces, "I've clearly seen my people oppressed in Egypt. I've heard their cry of injustice . . . I am sending you to Pharaoh to bring my people, the Israelites, out of Egypt" (Exod 3:7-10) we are not surprised that Moses objects. Is God seriously proposing to send an anonymous, unarmed, single sheepherder to make an impossible demand of the Egyptian powers-that-be? Wouldn't it make more sense to advise Moses on how to rally some support, gather up some numbers and make a show of strength for his bid to free the Israelite people? Wouldn't it make more sense to let Pharaoh know up front that Moses is ready to give tit-for-tat? The Israelites are oppressed and suffering—there's a lot of vengeance to be had. Why not give Moses the divine handbook for revolutionary insurrection?

In the same way, Jesus' counter-intuitive insistence that he must go to Jerusalem, suffer, and die, is met with incomprehension and resistance. Peter's refusal to accept this results in a horrifyingly stern rebuke from Jesus: "Get behind me, Satan. You are a stone that could make me stumble" (Matt 16:23). But Jesus offers an explanation for these harsh words; Peter's mistake is clear: "for you are not thinking God's thoughts but human thoughts" (Matt 16:23). Divine logic breaks the cycle of escalating retaliatory violence; human logic only completes it. But divine logic is un-humanly counter-intuitive.

The fact that it is counter-intuitive does not mean that we get to shrug and walk away from this ethic because it is definitively impossible. Lest we suppose that the break from human tit-for-tat is something we can conveniently relegate to the category of things only Jesus, the divine Son of God, can do, Paul slams shut our theological escape hatch. Yes, this is divine, and not human—but it is not for that reason beyond our reach. Rather, it is for that very reason our calling and the measure of our expectations for ourselves. "Love should be shown without pretending" (Rom 12:9), Paul says. This means not simply caring for each other but reaching out beyond the Christian community to extend hospitality to strangers, and, incredibly, blessing those who persecute us. A divine, arbitrary, extension of forgiveness to interrupt the human cycle of tit-for-tat.

Even for those who earnestly desire to live out a divine ethic that mirrors the action of God and the life of Jesus, this calling is not easy. Paul's final words in this passage perhaps demonstrate this—an echo of the difficulty of eradicating fully, rather than simply deferring, the human desire for retribution. Paul writes, "Don't try to get revenge for yourselves, my dear friends, but leave room for God's wrath. It is written, 'Revenge belongs to me; I will pay it back, says the Lord.' Instead, 'If your enemy is hungry, feed him; if he is thirsty, give him a drink. By doing this, you will pile burning coals of fire upon his head'" (Rom 12:19-20). Yet the last word leaves no room even for this deferred human expectation. The last word is simply, "Defeat evil with good" (v. 21).

Theologically, this leads us to a question of anthropology: are human beings capable of this kind of divine ethic? Aren't we, after all, a fallen creation? Didn't Paul himself so memorably describe the human experience as one of longing to do what is right and finding oneself simply unable to do it? (Rom 7:15-19).

If vengeance is not a Christian response, what is the alternative? While these passages do not speak directly of empowerment by the Spirit, they do explicitly name God's presence as the repeated, steadfast counter to the doubtful appraisals of human ability. God enters human suffering. God's answer to Moses is nothing more or less than this: "I will be with you." Jesus' insistence to the disciples that his suffering and death are necessary and unavoidable is the Christological reiteration of divine presence both with God's envoys and with suffering creation; this is the means by which the cycle of retributive violence and suffering is broken. Read within the larger context of these accompanying lectionary passages, Paul's instruction to "leave room for God's wrath" (Rom 12:19) can now be seen, not as deferral of human vengeance in expectation of divine retribution, but an invocation of God's presence. Christians can resist the human cycle of violence, because in leaving room for God, we are assured that God is indeed with us, even in circumstances defined by suffering, violence, persecution, and the desire for revenge.

A Pastoral Need

In a world in which power is exercised most often for violence and coercion, it is hardly possible to move through life and not find oneself the recipient of acts of violent, coercive power. The wounds inflicted upon us are sometimes surface wounds—a friend betrays trust nurtured over the long years of a relationship; a careless word spoken by another rests heavily in consciousness; a co-worker seditiously manipulates relationships in competition for a promotion. Other times the wounds cut deeper—domestic and sexual violence become commonplace; a life-time of systematic discrimination lies beneath subtly veiled threats; nations devise even more efficient ways to wage war against one another.

Our response is often self-defense or self-preservation. We learn this response at a very young age and are conditioned to conceive of the other person first and foremost as a potential threat. "No one is going to look out for you, but you." As a result, it is hard to imagine the world any other way. *The need to be known and loved* is hidden beneath the fear that the world may be nothing more than a series of violent and coercive power plays. Having experienced this form of power and the resulting wounds, we perpetuate the cycle. Christians are not immune from the cycle that occurs when power is exercised as violence and coercion. In fact, they too often become tragic expressions of power expressed as violence.

ETHICAL IMPLICATION

The story of the suffering, death, and resurrection of Jesus bears witness to an alternative form of power, a truer and greater form of power. The cross of Jesus exposes violence and coercion as false power, and the invitation of Jesus to join him in the way of the cross means that followers of Jesus will confront and expose violence and coercion construed as power in the same way.

The cross of Jesus is for us, then, both gift and invitation. It is the gift of God's gracious, self-giving life for the salvation of the world, and it is also the invitation to a way of life. The cruciform life is the way of self-emptying, self-giving power. The sermon may explicitly point to or subtly refer to the practice of the Eucharist as a means of telling and enacting the story of divine self-giving. The Eucharist is a means of receiving a world in which true power is found in weakness. In the breaking of bread, we give thanks for Jesus, who was broken and given. At the same time, we are offering ourselves to one another and for the sake of the world, broken and given. In sharing the cup, we give thanks for Jesus, whose own life was poured out for the sake of the world. At the same time, we say that we will pour out our lives for one another and for the sake of the world.

The story of God's self-emptying willingness to enter into the suffering of the world and the liturgical embodiment of that story in the Eucharist form us into a certain kind of people and send us into the world to enact this alternative, true form of power. The people of God are able to live this way because they are empowered by God's Holy Spirit.

GOSPEL IMPLICATIONS

When God might well have chosen to respond to human disobedience and sinfulness with vengeance and destruction, God chose instead to come to us in human form. The lessons for this week are held together by a gospel lens that reads the story of Exodus as a foreshadowing of the death and resurrection of Jesus, a move made by Gospel writers. Paul's exhortation to the life of genuine love emerges from gospel instincts growing out of the death and resurrection of Jesus. The invitation of Jesus in the Gospel lesson to follow in the way of the cross is possible only because of the assurance of the resurrection and the enabling accompaniment of the Holy Spirit.

The challenge for the preacher will be to bring this gospel lens to bear in the living context that holds the sermon. To do so, the sermon may first name false power exercised as violence and coercion in the world in which we live. The capacity to name the "bad news" implied in these readings is necessary in order for the sermon to announce the alternative form of self-giving power as good news. This is the story we tell, and it must be told in a way that names those ways life is already emerging in the midst of death. In order to do so, the sermon must move to make concrete the gospel claim in the life of the congregation.

STEPHEN C. JOHNSON
JENNIFER JEANINE THWEATT-BATES

PROPER 18 [23]

THE LESSONS IN PRÉCIS

Exodus 12:1-14. Instructions for the Passover are given to Moses and Aaron for the deliverance of the people from oppression in Egypt. Certain foods are to be eaten in a certain manner as a means of remembering God's deliverance.

Psalm 149. The psalm praises God for delighting in his people and invites Israel to exult in God's judgment and deliverance.

Romans 13:8-14. Paul instructs, love one another and so fulfill the Law. All the Law can be summed up in the ethic of love. Because the salvation of God is near, the people are to live in love toward one another and so put on the Lord Jesus Christ.

Matthew 18:15-20. Matthew offers guidance for life in Christian community when one sins against another. Reconciliation should be sought between individuals. If this is not possible, one or two others should be consulted and, if necessary, the matter brought before the entire church.

THEME SENTENCE

God frees God's people to live in love. Read together, the lessons present the church with movement *from* oppression and bondage *toward* life and love. The Christian community lives within the tension of this eschatological horizon ("The night is almost over, and the day is near" [Rom 13:12]), embracing the deliverance of all things and embodying it in communal life.

A KEY THEOLOGICAL QUESTION

In these texts, God's intent for human beings to live in community comes to the fore. In what ways may we understand God's freeing us to community living? Framing everything is the exodus narrative, in which God once again chooses a people as God's own, and acts decisively among them to deliver them from exile and slavery. This act both reaffirms and redefines God's election of the nation of Israel, providing a new historical reference point for the communal identity of Israel as God's own people. This new reference point is ritualized as the Passover, providing a way to solidify and commemorate this communal identity across the generations.

The communal nature of this identity is the basis upon which the gift of the Law rests. Without God's election and deliverance of Israel in the Exodus, the subsequent provision of Mosaic Law would be incomprehensible. The Law is for the people of God; without communal identity, the Law makes no sense. But given God's election and salvation of God's people, providing a vision of how that community should organize its common life together is an obvious next step. It also frames the way that God's people—then and now—should regard moral instruction, as a continuing form of God's original and unceasing concern for the welfare of God's people in community.

Paul echoes Jesus' summation of the Law in this Epistle reading. To love is the fulfillment of the Law, for "love doesn't do anything wrong to a neighbor" (Rom 13:10). The commandments Paul enumerates logically fall within this broad ethic of love—but again, we see that Paul is urging a shift in perspective for his hearers. "Don't be in debt to anyone," he writes, "except for the obligation to love each other" (v. 8). This shift in perspective echoes the original framing of Mosaic Law, one in which gratitude and not obligation forms the basis for the communal ethic. Having been formed as a community through God's act of election and deliverance, loving one's neighbor is the free and grateful mirroring of that act of love.

And yet, the reality of living together in community is not that easy. Paul turns swiftly to an admonishment: Wake up! Stop living like nothing's changed; stop gratifying yourself, harming and provoking each other. You know better! It seems that the Christians in Rome understood the concept—after all, loving one's neighbor is an easy enough concept to understand—but they were having a bit of trouble living it out. Paul names drunkenness, revelry, sleeping around, fighting, and obsession as problematic behaviors preventing the expression of neighbor-love in the Christian community in Rome. The self-referential nature of such behaviors betrays the fundamental way that love-of-neighbor has been forgotten.

Yet it's not just personal failures and selfishness that get in the way of living out the ethic of love in our communities. The Gospel text provides an even more problematic scenario: What happens when you're not the problem, but someone else is? When your neighbor sins against you, then what? The Gospel text provides a simple template for action. Don't sulk, don't gossip, don't avenge, don't avoid. Instead, love recognizes and maintains relationship even when put under the strain of sin. So go talk to your neighbor—that might just work.

And, it might not. In which case, try again, and try again, each time invoking the reality of the community, the basis of relationship and the communal ethic of love. Step two, bring a couple of people with you, and try again to communicate with your neighbor. Step three, bring the entire community in, and try again to communicate with your neighbor. But finally, there are no guarantees. In the worst-case scenario, the Gospel of Matthew tells us, "Treat them as you would a Gentile and tax collector" (18:17).

What does this mean? That "such a one" is "out"? Is this a prescription for excommunication, or shunning? We have, indeed, historically based such practices on this passage. But perhaps we might consider that provisions for welcoming the alien and stranger are strong in the Hebrew Bible, and that Jesus himself quite notoriously called and ministered to tax collectors. These people, no matter how unrepentant, are not ultimately outside the community and out of reach of the communal ethic of love—as indeed no one is. Jesus' instruction here may need to be put alongside his words (just beyond our lection), "Not just seven times, but rather as many as seventy-seven times" (Mat 18:22).

But love does not, cannot, coerce repentance or conformity to communal expectation. If the offender refuses to listen, love must honor even that. This is unsatisfactory insofar as it falls short of the communal identity of God's people and the ethic of love that this communal identity upholds. And yet this unsatisfactoriness itself testifies to the ultimate reality that, even when strained and broken, love of neighbor recognizes relationship—a relationship ultimately derived from the communal identity that all share as chosen and saved by God. As such, community is empowered by the Spirit. As Paul said, we are "transformed by the renewing of [our] minds" (Rom 12:2).

In theological anthropological terms, we learn from these texts that no one is singly chosen by God as a separate, autonomous individual. God chooses people, creating and recreating community. Being chosen by God is synonymous with finding oneself surrounded by neighbors—others who have also been chosen and saved, others to whom you now relate in an ethic of love founded on the originating act of God and the continuing sustenance of the Holy Spirit.

A PASTORAL NEED

Paul's words instruct us to "love each other" (Rom 13:8). In doing so, he identifies the deep need to love and be loved in true human community, made possible by the love of God. The need for meaningful community is often experienced as loneliness. Loneliness may be experienced as isolation from other human persons, but can also be experienced in the company of others. Even though other people may surround our lives, we may feel lonely or isolated, thus pointing out the need not only for human community but also for human connection.

The experience of loneliness and isolation can be considered byproducts of a Western worldview that emphasizes the individual. The need thereby intensifies for an ethic of love broad enough to sustain true human community. A worldview that holds the autonomy of the individual to be the chief virtue too often produces a narcissism that cannot extend human relationship beyond the vested interests of and the pragmatic benefits to the individual. From this perspective, descriptions of a truly interdependent community that is rooted in the well-being and care of the other at great cost can only be construed as an affront to the freedom of the individual. Such a worldview leaves us cut off from each other at the most significant level. We settle for cheap substitutions for love and for authentic, self-sacrificing, self-giving community.

ETHICAL IMPLICATIONS

The nature of God's love as manifest in scripture is love that holds in tension divine risk and vulnerability with divine justice and judgment.

These characteristics are the essential components of a community rooted in the ethic of love.

The act of creation is itself an act of love involving divine risk. That God creates human persons in God's image for relationship, placing within them the capacity to give and receive love, implies the possibility that the created beings might not choose to return the love of the Creator. God, in the act of creation, yields to the possibility that God might be wounded and rejected by the ones God has created. Indeed, this becomes the case. In the course of time humanity rejects the divine Creator, and as a result of this the divine experiences deep sorrow and pain. The culmination of this story, of course, is the rejection of Jesus to the point of death. Community in the image of the Creator is community that acts in love in ways that are vulnerable and require risk. Christian communities that bear the image of Jesus and go in the way of the cross are places of mutual self-giving in which we offer ourselves in love to one another at cost. Christian communities hold at bay the self-interest and self-preservation that closes one off from the other, or at least holds each other at a safe, convenient distance.

If in the act of creation and in the story of the cross divine love is characterized as self-giving love requiring risk and vulnerability, then it is also true that the justice and judgment of God mark such divine love. By this, we understand that God's purpose to draw all things and all people into life and wholeness, to reconcile all things, is sure. God will set the world right and bring all things to completion in love. Justice and judgment are coupled with God's self-giving risk. Christian community lives out God's justice in judgment in unlimited liability and accountability to one another.

GOSPEL IMPLICATIONS

The good news is that God has not left us to ourselves, but has drawn us up into God's life in community. The preacher will attend to God's work to call forth life in community rooted in divine love and to proclaim the divine empowerment we have to accomplish it.

The particular narratives of today's lessons provide language and imagery to name our own deep need and experience a word of God's grace. Exodus 12 suggests that meals are not merely about sustenance for our bodies, but that they ground the life of God's people in God's gracious and sure deliverance into life shared together. The language and imagery of the meal table is offered as the backdrop for a gospel moment in the sermon. Likewise, the image of the "day" dawning, of awakening to God's salvation, of participating in the new creation, provides language to name the good news of the life we share with one another in love. Glimpses of divine love in Christian community can be painted with the language of the "dawning day." Or the hard work to pursue right relationship with one another described in the Gospel lesson mirrors divine love. In each instance, as the particular language and imagery of the text meets concrete expression in the experience of the gathered community, good news is announced and received.

STEPHEN C. JOHNSON

JENNIFER JEANINE THWEATT-BATES

PROPER 19 [24]

THE LESSONS IN PRÉCIS

Exodus 14:19-31. God went before his people leading them out of Egypt and now moves behind his people to deliver them from the army of Egypt. Israel passes through the sea on dry ground.

Psalm 114. The Psalmist declares that as Israel went out of Egypt, God's dwelling was among them. The sea, the mountains, and the earth tremble at the presence of the Lord.

Romans 14:1-12. "We don't live for ourselves and we don't die for ourselves." Paul says that those who live and die for the Lord do not pass judgment on one another even if they believe and practice their faith differently.

Matthew 18:21-35. Matthew grounds the life of Christian community in the ethic of forgiveness telling the story of a merciful king who forgave the debt of one of his servants. That servant refused to forgive the debt of one who owed him and was called to account.

THEME SENTENCE

God leads us in the way of mercy and life. God goes before and behind God's people to lead them into a new life and a future marked by God's gracious life-giving mercy. The old order of things, represented in the first reading as Egypt, is overcome by the life that God gives. God's mercy is manifest in God's people who now live mercifully toward one another.

A KEY THEOLOGICAL QUESTION

What is the nature of God's mercy? What does it mean to live mercifully toward one another? In these readings we have both positive and negative examples—unsurprisingly, more negative than positive. Most of the time, human beings provide each other with excellent examples of what not to do. The Egyptians, determinedly pursuing the fleeing Israelites, showed no inclination toward mercy. The servant in Jesus' parable showed no inclination toward mercy, even after receiving it himself. The Christians in Rome showed each other no mercy in judging each other's divergent beliefs and practices.

There is more to the cultivation of mercy than simply mirroring what we have received, out of gratitude. That, perhaps, is the lesson of the parable of the ungrateful servant. After all, this man had a model and an example to follow. He had personally benefited from another's inclination toward mercy. We can assume that this man would feel relief, joy, and gratitude toward the king who forgave his debt. The contrast in the narrative between what he has received and what he dishes out is shocking.

We receive this story as though it is staggering that this man failed to "pay it forward," because we know that this is the moral expectation of the story. But is it so surprising? The servant owes a debt of gratitude to the king; this other man has nothing to do with that. Perhaps if the king had requested some special service or favor, this servant would have gratefully obeyed, reciprocating as best he could the mercy he had received in that relationship. But this other servant . . . what has he got to do with anything? That is an entirely different situation, and an entirely different relationship.

What, exactly, is the failure of this ungrateful servant? How does he fail to make the connection, which is obvious to us and would have been to the original audience of Jesus' parable, that he should treat this unfortunate fellow slave with the same mercy that he has received?

The failure of the ungrateful servant is both moral and epistemological. It is a failure of what we might call "empathetic imagination," the ability to place oneself in another's situation and understand that their lot might just as easily be one's own. To act mercifully toward his fellow servant, the ungrateful servant must be able to see himself as both the debtor and the debt-holder, as both his fellow servant and the king. He has been the debtor; he should be able empathetically to imagine what the fellow slave feels like. He has received mercy; he should be able empathetically to imagine himself as the forgiver of the debt. He does not do this. Instead, his actions are only self-referential. The ungrateful servant is not capable, or not willing, to see through the eyes of any other.

The other examples in the accompanying texts give us scenarios of the same human failing. On a social and systemic level, the Egyptians pursue their former Israelite slaves without mercy, determined to keep them enslaved—a sin that can only exist through an entire society's willful refusal to understand what slavery is to the slave. And on a very familiar, personal, quotidian level, the Christians in Rome cannot extend mercy toward each other over something as petty as differences of opinion and practice.

In the Gospel text, the moral dimension of mercy is the focus, but in the Epistle text, the epistemological dimension of mercy is the focus. Paul is writing to the Romans about what to do in the face of their different understandings of the Christian faith. Interestingly, not only does Paul refuse to adjudicate between these different understandings, he actually says that everyone "must have their own convictions" (v. 5). Paul does not pick sides, and his advice is for everyone to be convinced that their side is right. How can this be anything but a recipe for disaster and schism? Or—perhaps even worse, to some minds in this postmodern age—how is this not the utter chaos of complete relativism?

Paul's reminder to the Christians in Rome that "all will stand before the judgment seat of God" reframes the doctrinal disagreements within the church in reference to the ultimate, and ultimately unknowable, arbiter of truth: God's own self. Implicit within this reframing is a reminder of human epistemological limitations. Human beings, however faithful and sincere, do not know everything there is to know about God. This demands of the faithful Christian a measure of epistemological humility—and a corresponding mercy to those who believe and practice differently than we ourselves do. This does not mean we must be in a paralytic crisis, unable to worship or act because we don't know for certain what is right or true. Rather, Paul tells us to be both humble and fully convinced. The only way to be both, simultaneously, is to extend mercy toward others who disagree.

The necessity of empathetic imagination, of the ability to place oneself in the position of another, is multi-dimensional. It means, of course, that we must be able to empathize with our fellow human sufferers. But it also means that we must be able to imagine ourselves as capable of more than we believe ourselves to be. When we refer to Jesus as our moral exemplar, fully and yet sinlessly human, we can set ourselves up for either living a series of repeated moral failures or for living into the fullness of what God intends for us to become. In the roles of the parable, we may imagine ourselves as the merciful king, in order to act toward others as the king acts toward the servant. That may seem impossible, yet with God at our side, all things are possible.

A PASTORAL NEED

We do not really want to live our lives by the aphorism, "You get what you deserve." What we really want or need is a merciful paradigm for our lives. Our lives are marked by shortcomings—our own and those of others toward us. We violate the trust of others and have our own trust violated. We wound others and are wounded by others. If we choose the language of the parable, our experience is marked by debt—what we leave outstanding is left outstanding toward us.

Sometimes the debt is great and there is much at stake. The mark left by what is owed is great. The wound is large. Other times the debt is small, but over time even the small debts add up. Sometimes the debt is personal and unique to our individual experience (like the debt of the servant in Jesus' parable). Other times the debt rests upon people collectively (like the generations of oppression perpetrated in Egypt). Sometimes we are the indebted ones and sometimes we are the debt holders. Put another way, we need mercy—mercy given and mercy received.

The preacher does well to name those ways our lives are interconnected in the web of human community. As Paul puts it, "We don't live for ourselves and we don't die for ourselves" (Rom 14:7). Because we are connected, we need to give and receive mercy.

ETHICAL IMPLICATIONS

In terms of the texts before the preacher, Egypt systemically holds these Hebrews in bondage. The Exodus text imagines a world in which systematic oppression is overthrown. The Exodus text names the exploitation of some by others in the production of goods. Egypt builds its empire on the backs of oppressed people and they do so in a way that is life-taking. In other words, Egypt builds up its own life at the expense of others. Such a text raises challenging ethical questions about our own participation in systems of exploitation, or debt-holding. In what ways do we participate in or benefit from large, systemic structures that choke life out of some to the benefit of others? Those who take up the Exodus text must wrestle with the question. Are we really just looking out for our interests or the interest of all people like us?

It is easy to distance ourselves from questioning systematic exploitation when individuals seem to have little influence over large systematic oppression. But the ethical mandate of the text invites the listening community to imagine how individuals might work together in ways that lead to liberation.

These texts call forth a merciful paradigm for life. But the world does not seem to be constructed in ways that reward a merciful ethic. We must choose whether we will live mercifully toward the other or toward our individual interest. Are we willing to incur the cost of the way of mercy?

GOSPEL IMPLICATIONS
God goes before and behind God's people to lead them into a new life and a future marked by God's gracious life-giving mercy. The old order of things, represented as Egypt in the first reading, is overcome by God's life. This is good news!

The way of mercy is for us. We have been set free. God in Christ and through the Holy Spirit has set us free. For some, this may mean allowing oneself to believe that this is indeed true. Because we have received God's mercy, we are free to forgive and receive others in mercy. God has placed us on the trajectory of life-giving liberation. We not only receive God's mercy as a gift, but with the help of the Spirit we extend it to others. We do not live for ourselves.

The preacher who aims to proclaim good news will allow these texts to name the bad news that is the way of no-mercy. The more concretely the preacher is able to name this bad news, the more powerfully the preacher will be able to declare the good news of God's way of mercy, forgiveness, and liberation. Even to speak of what we are required to do is to speak of what God enables us to do.

STEPHEN C. JOHNSON

JENNIFER JEANINE THWEATT-BATES

PROPER 20 [25]

THE LESSONS IN PRÉCIS

In ordinary time, most lessons move in different directions. Underlying all ordinary time, however, is the extraordinary promise of God.

> *Exodus 16:2-15.* The people complain of hunger in the desert. God assures the people with daily signs that the One who freed from slavery also helps them through the vulnerability of freedom.

> *Psalm 105:1-6, 37-45.* In thanksgiving, the psalmist invites us to remember the mighty deeds of God, who remembers the desert promise and brings the people "out with rejoicing" (v. 43).

> *Philippians 1:21-30.* The promise of the gospel means everything, whether the Apostle lives or dies. For the struggling Philippians, it means the privilege of believing in Christ, even in their suffering.

> *Matthew 20:1-16.* Some workers in the vineyard agree with the owner for a fair day's wage. Yet God gives all workers, regardless of how long they work, the promise of "whatever is right" (v. 4) at day's end.

THEME SENTENCE

God gives us promise in vulnerability. The promise assures us in difficulty, peril, and suffering. In Philippians and Matthew, this promise is linked to Christ's gospel and the kingdom of heaven. In all four texts, the promise underlines God's commitment to see us into fragile freedom in view of God's good purposes for us and for creation.

A KEY THEOLOGICAL QUESTION

What exactly is the promise God gives us, that God makes to us particularly in the crucifixion and resurrection of Jesus? What does it mean to follow the God who makes this sort of promise?

In a consumer society like ours, considerable confusion can arise about what exactly God has promised to us. Some would argue that God promises health and prosperity. Others might argue that God promises things will be fair and just. Some claim that God promises that those who are faithful will be rewarded for their work.

One perspective from which to approach this question is often called the "Theology of the Cross." From this perspective, the cross is not primarily about blood, substitution, or imitation. It is a way of looking at theological questions that asks whether our interpretations are consistent with the fact that the central event of the Christian faith involves the execution of a common criminal—a common criminal whom Christians claim is the Son of God.

From the texts given in the lectionary for today, we can see several ways in which a theology of the cross helps us understand what God's promise might and might not be.

In the opinion of the Israelites, God's promise of freedom meant that they could at least keep their connection to the fleshpots and bread that they had as slaves. God feeds the complainers in an odd sort of way—giving them something like bread, but not something that keeps without spoiling. God's promise does not extend the old patterns of slavery but opens new ways to understand our needs as we wander toward freedom. These new ways will sometimes leave us feeling abandoned ("You've brought us out into this desert to starve this whole assembly to death" [Exod 16:3]) and sometimes confuse us ("What is it?" [16:15]). They will never be the old fleshpots of health and prosperity. The God whose promise is our salvation is a crucified God for whom the walk to freedom involves entering into rather than avoiding the desert.

The Philippians were faithful followers. They had maintained their unity and held steadfast against false teaching. They might have expected their faithfulness to carry them beyond suffering. Not so, says Paul. In fact, God has graciously granted them not only faith but also the privilege of sharing in Christ's suffering and struggle. The promise is not about earning rewards or avoiding the reality of life. Just as Jesus was immersed in human reality to the point of suffering capital punishment, so followers of Jesus, recipients of the promise, are called by grace into the world to experience the world fully. As Dietrich Bonhoeffer said, "[I]t is only by living completely in this world that one learns to have faith" (Letter to E. Bethge, 21 July, 1944).

You would think that we could at least expect this promising God to be fair. Maybe not. In the parable of the workers, those who work an hour receive the same pay as those who have worked all day. This obviously contradicts our usual standards. This is the sort of fairness you might expect from a God who somehow thinks that it is a good idea to get crucified as the answer to human sin!

The promise is not inside the cocoon where all are safe and sound, where we can fill ourselves with bread and keep a tight grip on the fleshpots of Egypt. The promise is not that those who work harder and longer will get more pay. The promise is freedom to be people of promise out there where the world really lives and dies. The promise is the freedom to strike out into the wilderness with nothing more than a food supply that will spoil before tomorrow, hoping against hope that there will be more "What is it?" before we starve. The promise is that Jesus is so rich he has enough struggle and suffering to share. The promise is that God's grace transcends justice to include all, even the lazy.

A PASTORAL NEED

The promise is not something laminated or hung on a wall to be observed from a safe, antiseptic distance. It is rather something grasped, and especially held closely during times of suffering. Many people remember the soaring language of Martin Luther King's "I Have a Dream" speech. The visionary words from the prophetic preacher at the Lincoln Memorial have proven inspiring over the years. Yet few remember how King earlier in that same speech used the image of the promissory note. The promissory note was the idea that African-Americans would one day be free and equal, but not just yet. For King, the promise spoke of something powerful in a time of suffering and need. In the face of injustice over many years, it may have even inspired, yet it was also a painful reminder that the promissory note itself had not yet been cashed. Suffering may be the home of promises given, yet suffering is also a profound test of promises not yet kept. Preaching that takes the promise seriously, will name it bravely into the heart of pastoral need: whether in the personal sphere of death and loss of job or in the public realities of injustice and corporate exploitation. It will speak of the way it points us to God's future, but it will never stop calling something what it really is. This is, pastorally, also the heart of a theology of the cross. Preachers today will want to speak of promise in a similar way—as a goad to lament and plain speech, and as something that can be held while moving forward.

ETHICAL IMPLICATIONS

The vulnerable promise is especially important for living lives of faith. Toward the conclusion of the Lutheran Sunday liturgy, worship shifts from Word and Table to the act of "sending." Having received God's promise given in Word and Sacrament, we are now "sent" into the world. One of the songs sung at this point actually puts it this way: "Send us with your promises, O God . . ." It is as if holding to those divine promises, we become aware that they are not just for us in our need, but for the whole world that God still "so loves." I once heard the story of one church where, when Eucharist is celebrated, people in the congregation actually bring smaller loaves of bread to the altar/table at the time of the offering. With so much bread at the table, there are always ample loaves remaining at the end of the service, with which the congregation then makes sandwiches to give away when the service is done. The promise is like that: it doesn't fix everything, but it is enough . . . and still is a sign of God's steadfast love sent into the world even in the midst of suffering. At the same time, God's promises are also not sent solely into moments of suffering in signs of compassionate solidarity. The promises also aid us in being steadfast in our call to live lives of justice as Jesus' disciple community. For us, the song of promise rings in our ears even when our eyes witness persistent injustice in our world. In those moments, the promise of God's presence helps us trust more deeply as we resist injustice. That's probably why the promise in song sings as it does: "Deep in my heart, I do believe, that we shall overcome some day."

GOSPEL IMPLICATIONS

The implications of this vulnerable promise for the gospel begin with Christ's own cross, as described above. The cross is more than just a place for atonement theories or pieties about sacrifice and shame. The cross is the revelatory place where the vulnerable promise calls into question all that we think we know. Some great preachers call this the scandal of the cross. Yet because the cruciform One is risen, the vulnerable promise points beyond itself to eschatology—looking forward to God's intentions. It thus invites us to proclaim the promise in places of suffering, precisely because God in Christ is not yet done with creation. Preachers in their imagery and illustrations will need to portray this gospel temporally. Speaking the promise activates in us even now eschatological grace, it bears witness to God's work among us, even now. The Bible talks about this with gospel language that presses metaphorically to the edges of speech: Christ is the *arrabon*, the down payment, the first fruits. Moreover, we know this by how Christ meets us even now: the risen Lord still bears the wounds of his crucifixion. And when Christ comes again, it is by those wounds that all will recognize Christ.

DAVID SCHNASA JACOBSEN
ROBERT ALLEN KELLY

PROPER 21 [26]

THE LESSONS IN PRÉCIS

God comes in ordinary time to do extraordinary things. In something as common as water, God's promise evokes incalculable life.

> *Exodus 17:1-7.* God's people complain to God yet again because of their thirst in the wilderness. God pours forth water from a rock and sustains them, even in battle, through the promise given in Moses' staff.

> *Psalm 78:1-4, 12-16.* The psalmist reminds the people of God's ancient deeds. God brings water from the rock.

> *Philippians 2:1-13.* Paul wants the Philippians to demonstrate the power of the gospel among them. Christ poured himself out for humanity, therefore we should discern the work of God, who enables us "to want and to actually live out his good purposes" (v. 13).

> *Matthew 21:23-32.* Jesus argues with the chief priests and elders over the significance of John's baptism as they question his authority. For Jesus, baptism is a sign of the promise producing belief even among tax collectors and prostitutes.

THEME SENTENCE

God pours out God's own life into us. Exodus memories recall life-sustaining water attending God's promise through Moses' staff in the desert. In Philippians, Paul speaks of Christ "emptying himself" (2:7) evoking life in praise to God. In Matthew, Jesus invites opponents to see God's righteousness in baptismal promise producing living belief among people seemingly opposed to God's purposes.

A KEY THEOLOGICAL QUESTION
God pours out Godself. . . .

Whenever we think of God's self-emptying (*kenosis*, in Greek), our thoughts almost immediately turn to the themes of incarnation and Christology. Certainly the meaning of the self-emptying of Christ in Philippians 2 has long been the subject of debate. What we may overlook in our rush to Christology is that the crucifixion of Jesus might reveal to us that self-emptying is far more deeply embedded in the being of God that we might think. In order for there to be a real incarnation and a real crucifixion, the Trinitarian relationship itself must involve some form of self-emptying in the core of the divine essence.

The social metaphors for the Trinity that are widely used in political, liberation, and feminist theologies enable us to see the communal nature of the Triune God. God is not a lonely, rugged individualist, but a communion of persons in loving relationship. The triadic relationship is the divine essence. If this is true, then each divine person self-empties in order to be in relationship to the other two divine persons. The self-emptying of the Logos in the incarnation is simply an overflowing of the ongoing dance of self-emptying that is the Trinity. This self-emptying is not a losing or lessening of the divine nature, but *is* the divine nature.

In this way, we can go even beyond the conclusions Paul draws in Philippians 2: "Adopt the attitude that was in Christ Jesus . . ." (v. 5). We are not just talking about imitating the mind of Christ here. Rather, if we are created in the image of God, that image is the likeness of a God whose very essence is a community of self-emptying love, whose "substance" is the sort of love that gives of itself for the sake of the other. Here, we are well beyond simply seeing Jesus as an example of someone who is self-effacing. At the core of human nature is the image of the community of the Trinity.

. . . giving us life.

The self-emptying love of the Trinity is poured out "for us and for our salvation" in the incarnation. God enters into the world in order to give the world life. That life was first given in creation, the first of the "outer" acts of the Trinity's self-emptying. God accepted the challenge of relating to an other. The universe did not have to be, but God chose to create the world as an act of loving, inviting relationship, encouraging wholeness. When that invitation was snubbed, the Trinity's self-emptying community focused on one person at one place in one particular moment of time as the Logos became incarnate. God accepted the inevitable result of self-emptying: death, even death on the cross.

In the "death of God" on the cross, God has given life back to creation.

To speak of the "death of God" in the context of both Philippians 2 and Jesus' debate in Matthew 21 raises some questions about just who or what is Jesus in the context of the Trinitarian community. Is he the self-emptying servant of Philippians or the assertive debater of Matthew? What sort of authority does he exercise whose source he is unwilling to discuss? If the Messiah is crucified, how can one speak meaningfully of "authority?"

The "upside-down" nature of Jesus' place is obvious in Philippians 2: Even though he has a plausible claim to equality with God, he chooses not to exercise the claim and empties himself to the point of execution on the cross. That self-emptying is not so obvious in Matthew. There, Jesus subtly confronts his opponents by asking them a question they would rather not answer. He seems more like a wily trial lawyer than an example of humility.

The question of authority provides a perspective for seeing these two pictures in relation to each other. Jesus' questioners in Matthew want to know the source of his authority; they want to know exactly what sort of authority it is. Or do they? Their question makes sense only if they already think they know what source of authority Jesus is claiming. They assume his authority is pretty much like theirs—that it derives from position, from collaboration with the ultimate social authority of their time and place; that it is backed up by the normal sources of power. Thus the source of their authority is clear—it is ultimately Rome—and getting Jesus to name his source will by necessity prove that he is illegitimate and an enemy of Caesar.

The reason Jesus will not answer their question directly is that the question distorts Jesus' authority in the very asking. His authority is a complete paradox. It does not involve the exercise of power, but the renunciation of power. The source of Jesus' power is not a claim to be god-like, but the very self-emptying of even a plausible claim to equality with God—precisely Caesar's claim. Jesus is not a rival of Caesar; he is a whole new paradigm for understanding authority.

This takes us back to our understanding of the Trinity. The doctrine of the Trinity is not about an Almighty Patriarch, like Caesar, who rules over all by coercion. The Trinity is a community of self-emptying love whose authority is in dying to give life. We who are created in the image of the Trinity and who are baptized into the church created in the image of the Trinity are swept into this upside-down authority that infuses the upside-down Reign of God.

A PASTORAL NEED

In the midst of crisis it becomes hard to see what matters and what really sustains us through parched times: whether personal grief at death or the grinding difficulty of an economy that can't produce enough jobs to thin the ranks of the unemployed. In such times, we feel isolated in our pain and cry out for someone strong enough to put the pieces back together. Precisely in crisis, we are tempted to look for someone authoritative enough to solve the problem and in ways that measure up to our own expectations of life until now. Our feelings help us name what we want: to be lifted out of crisis and to be returned to the way things were or to be set on a new path. Whether the reigning authority is Egyptian or Roman, it conditions our feelings in the midst of crisis. Yet this is not how God in Christ deals with us. The mystery of God's "pouring out" for us in Jesus' crucifixion is an upside down authority, but only such authority as to bring every human pretension or assumption down to earth. Yet, in the midst of such cruciform impossibility, we nonetheless discover the sustaining presence of God—like water giving us life in the desert. A young artist has pictured it well: two hands are struggling with chains as they reach up toward water flowing from a spigot. The picture paints our need.

ETHICAL IMPLICATIONS

The sustaining presence of God in the midst of our parched difficulties of crisis, grief, and suffering is a powerful ethical force. It helps us to remember God's "pouring out" for us so that we in turn can be available to meet the needs of our neighbors. The difficulty, of course, is when our desire to be ethically engaged for our neighbors negates them in some way. In such moments, our desire to "help" others leaves others unable to discern God's sustaining presence for themselves in their own desert moments of gracious resilience in pain and suffering. Again, God's "pouring out" is our ethical guide. Just as the Trinity of God's communion is a constant pouring out in love, so also the mode with

which we ethically engage others in their needs does not negate them
or anyone, but empowers others precisely in their need and in their
moments of crisis. God's pouring out sustains for just this reason—it
does not negate or overcome the suffering of another, but rather uncovers
a presence deep within that graces humanity. A strange resilience helps us
recognize the grace of God even while we see the true humanity of each
other. Judging by Jesus' connection with the unlikely persons of sinners
and tax collectors, this may just be what God's kingdom looks like. It's
a little like a shared banquet. When the party is done well, we are not
constantly reminded of who is the guest and who is the host. In times of
such radical pouring out, we forget ourselves for the sake of each other—
and share even now in a foretaste of the kingdom.

Gospel Implications

The gospel is good news of God's promise. In this case, the good news
focuses on God's action of "pouring out" Godself for us—in the life of
the Trinity in which we are invited to participate, in the Incarnation, in
Jesus on the cross, and in the gift of the Holy Spirit. We may experience
this particularly in the midst of the desert wanderings and struggles
over authority. Good news, after all, is not God's way of pretending that
suffering does not exist; it is rather God's way of offering promise and
hope in the midst of suffering. In that sense, the good news of God's
"pouring out" meets us at our greatest depth: our thirst and our inability
to slake it ourselves.

When you travel through the desert in the Southwestern United
States, there's not much to break up the landscape. As you travel along,
you see miles and miles of just miles and miles. And yet it is precisely in
that place where the cross seems to stand out: sometimes as a memorial
marker, other times as a vestige of an old mission site. When you see such
a cross, though, it stands out not in denial of the loss and the struggle for
life, but precisely in the midst of it. It sets the desert in relief, even as it
provides its own cruciform relief. There is no place so deserted, so lifeless,
so godforsaken, that God is not already there, poured out in love.

David Schnasa Jacobsen
Robert Allen Kelly

PROPER 22 [27]

THE LESSONS IN PRÉCIS

In ordinary time, we explore the extraordinary relationship of law and gospel, judgment and grace.

> *Exodus 20:1-4, 7-9, 12-20.* In this abbreviated version of the Ten Commandments, we learn the basics of God's Law. Yet even the Law is framed by the liberating grace of the God "who brought you out of Egypt" (v. 2).

> *Psalm 19.* Here, the psalmist hymns the same Sinai God whose glory is disclosed both in creation and law.

> *Philippians 3:4b-14.* The Apostle Paul sees the righteousness of God by faith as a surpassing gift. Though Paul values his life "under the Law" (v. 6), through faith he presses on toward "the prize of God's upward call in Christ Jesus" (v. 14).

> *Matthew 21:33-46.* In this judgment parable, Jesus discloses that God's kingdom will be given to those who see the son as the rightful heir, not as a stone to be rejected—as do the official interpreters of the law.

THEME SENTENCE

God's grace helps us receive law as gift. Exodus and Psalm 19 describe the law in relation to God's redemptive and creative grace. Paul celebrates divine grace that doesn't negate law, yet offers "superior value" (Phil 3:8). In Matthew, some teachers' self-serving interpretation of law renders them unable to see Jesus, "the heir," as the kingdom's gracious cornerstone.

A KEY THEOLOGICAL QUESTION

One theological question raised by these lessons is what Martin Luther referred to as "the proper distinction of Law and Gospel." If we are to understand the law as a gift of God's grace, we must tread carefully so that we do not turn the law into a scheme for self-achieved righteousness.

Properly distinguishing between law and gospel is the crucial hermeneutical skill, necessary in interpreting Scripture, preaching, and theologizing. The one who can exercise this skill artfully and accurately is the preacher and theologian par excellence. That person can preach and teach the word of God so that the gospel is clearly spoken. John Wesley (probably drawing on Luther) called the preaching of both judgment and grace in every sermon, "the scriptural way, the Methodist way, the true way." Luther understands the law as God's command, which reveals God's will and both reveals and limits human sinfulness. The "first use of the Law," the political use (*usus politicus*), is the divine energy behind human institutions that serves to limit sin by punishing those who do evil and rewarding those who do good. The "second use of the Law," the theological use (*usus theologicus*), reveals the extent of human sin and demonstrates conclusively that we cannot save ourselves by our own efforts. In these uses the law is indeed one of God's gifts and is necessary for human flourishing. The command is also a conditional promise: If you do what the law requires, you will be rewarded; but if you fail to do what the law requires or do what the law forbids, you will be punished. Our utter inability to fulfill the conditions reveals our need for the gospel.

The gospel is God's unconditional promise, made in the death and resurrection of Jesus: Because of what God has done in Christ, the ultimate destiny of creation and the human community is good. Whereas the law is about us and our ability or inability (if you . . .), the gospel is about God and what God has done and promises to do (because God . . .). Hearing the gospel creates the relationship of faith. This relationship of promise is central to understanding justification. Justification is by grace—it is founded in and created by the unconditional promise. Justification is by faith—it is brought to us through a relationship in which Christ is present by Word and Sacrament in the community and in the person.

The point of properly distinguishing law and gospel is so that the promise of the gospel can be heard in all of its power. By distinguishing them, preaching the gospel does not slide into legalism (harsh law) or moralism (nice law). This points us ahead to God's promised future.

At the same time, gospel does not deteriorate into something that we humans can do to save ourselves.

The objective is to hear the law when the law needs to be heard and to hear the gospel when the gospel needs to be heard. Distinguishing them is not to differentiate one testament from the other, or even one passage from another. Properly distinguishing law and gospel in reading Scripture is a dynamic and existential process that involves a sense of the connection between what the text is saying and the freeing promise that the Holy Spirit wants the reader to hear. The biblical interpreter must be skilled at discerning the meaning of the text, using all of the scholarly tools available, and must also be skilled at discerning the needs of the hearing community.

Preaching and theologizing use the same set of law and gospel hermeneutical skills. The preacher speaks the biblical message so that the self-righteous hear the word of God confronting their illusions about themselves and the troubled hear the word of God bringing them the comfort of God's promise. Interestingly, in Luther's opinion, self-righteousness and despair spring from the same roots: failure properly to distinguish law and gospel, which causes people to look to their own achievements (whether achievements of works or of belief) as the source of their salvation. In a sermon that fails to distinguish law and gospel, the primary subject is me and us and what I and/or we do. In a sermon that properly distinguishes law and gospel, the subject is always God and what God has done, is doing, and will do in Christ.

It is also crucial for properly distinguishing law and gospel to remember that both come to us as a word from outside of ourselves. The word of command puts objective limits on us. The word of promise is concrete, external, and connected with oral proclamation and physical sacrament ("I baptize you in the name of the Father and the Son and the Holy Spirit"). Otherwise what we hear becomes a confused mixture of law and gospel ("If you believe, then you will be saved"), which drives us to either self-righteousness or despair.

A PASTORAL NEED

The pastoral need on this Sunday might be to help the congregation understand the if/then nature of our living. Many people suffer from a sense that they must do it all, that their salvation depends upon what they can accomplish. Yet this burden is contrary to the gospel.

A lot of forces in the world tell us who we are: they discern in us a lack, a deficiency, an insufficiency that calls for action. Given the fact that these forces often have a stake in the game (marketers, salespersons, etc.), the action they call for usually works to their benefit. At the same time, the damage is done. We get accustomed to living our lives by the if/then view of the law. If we do X, then Y will happen; if we get our life together, then God will love, save, or be with us.

I suppose it goes back to "Grandma's Rule." In the parenting literature, Grandma's Rule is set out as a conditional clause: If you do X, Grandma will give you a cookie (or some other substitutable item from Grandma's amply stocked, homemade pantry). The message is one of control and obligation. Because it's Grandma, it sounds nice. And yet it is a way of getting us to comply out of a sense of lack or deficiency.

This view of our humanity runs deep. It is the narrative of our commercials and haunts the advertising jingles we hum to ourselves as we sit in the car. The danger is that it deforms our humanity and our relationships with others—especially with God. In our texts, this deforming view of law forgets God's goodness and, worst of all, God's unconditional promise.

ETHICAL IMPLICATIONS

The ethical implications of living within the gospel promise are important for our humanity. The vision of the gospel is that God's promises ("Because God . . . ," not, "If you . . .") free us for one another. The law is a gift, to be sure. And yet it is the gospel that frees us to engage for the other.

In the movie "The First Grader," an elderly Kenyan man of more than eighty years of age comes to school to learn to read and write. The post-colonial government has announced that there is now "education for all"—it is no longer about privilege or wealth. The elderly man, Meruge, had himself been a fighter for Kenyan independence years ago when it was still under British colonial influence. When he heard the announcement about free education, he walked all the way from his humble home to the overcrowded school where he was first turned away as too old. Yet through it all, he persevered. He bought books and pencils as the other students had, and was turned away again. He even bought a school uniform so outwardly he dressed like the children, and that was not good enough. While most of the authorities viewed the announcement from the government as a matter of law (education is for little children only), Meruge heard it for what it was—a promise— and began living through it already. In the process, he not only learned to read and write in this school, together with all its children, but also helped the children to claim their own learning and dignity by the way he lived out that promise.

GOSPEL IMPLICATIONS

Our theme invites us to read law in terms of the gospel, not gospel in terms of law. This is what helps us to discern God's promise and frees up humanity in the presence of God.

The American Civil War was in many respects framed as an argument over law. Both sides appealed to the constitution for legitimacy concerning states' rights. For many bloody months and years, the war proceeded from these competing principles of constitutional law—as if all that mattered were certain overriding laws that governed the case and, in the end, existed to justify one bloody battle after another. What changed? One key turning point was Lincoln's speech after the Battle of Gettysburg. In this speech, Lincoln acknowledged the tragedy and loss, but reframed them. In the introduction, Lincoln elevated the moment not by appeal to law, but by reading the constitution through a prior founding document, the Declaration of Independence: "that all men are created equal." In a moment the struggle is lifted beyond constitutional law to the realm of a promise still being fulfilled in the midst of struggle.

The gospel is like that. As promise it helps us see the law for the good that it is—even while it is the promise that continues to set us free for one another.

Notes

John Wesley, "Open Letter," in Albert C. Outler, *John Wesley*, 1964, 237.

DAVID SCHNASA JACOBSEN

ROBERT ALLEN KELLY

PROPER 23 [28]

THE LESSONS IN PRÉCIS

Exodus 32:1-14. God's people make an idol from their own gold. Moses persuades God to remember the ancestral promise to forestall God's wrath.

Psalm 106:1-6, 19-23. Though the psalmist recalls how God's people have been sinning from the get-go, the psalmist trusts God, who shows favor and delivers God's people, even from their idolatry.

Philippians 4:1-9. Toward the end of his letter, Paul makes an appeal to the church to move beyond disagreement. Paul reminds the Philippians to stand firm in the Lord and rejoice always. God's peace will be with them.

Matthew 22:1-14. Jesus' parable compares the kingdom of heaven to a wedding banquet. Although the joyous invitation is given widely, some refuse while others fail to let it shape their lives outwardly—to their own judgment.

THEME SENTENCE

God's love is for the unworthy. Exodus and Psalm 106 recall Israel's idolatry in light of God's wrath *and* God's strange, "faithful love" (106:1). Paul assures the Philippians of God's peace, even as some struggle with disagreements. Matthew's Gospel describes a parabolic God whose banquet invitation is rejected and responds not just in wrath but also by inviting far and wide.

A KEY THEOLOGICAL QUESTION

God's wrath is not something we like to think much about, and rightly so. We often have the impression that sometimes our ancestors in the faith spent too much time meditating on and fearing the wrath of God. We emphasize, and again rightly so, God's grace and avoid God's anger. What are we saying theologically?

One way to understand the wrath of God is that suggested by Martin Luther's distinction of the hidden God and the revealed God. The hidden God becomes an item of speculation when we are alienated from God. We think about the God of absolute majesty and sovereignty, the hidden God. This hidden God is the source of frightening possibilities. We speculate about God as an almighty, unchanging, unfeeling ruler of all, and we fear that God might be pure, unbending wrath. We become locked in mortal combat with this God, never sure whether we fight against God or the devil. Yet such a God is not what is revealed in the Word of the gospel. In Jesus what is revealed is the God of faithful promise who is gracious, merciful, and slow to anger. This God enters into dialogue with and justifies sinning humans. This revealed promise is the God who is preached, not the hidden monster of our speculations.

Japanese theologian Kazoh Kitamori (1965) suggests that God is wrathful over sin yet loves the object of God's wrath. As a result, since loving the object of one's wrath always involves suffering, both the wrath and the love are taken up in the pain of God. The paradigmatic place where God's pain is "seen" is in our execution of Jesus for the audacity of his love for the unloveable. No doubt our attempt to murder Jesus excites God's wrath, yet the murder goes ahead. Because God loves us, God's wrath is expressed in, with, and under the pain of God on the cross.

The cross shows us the true complexity of talking about the wrath of God. In the crucifixion of Jesus, God becomes a victim of what may be called the wrath of God. Part of the problem is that we use the phrase "wrath of God" to give a religious patina to our own wrath channeled against anyone who points out our golden calves for what they really are. At this level, Jesus is a victim of human wrath disguised as the wrath of God. Yet there is also a deeper level in which God is truly angry at our idolatry and yet loves us and so allows us to succeed in turning the prophet into a scapegoat. Our very success in murdering God hides from our eyes what is really happening. The fulfillment and the future of God's saving promise are hidden in the crucifixion of Jesus.

We are back again to Luther's hidden God, only this time the hidden God is not the God of human speculation, as opposed to the God revealed in the gospel. Now the hidden God is the real God whom we have murdered. The crucifixion both reveals and hides the God of unconditional promise. Only the ears of faith enlightened by the Word of gospel can hear the message of grace even as our eyes perceive the opposite of grace. Just when we think we have replaced God with something better, the gospel proclaims that God is still God and the promise still stands.

When we are open to the possibility of the pain of God, we can be less reticent about the possibility of God getting angry. When as pastors we encounter someone who has come to believe that they are living under the shadow of God's frown, it might be more helpful to acknowledge that, rather than to try to prove to the person that there is no need for them to feel that way. When someone has lived through hell, it is useless to try to convince that person that hell doesn't exist.

There is also a certain existential truth in the recognition that God is a bit—more than a bit!—dangerous. Touching the chest containing the covenant or getting too close to the mountain could be deadly. Attempting to replace God could be more deadly still. As we face the consequences of our misuse of the environment and our profligate exhaust of CO_2, we need some theological understanding of God's reaction to our activities. It is not that God gets mad at us and sends extreme weather to punish us, but that God is willing for us to get our way and allows us to live with the consequences of getting our way. God lives, I think, with hope that we will see that our attempts at being our own creators are deadly and may kill us, but God may not bail us out before the consequences really kick in. When we create gods in our own image, there is a cost beyond the gold we melt down.

In the end, the point of recognizing the cost of idolatry is not to fear the wrath of God but to understand that God's wrath and God's love come together in God's pain. Our addiction to fossil fuels will create suffering in the world, but that suffering gives God no pleasure. The same God whom we tried to murder on the cross feels deep pain when we create suffering for creation. Even in pain, God is faithful. God will not rapture us out of creation because the promise is made to all creation: In Christ your ultimate destiny is good.

A Pastoral Need

The idea that God's love is for the unworthy is more than just an idea—it is deeply about life lived in the midst of estrangement and wrath. There is a futility of human life through which God's steadfast love in all its ambiguity breaks through in bits and pieces, though we struggle to see it.

The movie *Temple Grandin* is about a remarkable woman who grows up with autism to discover her giftedness in the midst of life's struggles. One of the ongoing difficulties Temple faces is her relationship to her own mother. In the 1950s world of Temple's youth, autism is viewed as the result of a mother's aloofness during a crucial time of the child's development. So when Temple's mother hears the diagnosis for her daughter, she can't see the merit of it. The movie itself bears witness to the mother's steadfastness to stay with and advocate for her daughter, even to push her so that she engages the outside world. After Temple has met with some academic success, against all odds, years later she attends a party where she is overwhelmed by the stimulation of all the persons present, and the old feelings rush back in. She finds herself unable to connect with others and believes they are looking at her as if she were a freak—along with all the pain that brings. Her mother comforts her nonetheless, and Temple recognizes what she's doing. Her mother points out that she, too, looks at Temple and is proud of what she's become. In a moment of great insight, Temple says to her mother that she'll never learn how to do that.

What God does in meeting us in such ambiguity and struggle is to see us for what we are in God's eyes. It is also just what we need.

Ethical Implications

The ethical implications of this theme sentence are most sobering for the community of faith. If God loves the unworthy, and this is revealed in and despite God's wrath, then the church finds itself at odds with the surrounding culture.

Our culture likes to distinguish, for example, between the "deserving" and the "undeserving" poor. The deserving poor are those who are trying hard. They are poor, but do not give up on the official narrative of goodness: they keep their noses clean, they scrimp and sacrifice, they work long hours at low wage jobs and never complain. They are, in other words, people whose existence does not challenge the story we like to tell of wealth and opportunity. The undeserving poor, by contrast, are the poor of our worst nightmares. Their existence seems to challenge our worldviews: that the arrangements of our lives are intrinsically right and fair. Their messy lives lead us to believe that harshness toward them is some kind of odd civic virtue.

How different this is from Jesus' view of God's love for the unworthy! Jesus does not love just the misunderstood sinner, the misdiagnosed leper, or the tax collector with the heart of gold, he also loves the unworthy, *the undeserving*. In the midst of their suffering, which others have interpreted as wrath (disease, exclusion, etc.), Jesus loves anyway.

There's a church in Kitchener, Ontario with a Wednesday night supper for all. The people who show up range widely: the homeless, sure, but also people who are trying to stretch their food budgets beyond food pantry hampers, and even some of the underemployed. This is the face of divine love—in the midst of our attempts at calculating worth and distributing wrath.

GOSPEL IMPLICATIONS

The statement that God's love is for the unworthy is a strong gospel statement for preaching. It indicates, in the midst of difficulty and wrath, what God's intention is. In many ways the gospel question is this: Where do we align ourselves? Are we among the worthy or the unworthy?

In baptism we discover the truth of both sides of the statement. To be baptized is to acknowledge that we share in our common humanity in unworthiness. In the waters of baptism, the gradations and distinctions with which we attempt to decorate our lives are graciously washed away. At the font, we confess ourselves for what we are: sinners all. Yet, at the font, we also hear the word of promise and the pure, gracious Word of God. At the font, God's love and our unworthiness meet in a strangely life-giving flood of tears and redemption, of death and new birth.

God doesn't love sinners because deep down God thinks they can be rehabilitated to be as good as the socially upstanding. God loves sinners, the unworthy, because that's all God has.

Notes

Kazoh Kitamori, *Theology of the Pain of God*, 1965.

DAVID SCHNASA JACOBSEN

ROBERT ALLEN KELLY

Proper 24 [29]

The Lessons in Précis

Although it is ordinary time, it is an extraordinary God who meets us even now. We who are God's people journey forward with a God who comes with us in strange holiness.

> *Exodus 33:12-23.* Moses wants the Lord to assure him and the people of God's presence in their journey. God agrees, yet God's glorious presence cannot be managed or understood on purely human terms.

> *Psalm 99.* This hymn celebrates God's kingship, and yet acknowledges God's holiness.

> *1 Thessalonians 1:1-10.* Paul gives thanks for the faith of the Thessalonians to whom the gospel came not only in word but also in power and Spirit. They have turned from idols to worship "the living and true God" (v. 9).

> *Matthew 22:15-22.* A coalition seeks to trap Jesus with a question about paying taxes in the temple. Using their own coin, imprinted with Caesar's image/head, Jesus invites them to give everything that likewise bears God's image.

Theme Sentence

God accompanies us in holiness. Exodus assures Israel of God's presence, but maintains Sinai's mystery. The psalm celebrates God as Zion's *holy* king. The Word comes to Thessalonians as they turn from idols to the living God. In Matthew, Jesus' dispute about taxes hinges ultimately on giving that which bears the image/head *(eikon,* 22:20): whether Caesar's or God's.

A KEY THEOLOGICAL QUESTION

The theological question in these texts and this theme revolves around the identity and nature of God. Who is God? What exactly do we mean by "holiness"?

As our guide for these questions, a simple place to start is Luther's explanation of the first commandment from the Small Catechism:

> You are to have no other gods.
> What is this?
>
> Answer:
> We are to fear, love and trust God above all things.
> (Kolb & Wingert, 2000, 351).

The question of God's identity arises in the Gospel text. The coalition of Pharisees and Herodians asks Jesus whether "the Law allow[s] people to pay taxes" (Matt 22:17), which is obviously a trick question, meant to corner him. Jesus, perhaps the ultimate trickster, turns the trick back by asking what they have in their pockets. This is where the identity of God comes in. In the language of the catechism, our god is that which we fear, love, and trust above all things. Paul Tillich said that our god is our "ultimate concern." Thus, what we have in our pockets often tells more about where our ultimate allegiance lies that where we go to church on Sundays, for what we have in our pockets is a clue as to our ultimate commitment.

Jesus' opponents are in a quandary, because they have Caesar's money in their pockets. This is problematic because it bears an image of him and he claims to be a deity. They have become enmeshed in Caesar's rule and have given enough of themselves over to Caesar that they cannot say for certain whom they fear and trust the most. Jesus in effect tells them to pay their god what they owe him.

So just who is God anyway? If our god is that which receives our ultimate fear, love, and trust, then what is it that we fear, love, and trust the most? Atheism and attacks on religion sell books and get in the news, but academic atheism is not the church's greatest problem. Our greatest problem is that we are not sure whom we fear, love, and trust the most. The real question is not whether God exists, but which god we worship.

This is the question of the identity of God. Do we fear, love, and trust the God who is revealed in the crucifixion and resurrection of Jesus, or is our allegiance to some other god whom we have created in our own image to serve our own purposes? Do we hear the Word of God in the execution of a criminal convicted of blasphemy and sedition? Do we pray for God's will to be done, or do we pray to get what we want? Do we teach people of a God who died for all while we were all yet sinners, or do we honor a god who blesses people like us? The answers to these questions give us a clue about where our allegiance lies.

If we talk about the God who is hidden and revealed in the crucifixion of Jesus, then we need to recognize that what we think of as "holiness" may not be the holiness of God at all. The "crucified God" is clearly not holy in the ways most gods are holy. In common parlance, "holiness" usually refers to "the sacred" in one way or another. Certain places, certain ways of behaving, and certain activities are holy and sacred, set apart from the ordinary and secular. If the most sacred place of all, though, is the site of executions, then our usual definitions lose all meaning.

Even in conceding to Moses' request to see, God expresses holiness in a very odd way. God says to Moses, "Well, I can't let you see my face, but, I tell you what, I'll let you have a glimpse of my backside" (Exod 33:23). What sort of God expresses holiness by showing God's backside to God's servants? If what we see of the holy God is "the hind parts of God," as Luther put it, then our definitions of holiness need to be rethought.

This brings us back to the money in our pockets. This is the symbol of what we think is holy—and if you doubt that just listen to how people talk about "the market." We believe that the market can "decide," can "determine," can "discipline." Are these not the functions of a god? In our culture and societies, we fear, love, and trust the market above all things. The holiness of the market is expressed physically in the way we treat money as the sacred symbol of the market. We are the Pharisees and Herodians, caught with our idols in our pants' pockets.

In this sense, holiness becomes a mystification that prevents us from seeing what is really going on. It conceals the real relationships that determine who gets to carry money in their pockets and who does not. This mystification cannot be the holiness of God, for the holiness of God cuts through the clouds of obfuscation to reveal the truth of the matter. The holiness of the crucified God is the two-edged sword that cuts to the bone in order to kill and to heal. The amazing truth is that the money in our pockets and the market it symbolizes are idols that orient our allegiance away from the real God and focus our commitment on false gods.

A PASTORAL NEED

Most of us associate God with one who caters to *our* personal needs: a new job, a suitable life partner, perhaps a parking space just when we need one. Of course, we recognize the fallacy of such popular views of a personal God. God cannot be a mere extension of our wishes and still be God.

Yet beyond these desires, we all have a deeper need to know that God loves us and is attentive to our difficulties. We actually need a holy God. God's holiness is far beyond merely keeping God "in our pocket." Just think about persons who occupy our thoughts. We all reflect, of course, on ourselves, yet we sometimes don't even understand our *own* motives. Our sense of personhood runs deep when we recognize depths we've barely begun to fathom. Now turn and think about others in our lives. Again, we spend the better part of a lifetime with family, friends, or a spouse. But then they say or do something, and we are stunned that the person we thought we knew was beyond our grasp. "I didn't know that about you," we say—flummoxed that someone we thought we knew so well could disclose something new.

How much more is this true of God, who meets us as person and yet is holy. God cannot and will not be reduced to an extension of our desires or fears. God is God. And yet that is the substance of the mystery as well, a mystery *for us*. For God cannot truly meet us in a personal way apart from God's holiness, God's *otherness* in relation to us right now.

ETHICAL IMPLICATIONS

An understanding of the otherness of God, the Holy One, also helps us to guard and protect the otherness of persons. If God is such a holy Mystery, how can we not embrace the otherness and irreducibility of other persons we meet in our pluralistic world?

In a community in Montana in the 1990s, some hate-filled thugs threw a cinder block through the window of a Jewish boy who portrayed a picture of a menorah at his home during Hanukkah. As rare as Jewish communities were in this part of the West, some had singled out even this small display as a threat. They were *different*. What might people of good will do in response to such a threat? They could have called for greater police protection—a good thing to do. They could have also sponsored educational events designed to foster greater tolerance—also helpful. What happened in this community was unique, though, in that it embraced the difference. In order to send the message to the thugs that no person's difference should allow them to be singled out for threats, many local churches and Christian persons in the area began displaying the Jewish symbol of the menorah in their windows, on their signs, etc. In embracing their difference the message was clear: differences are neither to be threatened nor reduced.

Is this not also the God we meet in holiness on the cross of Christ? This God does not divide and conquer, but meets us all, different as we are, with the breathtaking solidarity of divine compassion. And this wondrous love is sufficient; it is enough to empower us to do the same.

GOSPEL IMPLICATIONS

The way such a view of God's holiness might be preached as gospel is a bit challenging. There are, underneath these notions of holiness, prophetic elements that are intrinsically challenging. God's holiness *sounds* more like law than gospel, whether at Sinai, in Thessalonica, or in the temple courtyard during a debate about taxes. Yet the gospel here is that the God of otherness, whose difference is irreducible to our needs and wants, is nonetheless for us. The theme here, therefore, is one of startling gospel solidarity in the face of difference: God comes *with us* in holiness.

John Wesley made part of an early reputation as an evangelist in eighteenth century England by insisting on *field preaching*. Part of what made Wesley's activity unique is that he would go out to the coal mines and preach in his clerical garments. The activity was shocking both to his hearers and to the church officials who rejected his mode of evangelical outreach. And yet in all its strangeness, his mission bore fruit. In an age when the poor and workers were being ignored in many ways, people heard the good news from this man who, in his clerics, was where he ought not be: among struggling people with the good news of the gospel.

Notes

Robert Kolb and Timothy J. Wingert, eds., *The Book of Concord*, 2000.
Paul Tillich, Systematic Theology, 1:12, 1967.

DAVID SCHNASA JACOBSEN
ROBERT ALLEN KELLY

PROPER 25 [30]

THE LESSONS IN PRÉCIS

God uses ordinary people in these ordinary times. The daily mystery of our life together is how God meets us there.

> *Deuteronomy 34:1-12.* God allows Moses to see the promised land, yet Moses will not cross over. Moses dies with great honor; yet to this day no one knows where he is buried.

> *Psalm 90:1-6, 13-17.* Ascribed to Moses, this corporate lament describes God as eternal amidst human frailty. It asks God to show compassion to God's fragile servants.

> *1 Thessalonians 2:1-8.* Paul reminds the Thessalonians how he and others came among them with God's gospel: not with greed or trickery, but sharing themselves as a gentle nurse.

> *Matthew 22:34-46.* Jesus is tested with a question about the greatest commandment, but he turns the table with a question about the Christ: how can the one whom David calls Lord also be his son? How can the lowly descendent be the greater?

THEME SENTENCE

God uses ordinary life for God's purposes. Moses, the great leader, is fallen before Deuteronomy's end—a celebrated life with an unmarked grave. Moses as psalmist laments human limitations and implores God's compassion. Paul recalls how the gospel shaped his dealings with Thessalonians in ordinary gentleness. Matthew's Jesus confutes opponents with a question that paradoxically gives greater status to David's *descendant*.

A KEY THEOLOGICAL QUESTION

Many people believe that Christian faith is about the supernatural, the extraordinary. Nothing could be further from the truth. The gospel affirms the ordinary.

To understand the gospel's affirmation of the ordinary, to use the phrase of Canadian philosopher Charles Taylor (1989), we need to begin with the first article of the Apostles' Creed: "I believe in God the Father almighty, creator of heaven and earth." In Luther's Small Catechism he gives the meaning: "I believe that God has created me together with all that exists. God has given me and still preserves my body and soul . . . . In addition God daily and abundantly provides . . . all the necessities and nourishment for this body and life. God protects me against all danger and shields and preserves me from all evil. All this is done out of pure, fatherly, and divine goodness and mercy, without any merit or worthiness of mine at all!" (Kolb & Wingert, 2000, 354-355).

The last sentence here orients us to the connection between the ordinary and Christian faith. Creation is an act of divine mercy. Just like justification, creation is not based on our merit. Just like the sacrament, the efficacy of creation does not depend on our worthiness. Creation is by grace alone, and faith alone understands creation as a gift of God's grace. God's grace is revealed in the daily, ordinary necessities of life, both as we receive those gifts and as we act as conduits of those gifts for our community.

The unconditional grace of God shows itself in the initial "creation out of nothing" and in the ongoing, gracious work of preservation. God remains involved in creation and continues to sustain the life of the world both by grace and through structures and institutions of worldly life. Day in and day out as we participate in the natural world and the political world, we are beneficiaries and agents of God's preserving work.

The importance of the ordinary is also revealed in the incarnation of God in Christ. The infinite God comes among us in, with, and under an ordinary, finite human being. This human being, Jesus of Nazareth, uses ordinary materials and objects to reveal God to us. He is baptized in water. He heals the blind with mud and spit. He gives his body and blood in bread and wine. He tells stories about everyday people using ordinary words. He dies the death of an ordinary criminal. Even after his extraordinary resurrection, he sits with his disciples for an ordinary meal of fish.

What this means is that creation is capable of communicating God to us, even though creation is finite and God is infinite. We do not often hear what creation is saying (witness our destruction of the natural environment), but the problem is not creation; the problem is our sin. We become "curved in on ourselves" (in Luther's words) and fail to hear the Word that God is speaking through nature.

Given creation by grace, preservation by grace, and the Incarnation, we Christians cannot legitimately divide the spiritual and the carnal, the body and the soul, the world and the church. Conversion to Christ and to the gospel cannot be conversion away from the world. To be a disciple is to be turned toward the world. The secular is the sacred.

We see this played out in the Gospel lesson from Matthew. When asked what the greatest of the commandments is, Jesus gives a simple and straightforward answer: Love God, and love your neighbor. In this answer Jesus directs us to the community of which we are a part as the locus for our love of God. We love God as we love our neighbor in the whole variety of everyday, ordinary acts by which we work for the health and welfare of our communities. In this sense discipleship is not about extraordinary heroics but about day-to-day, ordinary faithfulness in service. For the Apostle Paul in the second lesson, even preaching the gospel is a rather ordinary activity, like a nurse caring for patients. Being a saint means doing the ordinary thing that needs to be done.

A PASTORAL NEED

It is far too easy to think that Christianity—the life of faith—is really about the extraordinary. When we get too attached to this idea, though, the ordinary seems to pale by comparison. We look at our everyday lives—punching the time clock, taking care of the kids, stopping to speak to someone on the street—and end up treating that which we do most often, and indeed most intentionally, as less than meaningful. We end up with a Christian faith that dreams of far off lands or unlikely situations, and assume that there faith can thrive—just not here, and now, in the ordinary.

We end up with a difficult disconnect between God and our lives. The loss of meaning is more than just a restless feeling, or a kind of listlessness about life. It leaves us with a void in the everyday—even though it need not.

God operates on a different calculation. God doesn't despise the ordinary, but embraces it. Just as with creation and justification, God works beneath our normal range of vision. In times when we feel like our lives don't add up to much, God begs to differ. God's grace is there, in the ordinary. Faith helps us begin to see it.

ETHICAL IMPLICATIONS

God's affirmation of the ordinary has huge implications for the living out of the Christian life. There may be other religions that require practitioners to leave behind ordinary life—to seek higher states, extraordinary ways of life, and elevated views of earthly matters. Christian faith is different. It calls us into ordinary life with the expectation that God is already at work there. This realization calls us more deeply into the world that God still so loves.

In the film "Of Gods and Men," a group of French monks find themselves in a changing world in North Africa—amidst the Algerian civil war of the 1990s. Jihadists have threatened the local community and its ordinary life. The monks are even asked more than once to leave. They refuse. They remain in the community, engaging in simple acts of solidarity with the Muslim people: visiting with families, providing some medical service. One might expect monks to flee such a violent world for a better one. We may often think of the monastic life that way. Instead, these monks enter that world more deeply, refusing to stop embracing the ordinary lives of the people.

Chances are, our vocation as Christians will be less heroic. However, there are profound ways we too can embrace the ordinary as a good thing, the locus of God's concern and love. We may not have the mettle to face down violence in some extreme form, but we do have a vocation to live out—a vocation tied to God's good creation and our lives in it.

GOSPEL IMPLICATIONS

Without the gospel, our embrace of the ordinary world would eventually overwhelm us. We may be called to embrace the ordinary, but we, too, are ordinary. We who are called in the gospel are fragile human beings.

The good news in the end, then, is God's own embrace of the ordinary—or, as we have put it, God's use of ordinary life for God's purposes. It is God's embrace of the ordinary that represents good news for us.

We see this most clearly in the sacraments. In baptism, we see and sense the ordinary: everyday people like us, gathered around a font filled with one of the earth's most common and basic elements—water. And there we see God's promise in the gospel is joined with the ordinary, and we celebrate the gospel's claim: washing, liberation through the sea, and even death/new life. Communion brings us to the same place. Though we come to receive the elements, they are gifts—*ordinary* gifts. In communion, we receive bread and wine, and yet we receive through these ordinary things the very promises of the gospel: covenanting, sustaining, feeding, and sharing. That's just how God operates in the gospel: through the *ordinary*.

Notes

Charles Taylor, *Sources of the Self*, 1989.

Robert Kolb and Timothy J. Wingert, eds., *The Book of Concord*, 2000.

DAVID SCHNASA JACOBSEN

ROBERT ALLEN KELLY

PROPER 26 [31]

THE LESSONS IN PRÉCIS

Joshua 3:7-17. Joshua learns he is God's next chosen leader after Moses' death. He leads the people over the Jordan River in a way reminiscent of Moses' leading the people through the Red (or Reed) Sea.

Psalm 107:1-7, 33-37. Remembering and bearing witness to God's leadership and deliverance from slavery and provision in the wilderness gives way to praise and the assurance that God continues to deliver constantly from many troubles.

1 Thessalonians 2:9-13. Paul reminds the church at Thessalonica that he and others have led with integrity and from a heart with familial tenderness. These leaders rejoice that the church receives their teaching as from God.

Matthew 23:1-12. Jesus' teaching reminds us that leaders must not demand what they themselves cannot or will not follow, and that humility is a primary mark of a great leader.

THEME SENTENCE

God equips whom God calls. Christian leadership is grounded in God's call, a community of faith's collective memory and willingness to follow, and the leaders' personal humility and willingness to inspire and direct the community toward God's future.

A KEY THEOLOGICAL QUESTION

This series of texts touches on an issue much in the air these days: the issue of leadership.

What is leadership? How ought Christians think about it? What does the question of leadership have to do at all with following Christ in today's complex world?

Each of our passages presses into this nexus of questions.

The Joshua text lodges the question of leadership inside of Israel's journey of following YHWH their liberator God. Their deliverance from bondage began in earnest when the people of Israel crossed the Red Sea. In the Exodus story, we journey with Israel through their Egyptian deliverance as it takes place through the guidance of a mediating figure, a leader, Moses. As Israel's leader, Moses was a servant to the people, and the people submitted to Moses' leadership because God was with Moses.

In Joshua 3:7-17, which takes place after Moses' death, we find ourselves once again inside the story of God's care and concern for and nearness to God's people. And once again, we come to the question of leadership, this time Joshua's.

The problem, however, is that he was untested. How was Israel to know that God was with Joshua, that he should be followed? But is this not the wrong question? For what Israel needed reminding of is that a leader's qualifications neither begin nor end with his or her skill set. What's most vital is God's promise and presence. On this Joshua's leadership will turn. "I will be with you in the same way that I was with Moses" (Josh 3:7).

God's presence is so vital that it is to lead the way across the Jordan River. This is what grounds Joshua's leadership, the presence of God. It is God's presence that cuts off the waters and allows the people to cross the Jordan on dry ground, the event that serves as Israel's second Exodus. And that is proof positive that YHWH is God both of the Exodus and of the land (Ps 107). No matter what Israel faces, the presence of God will keep them, a presence that is beyond their (and our) control. We can only receive God's presence as miracle.

In all of this we see a mode of leadership that points away from itself. It is leadership that dares, even risks, following God into God's work of creating a new social reality, a reality that only God can bring to pass but that we can participate in. Leadership aims towards this: participating in God's work of realizing a new community of belonging.

The Joshua story itself points in this direction, though the story of leadership towards new community grounded in God and realized by God is shrouded in a "warrior God" nationalism built around subduing "enemies."

Sadly, many today take the wrong lesson and attempt to lead in these terms, the terms of nationalism, both political and cultural, that require outsiders and enemies to subdue. This is the strategy of the modern-day Tea Party movement in the U.S. and the nationalist wave against immigrants, especially Arabs and Muslims, in the U.S. and in several European countries.

But in Jesus Christ, who culminates (not throws away) the Moses-Joshua leadership tradition, we go beyond this social imagination. In "his kingdom and glory," as Paul puts to the Gentile Christians of Thessalonica, Gentiles are no longer enemies. By grace, they are adopted into the story of YHWH's dealings with the Israel. And with Israel, they too are "children [of God.]," recipients of "God's good news" (1 Thess 2:7-9). Barriers of in-and-out and the relationship of enmity between the Jews and Gentiles are overcome.

This is only possible because it takes place in Jesus Christ. As the gospel of God, a new social order is being realized around him. This is Matthew's message (23:1-12), which he profiles through two contrasting leadership types and two differing social visions.

The first leadership type centers on communities of exclusion. Seeing that the legal expert and the Pharisee are the archetypes of this first style of leader, religious leaders are uniquely susceptible to leading in this way. Being lovers of honor, being called great teachers and leaders, and taking themselves to be protectors of spiritual truth (for they "sit on Moses' seat"), the scribes and Pharisees built communities that did not allow the reconciling presence of God in.

In short, such leaders reproduce political and cultural nationalisms and communities of exclusion. Arguably, much of Christianity in the Western world and in the U.S. today and many Christian leaders today perform this kind of leadership.

Indeed, it was just this kind of problematic leadership, with its Christian trappings, that the Rev. Dr. Martin Luther King Jr. challenged. A group of pastors wrote a public letter to King, imploring him to cease protesting and agitating for Civil Rights. But King responded in his famous "Letter from a Birmingham Jail" by calling out their failure of Christian leadership. True Christian leadership strives to exemplify God's community-transforming presence, which leads to the "Beloved Community."

King understood that realizing this kind of community requires a different kind of leadership, the kind that contrasts with the legal experts' and Pharisaic leadership recorded in Matt 23:1-7. This is the model of the leader as the servant, which only one person has exemplified: Jesus Christ. As the Redeemer he *is* the Leader, the Lord who as servant builds a new community of embrace just as, in Christ, God has embraced us.

Leadership that would be Christian is discipleship, following Jesus on this path and participating in his work of building a community of belonging beyond exclusion.

A PASTORAL NEED

Congregations and individual members in them deserve to be safe under leadership that is not abusive or corrupt. Because people's spiritual lives are at the deep core of who they are, spiritual integrity becomes crucial to soul care so that those who sit alongside or under leadership may trust they are being led under God's inspiration. While the familial analogy Paul offers in 1 Thessalonians may be problematic, given the incidences of sexual, physical and verbal abuse inside family systems, it is a way of understanding at least some of what he believes people need in a spiritual community: clear boundaries and loving instruction. These things only happen as leaders yield themselves to God who equips them for these tasks. In order for the work of ministry to happen, there needs to be a constant reminder of God's part in building and maintaining a community of faith, so that members will not conflate their leadership with God's role. Humans are relational—a spiritual concept. The need for leadership to be connected to God puts the leader in the role of mediator and the people are led into this mediation ("call no one Father"). Of course, to call a leader *rabbi* or *father* is to point to the ultimate teacher/parent paradigm. That pointing is an ongoing need for congregations so that members are never stuck on the human side of the equation, but learn to trust God's care.

ETHICAL IMPLICATIONS

We cannot overstate the role of a good leader. There have been too many examples of leaders across the church's history who abused their authority or influence. Or leaders like the Pharisees in the text from Matthew who demanded more from the people than the leader was willing to bear. Congregations are vulnerable to such abuse of powers. Congregations have been torn asunder by such abuse. People have left their faith in Christ because of it.

It is not enough to claim authority. Authority without responsibility is dangerous and leaders must take into account the impact of their authority in the lives of those who follow them. That seems to be central to Paul's appeal in 1 Thessalonians: he has dealt faithfully and taken seriously his responsibility. Congregations must be discerning and careful listeners for God's Spirit as well. But in order to be effective, leaders must—in my estimation—commit themselves to a style of leadership that bows to the call and equipping from God. This leadership not only acknowledges God's part, but also leans on God's history of leadership and God's design. Reminding oneself of the story recounted in Psalm 107 is a good start. Congregations deserve leaders who believe they must serve the congregation at God's behest.

Finally, people will make missteps and mistakes. It's called being human. So leaders and congregations are called into relationships that are infused with humility and the ability to forgive one another. Otherwise, the waters of leading and following will be near impossible to navigate.

GOSPEL IMPLICATIONS

The biblical texts under review in this section lead us easily to the proclamation that God is the ultimate leader, that God calls leaders. There are seemingly trite sayings like "God doesn't call the qualified; God qualifies the called" that come to mind as we consider Joshua, untutored and untried in the role of the leader. But it is a truth. God equips whom God calls. God's own desire to lead us into freedom provokes the Divine Leader to call and qualify those who will yield in humility to God's way. It is the leadership Jesus shows in his ministry on earth and in his ultimate commitment to give himself completely over for the sake of our salvation. The social order that the gospel ushers in allows for relationships that are infused with God's reign and God's glory. And we are heirs to it all.

VALERIE BRIDGEMAN

J. KAMERON CARTER

Proper 27 [32]

The Lessons in Précis

Joshua 24:1–3a, 14–25. Joshua leads the people into a renewed covenant with God, calling them to denounce other gods and to recommit to God's severe grace that is jealous and unsparing.

Psalm 78:1–7. The psalmist's song prods the people to remember God's mighty acts and to share them with the generations to follow, so that every generation will set their hope on God.

1 Thessalonians 4:13–18. Paul describes the second coming of Jesus for those who are alive as a way to help them cope with the death of others. He tells them to let his words encourage them.

Matthew 25:1–13. The parable of the ten bridesmaids is a cautionary tale about being ready for an anticipated arrival of the Bridegroom, but one whose date is not announced. The parable calls believers to be alert and ready.

Theme Sentence

God fills life with meaning. The God-filled life is lived between memory and hope, and we are cautioned not to tether ourselves to the past or to lean only into the future. We live in gratitude for what was and in hope of what is to come, but we live in Christ now.

A Key Theological Question

This week's texts remind us that the Christian life is lived between memory and hope. Moreover, they remind us that the ethics of such living is to live a radical identity. It is to live as a disciple. It is a life lived in freedom—freedom for God and therefore for the stranger and the neighbor, or in short, for the world. In these in-between times, God fills life with meaning. To live between memory and hope and therefore as a disciple is to live in expectation of the often surprising and unexpected presence of the Lord in our midst, the Lord who calls us and equips us for action.

This is the lesson Christians over the centuries have sought to live out, sometimes successfully but too many times in failure. This is the lesson that Christian theologians and ethicists have tried to think through with such notions as tradition (from the Latin word *traditio*, to hand down or pass on) and eschatology (from the Greek words, *eschaton* and *logos*, the study of last things). And this is the lesson before us now.

It begins in Joshua 24 and is carried through to Psalm 78:1-7. As Joshua approached the end of his ministry, he gathered Israel together with a singularly focused message: Remember. Into the future, they were to be a congregation of remembrance; but not just in the future, in the present as well—most especially in the present. They were to remember that their life is rooted neither in the fragility of blood nor of kinship. When they are commanded to remember the patriarchs, the point is only secondarily about the patriarchs. What is primary is that Israel lives faithfully to God who called them into existence and accompanies them as a people. This faithfulness translates into serving God.

A life of service follows from the specific memory that God secures their origins and has been faithful to them. This memory, the dangerous and liberating memory of God, is what they are to pass down through the generations.

Is this not the meaning of *tradition*? In its more common usages, tradition has come to mean securing or codifying the past, be it a past body of knowledge or a set of accepted ways of doing things. On this understanding tradition protects us. It protects us from the corrosions that disintegrate "traditional values," etc. But at the root of such an understanding of tradition is fear and distrust.

Our current politics in the US and across much of the West is gripped by such fear and distrust—for example, over immigrants and non-Christians, especially Muslims, in our midst. Many people are calling for a return to the Founding Fathers, to a more robust constitutionalism, to restore "traditional Western values."

But in these texts, tradition is less about securing the past or building boundaries. Rather, tradition is tied to God's covenant and ongoing faithfulness. As such, it points to what each generation must draw to confront the challenges to and the new possibilities of faithfulness to God in its present. That is faith and trust is in a God whose covenant reconciles us to Godself and to each other to the stranger and the neighbor alike. This reconciliation may be especially to the stranger because God has come to us as the stranger to us to make us neighbors.

Our Old Testament texts advise us against the temptation to seize the past, and the texts of 1 Thessalonians and Matthew 25:1-13 warn against securing or seizing the future in our image. As God is our origin, so also beyond death and in Jesus Christ, God holds the future and fills it with meaning as well. Thus contrary to the obsessions with the future in so much of popular Christianity today, as for example in the *Left Behind* book series, living between memory and hope does not mean obsessing over the future, trying to secure it with schemes about when Jesus is coming back, when every wrong will be righted with some going to hell and others to heaven.

The message of 1 Thessalonians 4 and Matthew 25 directs us away from the future and toward Jesus Christ. The message here is that Jesus himself obsessed neither about his origins nor his future. Freed from obsessing over the past and future, Jesus' hope is in God. Because his origins and his future were God's, he was free to follow God's command now, to embrace tax collectors, sinners, and outcasts. The Christian's life of hope, Paul tells us, follows from Christ's hope, from a form of life that continues in his resurrection from the dead.

The challenge before us then is this: How will we live now, *in the present*? The question of when Christ will return is secondary to living in constant readiness to do God's will, however that may present itself to God's people. The challenge is being prepared for Christ's unpredictable presence and the command to follow him that arises from his surprising presence. The grace is that the Spirit makes us ready for his presence as we live between memory and hope.

A Pastoral Need

In uncertain times and volatile geo-politics, people need to feel anchored. They need to know that life is meaningful, and that God fills life with meaning. That need sometimes gets couched in statements of assurance, dogmatic faith claims, and creedal statements. This pull to concrete faith belies the ongoing human struggle to grow and mature and to be comfortable with what one may never be fully able to know. It also belies the truth that no one's spiritual journey is as clean cut as creedal faith suggests. There is the ideal and then there is the lived reality.

A competing need, however, is to feel the freedom to explore one's faith, with its boundaries. The intersection of exploration and boundaries is fraught with uncertainty. What will happen if I go "too far," a person may wonder. No one wants to feel foolish. No one wants to think or believe she or he has gone down the wrong path or slept through a great spiritual awakening. People need some hint, some divine guidance that they are pursuing God rightly. Without this guidance and assurance, the tendency is to live either in a mythic past or a supposed glorious future, dulling oneself to the present. And so the call in 1 Thessalonians to give believers a preview of future things comes to ground them in an earthly expression of faith.

Ethical Implications

At least two implications present themselves in these readings. The first one is how to be faithful to one's own history and traditions, one's own experience with God, without denigrating or demonizing the faith traditions of another. The zealousness with which Joshua calls the people to a new covenant is fraught with dangerous xenophobia and religious bigotry. In his time, of course, these concerns would not have been apparent or considered. There is no room, at least not in Joshua's accounting or in the Psalm under review, for faithful syncretism or interreligious dialogue. But we live in the twenty-first century and in the presence of people who accept differing religious belief systems and worship practices. And, if we are honest, our faith has been influenced and most often strengthened by this contact. We must be cautious in our condemnation, even as we embrace God's historical claim on our lives as Christians.

The second ethical concern that presents itself is that the desire for God's future could lead us to living in denial or not living faithfully in the present. I heard a Jewish saying once: "If you are going to plant a tree, and hear that Messiah has come, plant your tree, and then go meet Messiah." One ought to stay connected to sustaining work, a life grounded in the present. First Thessalonians actually supports this sentiment. The writer wants to assure those who await Christ's return of the way the future will unfold. But the point is not to head to a bunker or some hilltop and wait on it; rather, believers are to use the story to encourage one another. God is already present with them in the Holy Sprit (4:8). In the context of the entire letter, this encouragement leads to faithful discipleship in the nascent community, a community still defining its boundaries.

GOSPEL IMPLICATIONS

Each of these texts offers possibilities that proclaim God's grace and God's intentions to be in covenant relationship with humans. Surely the first testament text, Joshua's personal testimony, "as for me and my household, we will serve the Lord" (Josh 24:15, NRSV), has found itself in a lexicon of faith statements. God has chosen a family among families and these are our ancestors. God has made covenant with them and with us. We may choose freely because of this choice. The psalm solidifies our choosing as we remember God's mighty acts. God has acted on behalf of our spiritual ancestors. These acts are our legacy.

The second testament texts lead us to a life of faithful attentiveness because God's promises are sure. God not only has filled our lives with meaning, God will continue to do so. We are invited to be ready for a coming future. It may seem cruel to imagine that some may be outside the realm of God's salvation, beyond the party of eternity because they were "foolish." But Matthew's word is cautionary and not prescriptive. No one has to fall into that category. In fact, it is not God's hope. These texts hint at expanding the boundaries and the invitation of God's love, as we see in the cross, resurrection, and ascension of Jesus Christ. We cannot know the day or the hour of this approaching final consummation of God's love, a wedding feast and a resurrection. But we can be ready, with the help of the Spirit and by God's grace.

VALERIE BRIDGEMAN

J. KAMERON CARTER

PROPER 28 [33]

THE LESSONS IN PRÉCIS

Judges 4:1–7. Deborah sits as a judge in ancient Israel when it falls under a repressive Canaanite regime, and she directs Barak, through a word from God, to rise up as a general to deliver the people.

Psalm 123. The psalmist watches God for directions, much as slaves watch their masters or mistresses for instructions. The psalmist's plea is for God's mercy in the life of God's people in the presence of contempt.

1 Thessalonians 5:1–11. Paul explains that the "day of the Lord" will come "like a thief in the night," with chaos and fear. He encourages those who "belong to the day" to trust God's salvation and to encourage one another.

Matthew 25:14-30. The parable of the talents, told to expound on the kingdom of heaven, expects those who receive a gift to use it. Losing that talent and being thrown off the master's land punishes the one who does not use the one talent.

THEME SENTENCE
God gives us talents with which to serve. This includes the grace to act out of trust rather than fear as we await Christ's return.

A KEY THEOLOGICAL QUESTION
The texts before us are unsettling, because they speak of the possibility of failed leadership. God gives us talents with which to serve and we may squander the very gifts we've been entrusted. The very possibility of this

failure most attends those who lay claim to doing God's will, to being disciples of Jesus Christ.

The above possibilities reflect the story of each of our texts, but it's the story uniquely profiled in the Gospel reading. It is a story of how the kingdom of God, in contrast to the kingdoms of this world, is to operate in the time between the times. This in-between time is not one in which our mandate is to calculate the exact moment of Christ's return. What these texts press upon us is this: We now occupy the space of trust in Jesus Christ who is ever coming to us in surprising and unpredictable ways, and responsibility toward the world that Jesus Christ ever loves.

We learn in our texts that none of us is talentless or without significance. None of us is without specific gifts. These gifts are themselves signs of God's care and love for us. They are gifts that signify our having been recognized by God. God does not recognize us *because* of our gifts and talents. Our gifts and talents come after God has recognized us, not before. One might say that our worth is the gift from which the other gifts and talents flow.

But this only partially captures the significance of the "kingdom" story Jesus tells in Matthew's Gospel. While this might seem like a kingdom or a politics like any other, while it might seem like just another consumer society driven by a "return on investment" ethic, we are presented with something strikingly different. For here the subjects of the kingdom, the Christ's disciples, have been given gifts neither for their own cause nor for their own increase. Neither self-interest nor a desire to calculate and control outcomes drives this kingdom.

We are confronted with a story of trust. It is important that we not confuse this story's call to "trust in God" with the similar words "in God we trust" that adorn the money that circulates in the U.S. financial system. Our financial system has tied the God-language of "trust" and "debt" or obligation (which is not to be confused with the language of "responsibility" I'm using throughout this meditation) to a capitalist order. The story of Matthew's text points in a different direction.

We get a sense of this new direction when the first two servants in the story speak. Master, they say, "you trusted me with two (or five) talents, and I have returned that trust in a specific way. I have resisted a life of calculations and manipulations in order to secure certain ends or results. I have not lived in the time between the times by making calculations about where and with whom I should invest my energies. I have not asked first and foremost: Is caring for this or that person, or being involved in this or that activity, worth it. Will such investments of my time and energies yield increases or profits that will raise my profile in the community or give me more respectable credentials?" These servants have given of themselves and of their talents and gifts. The servants recognize that controlling the increase, and thus securing the results, isn't their job at all, for this is a sign that one is living in the will to mastery or to being a master. Dietrich Bonhoeffer, in his book *Creation and Fall*, called this the will to be like God (*sicut Deus*).

It is just this lesson that the third servant had not learned, for he was moved by fear. He ran the calculations and determined that being conservative was the way to go. He refused to return God's entrusting of talents to him with trust in God. He lived by an ethics of possession. He wanted to wait for a safe environment in which to follow God. But he was deemed an unfaithful and irresponsible disciple.

With this story or parable, the Matthean text presses upon us an ethics, not of good and evil or of right and wrong. It is a story of the ethics of fear (because of trust in ourselves as a false god) and trust (in the true God or not ourselves). It is a story of faithful and unfaithful discipleship.

Faithful discipleship is precisely what is dramatized in the story of Deborah, who becomes the Old Testament model of the faithful Christian servant in this time between the times. After Joshua's death, Israel was challenged to trust and serve God. They said they would trust and serve the Lord, but they quickly started to live out an ethics of fear and not of trust. The Deborah story is about one such episode of increasing unfaithfulness in Israel.

Full of gifts of leadership, Deborah is a witness of what it means to follow YHWH. She, in effect, announces in her life just what the psalmist (Ps 123) utters: "I raise my eyes to you—you who rule heaven . . . our eyes attend to the LORD our God, until he has mercy on us." In this Deborah is the model God-follower, the one who embodies and thus performs what is called for in 1 Thessalonians 5:1-11. She wears the breastplate of faith and love, and dons the helmet of salvation. She is not paralyzed by fear, but looks to the coming of the Lord. This enables her to act in obedience towards God and thus be true to herself and the gifts she has. She therefore is the one who hears the words, "Well done, good and faithful servant."

In these times between the times, or in the time that remains for each of us, may we follow the witness of Deborah and not squander the talents entrusted to us. May we live in responsible generosity in the world as a sign of the love and extravagance of God toward the world.

A PASTORAL NEED

God gives us talents with which to serve. God's claim on our lives comes with responsibility. It takes courage to follow God into unknown territory like Deborah did or to launch into an extravagant bet on one's gifts, as two servants in the parable of the talent did. Still, we must not be so hard on Barak, who did not want to go to battle without Deborah, or on the servant who judged his master as a hard man and tried to preserve what he had been given, so as not to lose it. But risk is a part of the human experience, if we are to grow in every way, including spiritually. There is no safety net. And escapism, the longing to leave the present for a romanticized or even sure godly future, is great. The pastoral role, then, becomes to preach a word of trust that helps people find the ability to turn their eyes toward God and God's merciful care. People need to be led gently into extravagant trust by sharing stories of both success and defeat. These stories, both sides, are the witnesses to human strivings toward God's gift. In the end, when people fail or succeed, they stand in need of a community that will encourage them in the between time, and who will remind them of God's future that, while it does not feel secure, does come with the promise of God's saving presence in Christ.

ETHICAL IMPLICATIONS

There are some troubling concerns for the use of militaristic and slave imagery in these texts. In the twenty-first century, when governments are able to wipe one another out in moments by nuclear or biological warfare, we must not behave as if (bloody and horrific as it is in the text) war in our times is the same as biblical war imagery. The same is true about slavery. Persons unconcerned about the annihilation of people, or about the horrors of slavery, write these texts as if war is desirable and as if servants/slaves serve with no repercussions. The servant who hides his talent gives us a hint to the severity of a taskmaster. And we generally overlook the fact that the servant didn't steal the talent or run off with it; he merely calculated wrongly that preserving it would spare his life. I would argue that this parable tells us something about human slavers, but I'm not sure what it tells us about the kingdom of God, exactly. Ethically, would we not at least need to offer a resistance to the notion that brutality is at the core of who God is?

GOSPEL IMPLICATIONS

In spite of the troubling aspects of these texts—the brutality of war, the slavery imagery, and the labor pains at the end of times—there is good news to mine from them. The preacher who would proclaim God's divine care for God's people would handle the landmines of language and remind us that in times of oppression, God does in fact hear the prayers of those who cry out and will, in fact, raise up leaders among us. And, we may be the leaders to whom God entrusts the call. But God never entrusts us with any call for which God does not also equip and encourage us. God gives us talents with which to serve. We are not slaves looking to a master, but we know what it is like to look earnestly toward God for instructions and what we need to carry out those instructions. We live into our call in the midst of uncertain times, always. The "end times" are all these in-between times while we await the coming again of Jesus Christ. There is fear and angst, turbulence in human affairs and natural phenomena. And yet, the greatest talent or gift that we have been given is Jesus Christ, and this is a talent that we can hold onto and who holds onto us. God is with us, cladding us with armor, yes, but the armor of faith and love, and the hope of salvation. We are, by God's grace, children of light. We are so because God has saved us through the word of Jesus Christ, for whom we long and for whom we wait. But in the meantime, we remain sober, alert, and awake so that we may live expectantly while we serve in trust.

VALERIE BRIDGEMAN

J. KAMERON CARTER

PROPER 29 [34] [REIGN OF CHRIST]

THE LESSONS IN PRÉCIS

Ezekiel 34:11-16, 20-24. As a good shepherd seeks and finds lost sheep to return them to the fold, God promises to gather God's people from the exile where they have been scattered and to restore them, make them safe, and strengthen them.

Psalm 100. All the earth is summoned to give thanks and remember that they belong to God, the great shepherd who is also the great creator. They are called to acknowledge God's goodness, steadfast love and faithfulness to every generation.

Ephesians 1:15-23. Paul gives thanks for the believers in Ephesus and commends them for their love for all the saints. He prays for their wisdom, for their inheritance, and for God's power to work in them as it did in Christ when he was resurrected.

Matthew 25:31-46. In this iconic text, Jesus distinguishes between the sheep and the goats, those who will and those who will not inherit God's reign. All who attend to the least and vulnerable in any way are blessed of God and have in fact done what they have done to Jesus, who identifies himself as every vulnerable person to whom help is offered.

THEME SENTENCE

God protects. As a true and just shepherd, God leads people and all creation in the face of threat and need. God cares for us because we are God's own and leads us to care for one another.

A Key Theological Question

At the heart of these texts are a series of images in tension that point both to the reign of God in Jesus Christ (what sets God's rule, reign, and politics apart from all others) and to the ethics of God's reign in Christ (how we are to live under God's reign). Our readings point us to how God has intervened in our fallen condition to restore and renew us and to call us to carry out our daily activities in affirmation of our dignity and sacred worth.

Ezekiel's prophecy uses the language of the shepherd to describe ancient Israel's situation. Ezekiel is to "prophesy against Israel's shepherds" (Ezek 34:1). Israel's leaders, from the kings to the priests, that is, the shepherds, are responsible and will be judged for the people not following God's law or heeding God's prophets. The leaders abdicated their role to instruct God's people in God's ways. The people were scattered and separated from the land and thus were in the midst of an eco-crisis.

At the heart of ecological crises, which Native Americans all too well understand, is disconnection from the land. The land of Israel was "resourced," converted into property to be seized or possessed (private property) through the activity of war. Consequently, food and provisions became scarce as the land came to be occupied by an enemy. Ultimately at stake in dispossessing the people from the land and in breaking the relationship between God and the people was the very humanity of Israel. The life of creation and of the people was at stake.

Into this situation Ezekiel prophesies that God will intervene as Shepherd, thus setting in place a different material reality for the flock. As the true Shepherd, God will search for the sheep. What we see in Ezekiel's prophecy is God committing to a promise, the quite material promise of salvation: "I will rescue my flock" (Ezek 34:10). What kind of words are these? They are the words of a God who takes our plight and condition seriously. For Christians, these words point to the incarnation of God in Jesus Christ, even as they point to the work to be accomplished in his flesh. This work is the restoration and affirmation of our humanity and status under God, no longer subject to false overlords.

It is just this message that the psalmist picks up and celebrates in praise. The psalmist recognizes that "we are [God's] people, the sheep of [God's] own pasture" (Ps 100:3), an insight that grows out of the psalmist's recognition of the restoration and affirmation of the dignity of creation.

In this moment, the psalmist's act of praise (and our acts of praise to the extent we join the psalmist) becomes a profoundly political act as well as a theological act. Our praise speaks back to the powers that would destroy the dignity of humans and of creation. Thus, perhaps in an unexpected way praise to God marks out our humanity and can be for us the platform from which further, material affirmations of our and others' humanity flows.

Paul also grasped this, for the hymn of praise that opens the letter to the Ephesians is an extended celebration of the gloriousness of God's grace. He celebrates that as human, as creatures, God has accepted us. What Ezekiel's prophecy yearns for (a new social reality constituted around God as the Shepherd) and what the psalmist praises God for (that we are God's people, and the sheep of God's pasture) is precisely, Paul contends, what is realized in Jesus Christ.

In Christ a different kind of pastorate has begun and therefore a different way of being human in relationship to God and in relationship to each other has been put in place. The love believers have toward each other is a demonstration of their faith in Jesus Christ. They interact with each other as belonging to God, and not according to the social scripts of the false lords—what Paul calls the principalities, the powers, the dominions or the social and political structures of his day. It is just this breaking up of social and political structures—structures that assign values to humanity according to certain markers of identity—that the Gospel text says happened in Jesus Christ. And it is here that we come face to face with a Christian social ethics, a new Christian social imagination opened up in Jesus Christ.

In Matthew 25, we again are at the precincts of the incarnation. But now we face the ethics of the incarnation, the humanization, of God in Jesus Christ. In taking up our human existence, God wills to be known through Christ and in all human life. The humanization means that all life is sacred and marked by human dignity and as such (which means there is no Christian prerequisite) witnesses to God. And this is to what Matthew's Gospel points. In Matthew 25, following Jesus means attending to the needs of the sick, the homeless, and the imprisoned, social outcasts. For their humanity is the humanity of God in Jesus Christ. "When did we see you hungry and feed you, or thirsty and give you a drink?" "When you took care of them," Jesus seems to say, "you took care of me, for my humanity is their humanity and their humanity, mine."

Jesus restores our dignity—the dignity of us all—and in so doing enacts a new social reality. This is the pastoral situation he establishes. May we, with joy, work in his sheepfold at the service of the Good Shepherd.

A Pastoral Need

God protects. As people, we need to know that our well-being is not just up to ourselves. If it were, most of us would mess up. The texts assure us that it is not too much to hope for God to seek after us and find us, even when we are in exile, the prescriptive consequence for disobedience of God's law. People need to experience a sense of being important enough for God to seek them, a sense of belonging to God, first, as the psalmist describes: we are God's people, the sheep of God's pasture. The belonging comes as we are reminded that God created us and cares for God's creation—all of it. People need to experience the kind of care described by the prophet Ezekiel where they are sought, their wounds are treated, and their strength is restored. The community of faith needs to believe that God does in fact act in justice and hold to account those who have mistreated and wounded the community, as Ezekiel describes in putting forth God's justice and as Matthew's Gospel calls out those who do not do justice. And people need to feel a part of God's work in the world.

Ethical Implications

If it is true that the role of each of these texts, to some extent, is to show us God's protection and care, then our business is also protecting one another. The risk always is that we will dehumanize others and not care for them. To do so would make war and devastation easier to do or to overlook since those who would suffer would be non-human or so completely enemy as to be monstrous and deserving. There is a thin line, sometimes an imperceptible line, between self-protection and revenge. I do not presume to know where that line is, but I do think that we must always try to put ourselves on the other side of any human equation before we act.

Additionally, the problem with not seeing the humanity in others is that we can stand by and watch them be in prison, homeless, naked, and hungry and not see the divinely reconstituted humanity in them and therefore not respond to alleviate the pain or to transform the systems that uphold such suffering. So the work calls for the kind of love and wisdom that Paul advocates in Ephesians.

GOSPEL IMPLICATIONS

These texts point to ways God cares for us and pursues us for the sake of our safety and our salvation. It is the pursuit of a shepherd for sheep who wander, who find themselves in harm's way because of such wandering or because danger is nearby. It's the pursuit of sheep who get caught away from community. It is the pursuit of those who break covenant. It is the vision of God (in the first testament) and God in Christ (in the Christian testament) who cares, protects, corrects, and instructs. These visions of God are compelling. We have come to the great Shepherd, the great protecting caretaker of our souls. Having been so loved and cared for, the gospel calls us to meet the world and the most vulnerable among us with the care and protection we have received, to hold ourselves accountable and responsible. The good news is that we may now treat all people as if we were serving Jesus. It is more than "what would Jesus do," but rather "who will we be because of what God has done for us." It is humane, yes. But it also is resisting the powers and principalities as the incarnational presence of God. It is the vision of pastors who know the character and will of God and call the people to the God who created them. These texts allow the preacher to work through questions of how God cares for us and why our allegiance to God is warranted. To hold allegiance to God is to hold allegiance to all that God loves—humans and all creation. As God's own, we are made fully human, in whom the resurrection power of Christ resides and works. "Ain't that good news!"

VALERIE BRIDGEMAN

J. KAMERON CARTER

ALL SAINTS DAY

THE LESSONS IN PRÉCIS

Revelation 7:9-17. John envisions a multitude that represents all nations, peoples, and languages around the throne of God at the culmination of times. The multitude witnesses to God's grace through the Great Ordeal and finds rest, provision, and praise for all they have suffered.

Psalm 34:1-10, 22. "I will bless the LORD at all times" begins a litany of why, in the face of tribulation, God's name ought to be praised. But beyond the provision for food, shelter, and freedom from shame, this psalm invites communal witness and praise. "Magnify the LORD with me" (v. 3).

1 John 3:1-3. This text witnesses that we are already the children of God and pushes us to an anticipatory joy that we are not yet all we will be. One day we will know as we are known.

Matthew 5:1-12. The Sermon on the Mount does not promise an easy life; it does, however, promise a life infused with God's blessings.

THEME SENTENCE

God empowers us to be witnesses in the face of persecution. The good news is that God is with us as we face struggles, especially for righteousness' sake. And that God gives us companions along the way. We are not alone.

A KEY THEOLOGICAL QUESTION

There is a phrase—really a question—that I often heard in the Sunday morning worship services in the church of my youth. "Have I gotta witness?" I remember the church mothers and deacons uttering it in their testimonies as they spoke, often with tear-filled eyes, of the difficulties of life they were dealing with and trying to make it through and trust God through. They would ask "Have I gotta witness?" "Does anyone know what I'm talking about?" Others in the congregation would often respond by nodding their heads or by raising a hand, swaying back and forth. They were witnesses offering their affirmation that God would sustain the one testifying because God had sustained them. As an adolescent, I had no clue as to the depth of this acclamatory phrase. I did not know that *martyr* in the New Testament means "witness," one who attests to God's faithfulness.

All Saints Day (also known as *Martyrs' Sunday*) is that day in the Christian calendar for pondering the question, "Have I Gotta Witness?" It's that day in which the Christian faithful consider those who have been witnesses or martyrs. Each of our lectionary passages offers food for thought on faithful witnessing today.

In Matthew 5:1-12, Jesus gathers together his disciples and begins his famous "Sermon on the Mount." Verses 3-12 enumerate Jesus' descriptions of what the blessed life consists. The hopeless—Luke's account simply says the poor—are happy because God's Kingdom will be their inheritance. Those who grieve will be made glad. The humble receive the earth itself as their inheritance. The hungry and thirsty for righteousness have God provide for them. The merciful receive mercy. The pure in heart might not see God now in their circumstances, nevertheless, they will see God. The peacemakers are best examples of God's children.

But then Jesus (as a hip-hop artist might) does a kind of "remix" on what he's just said. In the remix he compresses into two descriptions of happiness (vv. 10–11) what he had just described with seven statements of descriptions in the first part (vv. 3–9). We know that Jesus is doing a remix because he "samples" or cycles us back to the notion of "the kingdom of heaven" that he introduced in v. 3. The difference this time is that Jesus introduces into his remix that key notion for All Saints Day: the martyr or the witness.

The happy one is the one persecuted for taking a stand for God's justice, freedom, and peace (v. 10) and therefore runs the risk of being reviled or castigated if not persecuted or tracked down for standing for justice (vv. 11-12). This justice is not a human-invented justice or righteousness. It is not *self*-righteousness. But nor is it a judgmental or condemning justice. It does not point the finger to condemn—to hell or otherwise. It is God's justice. But even in saying that it is God's justice, note God does not seek to justify Godself or to establish that someone else is wrong. Even God's justice does not seek to condemn the world. This is the unique justice of God.

So Jesus' remix says, "Happy is the one who stands for God's unique kind of justice, God's righteousness. This is a justice that judges in favor of peace not war, love not hate, mercy not condemnation, and so forth." But one can only stand firm in a justice that refuses condemnation and that executes a new kind of judgment—the judgment of love, the judgment to embrace as God embraces—only as one seeks or "hungers and thirsts" for this unique kind of divine righteousness. As the psalmist says, "Even strong young lions go without and get hungry, but those who seek the LORD lack no good thing" (Ps 34:10).

Having described this multifaceted condition of blessedness and remixed it in the direction of those who would stand up for and bear witness to God's righteousness, Jesus culminates this part of his sermon by offering a celebratory word of encouragement: "Be full of joy and be glad [if you're persecuted for God's justice], because you have a great reward in heaven" (v. 12a). Jesus offers this encouragement because it's not always easy to stand for God's righteousness. Jesus offers his culminating assurance that if we are persecuted for standing for God's justice, we can draw strength from the fact that in response to the question, "Have I got a witness?" there are many who have gone before us who are standing with us on God's promises, happy that even in persecution "now we are God's children, [though] it hasn't yet appeared what we will be" (1 John 3:2). In other words, "Yes, there are witnesses. We do not stand alone."

We stand amid a great multitude that no one can count, from every nation, from all tribes and peoples and languages (cf. Rev 7:9). We stand with prophets before us who were persecuted (cf. Matt. 5:12b). Among the prophetic witnesses surely is Dietrich Bonhoeffer who stood against the Nazis, Martin Luther King Jr. who was gunned down standing up for poor folks and working for civil rights, and host of others whose names history has and has not recorded, though God knows their names.

"Have I got a witness?" An answer comes from an angel in answer to the question, "Who are these people wearing white robes, and where have the come from?" "These people," the angel says to John of the

Apocalypse, "have come out of great hardship. They have washed their robes and made them white in the Lamb's blood. . . . [A]nd the one seated on the throne will shelter them. . . . [A]nd God will wipe away every tear from their eyes" (Rev 7:13-17).

A Pastoral Need

Some of the most beleaguering questions for people of faith arise in times of struggle. "Am I alone in my suffering?" "Where is God in this struggle?" "Will all this being persecuted for my faith pay off?" It is easy to become weary in the face of opposition, even when one believes his or her cause is right and on the side of God. It seems that feeling alone also is a constant reality. Our pain and isolation can feel uniquely ours. When in want or in need, it can seem as if no one else would possibly understand. And yet, these texts give us a glimpse of the human struggle, not merely the individual struggle. We are a part of the human experience. We lack, we want, we struggle, and we desire. And we have those who have gone before us and those who walk beside us who are witnesses to the struggle and to God's blessings in the struggle. The pastoral challenge is to make John's vision plain, so to speak. Our work is to help people see what John saw: a great cloud of witnesses from all walks of life who have not only endured the suffering life has given, but who have come out of it with praise on their lips. This vision is not an "easy fix," as in forget the pain. It is an acknowledgment of the pain as well as of God's sustaining presence, and the presence of human companions along the way.

Ethical Implications

Set against the backdrop of overwhelming poverty, of global war, and continual rape culture against women and girls around the globe, these texts are challenging. The biblical witness must never stand alone, but always be in conversation with lived flesh-and-blood stories. There are people who are suffering because they are poor, hungry, and under constant threat of annihilation: bombs and bullets are their daily reminder of danger. There also is the reality that these people come from "every tribe, tongue, and nation." It sometimes is easy for people to think only of their nation or their kin or language group. Xenophobia might keep us from choosing to suffer for righteousness' sake. But these texts beg a more global vision; actually, the Revelation text begs a cosmic vision.

The implications it seems are that in order to really partner with God's blessings, one must be willing to embrace the struggle for those who are outside of worldly favor. God—at least in these texts—sides with the poor person who calls when in trouble (Ps 34:6).

One must be willing to be a martyr for what is right and be willing to die for one's beliefs. In a culture of comfort, where comfort often is the highest value, suffering does not ever sound like good news. And yet, the reward for righteousness is its own reward. Knowing that one has taken God's side means that one can depend on God to protect and provide. And if death comes as a result of one's stance, then one joins a multitude of witnesses who do not cede to death the ultimate victory. In this kind of witness, it does not yet appear what we shall be, but are unveiling with it the full revelation of God's grace (1 John 3:3).

GOSPEL IMPLICATIONS

If there is one overwhelming gospel message in these texts it is this: we are not alone. We have companions along the way and those who have gone before. We have a witness in our own lives of God's presence and in the lives of those with us. Their testimonies help us through difficult times and hard choices. The biographies of the faithful read like gospel. They are what the Apostle Paul once called "living letters." But more than that reality, we have God. In death and in life, we belong to God. Life is full of struggle, true. Sometimes we take stands that put us in the direct line of opposing forces that could very well end our lives. It is God who makes it possible for us to stand, who strengthens and feeds us for what we must face. Blessings come from God, not because we are perfect or get it right. Blessings come when we most need them: when we hunger and thirst for food, and when we hunger and thirst for God (Ps 34:8; Matt 5:6).

VALERIE BRIDGEMAN

J. KAMERON CARTER

THANKSGIVING DAY

THE LESSONS IN PRÉCIS

Deuteronomy 8:7-18. God is bringing the people to a good land where they are to remember the source of their abundance and keep God's commandments.

Psalm 65. The "God of our salvation" answers prayer, has provided the people with grain and crowned the year with goodness.

2 Corinthians 9:6-15. "God loves a cheerful giver" and will make the generous rich in righteousness. Generosity will produce thanksgiving to God in others.

Luke 17:11-19. Jesus heals ten lepers and the Samaritan is the only one to give thanks. His faith makes him well.

THEME SENTENCE

God invites and empowers our thanksgiving. Our thanksgiving is in return for what God has given freely by grace, without exacting price or demanding anything from us. We know God by grace, and thus give thanks.

A KEY THEOLOGICAL QUESTION

Why give thanks? Is it to be polite? If we follow Luke's story, it is a way to reciprocate a relationship initiated by God, and to know one's Savior. The ten lepers are the least of the least, unnamed people outside an unnamed village, in a place known by where it is not, Samaria or Galilee. The Samaritan is the least of the lepers who all call Jesus for any mercy he might give them. They do nothing to earn the healing he gives them, Jesus simply responds to their need. He heals and restores them to their community and families.

Typically as preachers when we engage this text, we barely take time to mark and honor the healing itself. We race to condemn the nine. In so doing, we may be as guilty as they are: like them we race to do what seems required. The miracle gets short shrift. Even as Jesus healed the lepers, God knows our needs and generously provides for them. God's providence and daily sustenance are worthy of endless thanksgiving.

However, at Thanksgiving we may be painfully aware that millions of people do not share in the bounty of material wealth or social benefits that many in our congregations enjoy. People who live in poverty are children, struggling parents, young people unable to find work, veterans, the elderly, members of our own families and circles of friends. Around the world, known to us personally or not, they are all our neighbors and God's children.

Is it appropriate to give thanks for the abundance we enjoy when others lack the basic necessities of life? From this perspective, Thanksgiving could seem oddly self-centered, in effect we thank God that we have too much while others have not enough. For the original pilgrims who fought hard with the land for their harvests, Thanksgiving was simpler. Global consciousness and the media have brought economic disparity and poverty into our living rooms, and Thanksgiving is more ethically complex.

From a theological perspective, Thanksgiving appropriately is not just thanking God for what we have, it is about God's generous provision and sustenance for all. It may be helpful to distinguish between the generosity of divine provision and those forces that work against God's purposes, preventing everyone from receiving their share. One way to give thanks to God is obedience, loving both God and neighbor so that people everywhere may enjoy their share of God's provisions.

Should we give thanks only when things are good, or when we feel like it? What if we are a community hit by hardship, tragedy, or disaster? Paul says give thanks in all things (1 Thess 5:18). Giving thanks can be a way of relating to and putting trust in God, regardless of circumstances. Failing to offer thanks may unintentionally affirm an untruth, God has departed and it is all up to us. Jesus said, however, "I myself will be with you every day until the end of this present age" (Matt 28:20), and Paul said, "nothing can separate us from God's love in Christ Jesus" (Rom 8:38). Of course as individuals in times of struggle or doubt, we may need to let the church do some of our thanksgiving and believing for us. Still we may lean on words of scripture, like, "Don't be anxious about anything; rather, bring up all of your requests to God in your prayers and petitions, along with giving thanks." (Phil 4:6.)

Innocent suffering may mark not the absence but the presence of God with those who suffer. Both Deuteronomy and the psalm praise and give thanks for the current fullness of harvest, and they allude to former suffering. Both imply God's care even in those former times. Various contemporary theologies note Jesus' earthly bias toward the poor and oppressed. Far from being at the periphery of God's care and attention, they are at the center. The incarnation and the cross proclaim God's entry to the deepest suffering, even death itself, to rob it of its power. The old creation is still painfully present, however, and one can never be glib in speaking of those who suffer, for instance suggesting that their consolation is in knowing God is with them. We can nonetheless uphold the mystery of God's presence in brokenness and hope that even in the worst of circumstances, we may be given the grace to give thanks. Joy in the midst of suffering and gratitude in the midst of sorrow are marks of the kingdom of God. As Paul says, whether we live or die, we are in God's care (Rom 14:8).

Do we give thanks to earn favors with God? Some scripture verses imply that God punishes and causes suffering. If that were in fact true then we would need to stay on the right side of God, and thanksgiving might be one way to do it. It is one thing to affirm that God is sovereign and has the right to do exactly as God wills, even to punish whomever God wants. That notion needs to be put in tension with God's love. God does not will or inflict suffering, but God may allow a disobedient people to suffer the consequences of their own actions, without necessarily abandoning them. The thanks we rightly give to God are for God's steadfast love in and out of season, especially when we do not deserve it. We do not give thanks in order to receive God's care, we give thanks because with all people we have received God's care. Thanksgiving is no down payment on future favors, for God's blessing cannot be bought. Thanksgiving is for gifts given to us by grace, not because of our merit.

Does God need our thanks? Not in the sense that God lacks in anything. But thanks is one way to give something in return for all God has given us. God may not need our thanks, but God delights in them and in being in relationship with us. Our thanks complete a circle of love begun by God, as happened with the Samaritan. He acknowledges Jesus who made him well, and in so doing receives faith and fullness of life. The key difference between him and the other nine is that he came to know his Savior. Jesus does not condemn the nine—they yet may know who saved them.

A PASTORAL NEED

Here we might name two needs. First, some people may wonder, Why should I give thanks? For them it is especially important that we paint the miracle of God's provision. A starting place can be with Luke. Focus on the healing so it is not just a drive-by miracle. Let it happen. For example:

> Before the lepers have gone out of shouting range, the text says they are made clean. It is God's delight to answer their prayers; it is God's delight to give them what they need. Their skin dries up. The scars on their skin smooth out. The white blotches of dead skin return to olive color. Wasted flesh returns to health. Limbs become whole. Disfigured faces return to normal. Movement returns to disabled feet. They will be returned to their families, to their friends, to society, to their jobs, to their homes, to their names, they returned to life. They receive the benefits that God wants them to have.

What if we could communicate the same sense of miracle about the provisions (and other things) for which we give thanks on this day?

A second need: Giving thanks can be a way to a more meaningful life. A man in his forties in Québec was recently surprised to receive in the mail an envelope from a lawyer concerning the death of his natural mother whom he had never met. Included in the envelope was a letter she wrote several years earlier telling him of the sad circumstances of his adoption, her love for him, and her desire not to interfere with his adult life. She had left him her estate. He said he was pleased to have her things, but he would have preferred to know her. He had the benefits of being her son, but he did not have the blessing of a relationship with her. "If I had the choice of one or the other, I'd choose the relationship any day."

Today we have a choice to know God through God's estate, the things around us, or to have a lively relationship with God. In personal relationships, giving thanks can be a way to deepen bonds. So it can be with God. The more thanks we give, the more thanks we have to give, for by grace our awareness of God's involvement in our lives increases.

Ethical Implications

At a dinner, a man refused to say grace because he did not think it right to thank God for food when so many people have none—the night never fully recovered. Thanksgiving is an important time to raise the subject of world poverty, but not to lay a guilt trip on the gathered community. They may have good reasons to feel guilty, but how much better it is if we can motivate them positively to thank God through their words and by their actions on behalf of others.

Preachers might motivate by modeling thanksgiving for all of those inside and outside of the church who dedicate time to easing hunger and poverty. The poor will always be with us, and we can never do enough, but we can nonetheless give thanks for what is done, and for all of those who participate. We might give thanks that the United Nations General Assembly set up targets aimed at reducing the proportion of people living in extreme poverty by 50% before 1215. We might give thanks for a growing global awareness that poverty is not solved by only sending money to buy food and clothes. Such awareness is apparent in the language of the World Social Summit that advocates "the empowerment of people living in poverty through their full participation in all aspects of political, economic and social life, especially in the design and implementation of policies that affect the poorest and most vulnerable groups of society." We might even give thanks on this day also for people like Bill and Melinda Gates (or others we could name) who dedicate so much their wealth and lives to helping others.

Gospel Implications

The best way to give thanks to God is by doing God's will. If giving thanks to God is righteous living, who among us is fully capable? We all fall short. Only Christ was capable of such love. By the giving of his life for us, Christ gives the perfect thanks by giving back to God in the same manner that God continually gives to us: totally, respectfully, selflessly, lovingly. Through our faith in him, our thanks are counted by God as sufficient. Through our baptism, we have received the Spirit who empowers and guides our best thanksgiving, our giving of ourselves for others.

Notes

United Nations Poverty and Social Development Division, "Poverty Eradication," <http://social.un.org/index/Poverty.aspx>

Paul Scott Wilson

CONTRIBUTORS

Valerie Bridgeman, Associate Professor of Hebrew Bible/Homiletics and Worship, Lancaster Theological Seminary

Gennifer Benjamin Brooks, Ernest and Bernice Styberg Associate Professor of Homiletics, Garrett Evangelical Theological Seminary

J. Kameron Carter, Associate Professor of Theology and Black Church Studies, Duke Divinity School

Jana Childers, Professor of Homiletics and Speech Communication, San Francisco Theological Seminary

David Schnasa Jacobsen, Professor of the Practice of Homiletics and Director of the Homiletical Theology Project, Boston University School of Theology

Willie Jennings, Associate Professor of Theology and Black Church Studies, Duke Divinity School

Stephen C. Johnson, Associate Professor of Preaching and Dean of the Honors College, Abilene Christian University, Abilene, Texas

Robert Allen Kelly, Professor of Church History, Waterloo Lutheran Seminary, Waterloo, Ontario

Henry J. Langknecht, Professor of Homiletics and Christian Communication, Trinity Lutheran Seminary, Columbus, Ohio

Gregory Anderson Love, Associate Professor of Systematic Theology, San Francisco Theological Seminary

Darren C. Marks, Assistant Professor of Theology and Jewish Studies, Huron University College at the University of Western Ontario

Sam Persons Parkes, Ordained Elder in the United Methodist Church and Th.D. Student in Preaching, University of Toronto

Luke A. Powery, Dean of Duke Chapel and Associate Professor of the Practice of Homiletics, Duke Divinity School

Melinda A. Quivik, Liturgical and Homiletical Scholar, Houghton, Michigan

Stephen Ray, Neil and Ila Fisher Professor of Theology, Garrett Evangelical Theological Seminary

Martha E. Stortz, Professor of Historical Theology and Ethics, Pacific Lutheran Theological Seminary

Jennifer Jeanine Thweatt-Bates, Theologian-at-Large, Greater New York City area

Todd Townshend, Canon Theologian for the Diocese of Huron and Lecturer in Homiletics and Contextual Theology, Huron University College at the University of Western Ontario

Eric Trozzo, Lecturer of Theology with the Lutheran Study Center at Sabah Theological Seminary, Kota Kinabalu, Malaysia

Paul Scott Wilson, Professor of Homiletics, Emmanuel College, University of Toronto, Toronto, Ontario

Scripture Index

Genesis

1:1-2:4a	*159*
2:15-17; 3:1-7	*79*
6:9-22; 7:24; 8:14-19	*165*
12:1-4a	*85*
12:1-9	*171*
18:1-15, (21:1-7)	*177*
21:8-21	*183*
22:1-14	*189*
24:34-38, 42-49, 58-67	*195*
25:19-34	*200*
28:10-19a	*205*
29:15-28	*210*
32:22-31	*215*
37:1-4, 12-28	*220*
45:1-15	*225*

Exodus

1:8-2:10	*231*
3:1-15	*237*
12:1-14	*243*
14:19-31	*249*
16:2-15	*254*
17:1-7	*91*
17:1-7	*259*
20:1-4, 7-9, 12-20	*264*
24:12-18	*68*
32:1-14	*269*
33:12-23	*275*

Deuteronomy

8:7-18	*310*
34:1-12	*280*

Joshua

3:7-17	*285*
24:1-3a, 14-25	*290*

Judges

4:1-7	*295*

1 Samuel

16:1-13	*96*

Psalms

2	*68*
8	*159*
13	*189*
15	*57*
16	*123*
17:1-7, 15	*215*
19	*264*
22	*112*
23	*96*
23	*133*
27:1, 4-9	*52*
29	*42*
31:1-5, 15-16	*138*
31:9-16	*106*
32	*79*
33:1-12	*171*
34:1-10, 22	*305*
40:1-11	*47*
45:10-17	*195*
46	*165*
47	*148*
51:1-17	*73*

Psalms (continued)

65	*310*
66:8-20	*143*
72:1-7, 10-14	*37*
72:1-7, 18-19	*7*
78:1-4, 12-16	*259*
78:1-7	*290*
80:1-7, 17-19	*19*
86:1-10, 16-17	*183*
90:1-6, 13-17	*280*
95	*91*
96	*25*
99	*275*
100	*300*
104:24-34, 35b	*153*
105:1-11, 45b	*210*
105:1-6, 16-22, 45b	*220*
105:1-6, 23-26, 45c	*237*
105:1-6, 37-45	*254*
106:1-6, 19-23	*269*
107:1-7, 33-37	*285*
112:1-9 (10)	*62*
114	*249*
116:1-4, 12-19	*128*
116:1-2, 12-19	*177*
118:1-2, 14-24	*118*
119:105-112	*200*
121	*85*
122	*1*
123	*295*
124	*231*
130	*101*
133	*225*
139:1-12, 23-24	*205*
146:5-10	*13*
148	*31*
149	*243*

Isaiah

2:1-5	*1*
7:10-16	*19*
9:1-4	*52*
9:2-7	*25*
11:1-10	*7*
35:1-10	*13*
42:1-9	*42*
49:1-7	*47*
50:4-9a	*106*
52:13-53:12	*112*
58:1-9a (9b-12)	*62*
60:1-6	*37*
63:7-9	*31*

Ezekiel

34:11-16, 20-24	*300*
37:1-14	*101*

Joel

2:1-2, 12-17	*73*

Micah

6:1-8	*57*

Matthew

1:18-25	*19*
2:1-12	*37*
2:13-23	*31*
3:1-12	*7*
3:13-17	*42*
4:1-11	*79*
4:12-23	*52*
5:1-12	*57*
5:1-12	*305*
5:13-20	*62*
6:16, 16-21	*73*
7:21-29	*165*
9:9-13, 18-26	*171*
9:35-10:8, (9-23)	*177*
10:24-39	*183*
10:40-42	*189*
11:2-11	*13*
11:16-19, 25-30	*195*

Matthew (*continued*)

13:1-9, 18-23	*200*
13:24-30, 36-43	*205*
13:31-33, 44-52	*210*
14:13-21	*215*
14:22-33	*220*
15: (10-20), 21-28	*225*
16:13-20	*231*
16:21-28	*237*
17:1-9	*68*
18:15-20	*243*
18:21-35	*249*
20:1-16	*254*
21:23-32	*259*
21:33-46	*264*
22:1-14	*269*
22:15-22	*275*
22:34-46	*280*
23:1-12	*285*
24:36-44	*1*
25:1-13	*290*
25:14-30	*295*
25:31-46	*300*
26:14-27:66	*106*
28:16-20	*159*

Luke

2:1-14, (15-20)	*25*
17:11-19	*310*
24:13-35	*128*
24:44-53	*148*

John

1:29-42	*47*
3:1-17	*85*
4:5-42	*91*
9:1-41	*96*
10:1-10	*133*
11:1-45	*101*
14:1-14	*138*
14:15-21	*143*

18:1-19:42	*112*
20:1-18	*118*
20:19-31	*123*
20:19-23	*153*

Acts

1:1-11	*148*
2:1-21	*153*
2:14a, 22-32	*123*
2:14a, 36-41	*128*
2:42-47	*133*
7:55-60	*138*
10:34-43	*42*
10:34-43	*118*
17:22-31	*143*

Romans

1:1-7	*19*
1:16-17; 3:22b-28, (29-31)	*165*
4:1-5, 13-17	*85*
4:13-25	*171*
5:1-11	*91*
5:1-8	*177*
5:12-19	*79*
6:1b-11	*183*
6:12-23	*189*
7:15-25a	*195*
8:1-11	*200*
8:6-11	*101*
8:12-25	*205*
8:26-39	*210*
9:1-5	*215*
10:5-15	*220*
11:1-2a, 29-32	*225*
12:1-8	*231*
12:9-21	*237*
13:8-14	*243*
13:11-14	*1*
14:1-12	*249*
15:4-13	*7*

1 Corinthians

1:1-9	*47*
1:10-18	*52*
1:18-31	*57*
2:1-12 (13-16)	*62*
12:3b-13	*153*

2 Corinthians

5:20b-6:10	*73*
9:6-15	*310*
13:11-13	*159*

Ephesians

1:15-23	*148*
1:15-23	*300*
3:1-12	*37*
5:8-14	*96*

Philippians

1:21-30	*254*
2:1-13	*259*
2:5-11	*106*
3:4b-14	*264*
4:1-9	*269*

Colossians

3:1-4	*118*

1 Thessalonians

1:1-10	*275*
2:1-8	*280*

2:9-13	*285*
4:13-18	*290*
5:1-11	*295*

Titus

2:11-14	*25*

Hebrews

2:10-18	*31*
10:16-25	*112*

James

5:7-10	*13*

1 Peter

1:3-9	*123*
1:17-23	*128*
2:2-10	*138*
2:19-25	*133*
3:13-22	*143*

2 Peter

1:16-21	*68*

1 John

3:1-3	*305*

Revelation

7:9-17	*305*